THE MIND MONSTER
SOLUTION

Photograph © Greg Funnell 2018

About the Author

Hazel Gale is a master practitioner of cognitive hypnotherapy, a former world kickboxing champion and a multiple national and open European ABA boxing-title winner.

Following a physical and psychological burnout during her first few years of competitive fighting, cognitive hypnotherapy helped Hazel to rebuild her physical strength and achieve a balanced, healthy emotional state.

Empowered by the changes she made for herself, Hazel trained as a therapist so that she could devote her time to helping others win their own emotional battles. She currently practises in London and specialises in performance-related issues and the pursuit of creative and professional goals.

hazelgale.com

mindmonsters.online

 @hazelgale

 hazelgalehypnotherapy

 @hazel.gale.therapy

THE MIND MONSTER SOLUTION

How to overcome self-sabotage and reclaim your life

HAZEL GALE

First published in Great Britain in hardback as *Fight* in 2018 by Yellow Kite,
an imprint of Hodder & Stoughton
An Hachette UK company

First published in paperback in 2019

3

Illustrations by Han-Ter Park

A CIP catalogue record for this title is available from the British Library

Paperback ISBN 978 1 473 66246 9
eBook ISBN 978 1 473 66245 2

Typeset in Miller Text by Palimpsest Book Production Ltd, Falkirk, Stirlingshire
Printed and bound in Great Britain by Clays Ltd, Elcograf S.p.A.

Hodder & Stoughton policy is to use papers that are natural, renewable
and recyclable products and made from wood grown in sustainable forests.
The logging and manufacturing processes are expected to conform to
the environmental regulations of the country of origin.

Yellow Kite
Hodder & Stoughton Ltd
Carmelite House
50 Victoria Embankment
London EC4Y 0DZ

www.yellowkitebooks.co.uk
www.hodder.co.uk

In loving memory of Mike Gale

Dedicated to Sue Gale and Tess Gale

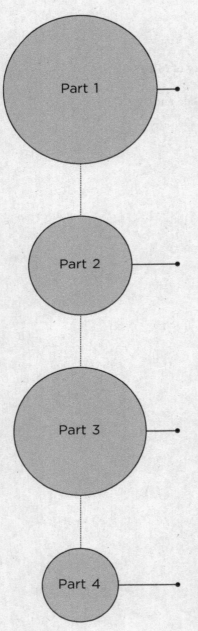

Perception
The most powerful changes start with understanding. What if you could really get to know the part of your personality that inspires anxiety, shame and self-sabotage and teach it a better way of thinking? It's time to meet your monster.

Power
Part 2 is about reclaiming your right to both internal and external command. Autonomy is the goal. We all need to learn how to take effective control.

Play
In Part 3 we'll bring everything from the first two parts of the book together by learning creative therapeutic techniques designed to generate unconscious change and bring your monster back onside.

Purpose
Part 4 guides you in applying all of the tools you will have developed over the course of this book to your life as a whole, so that you can move forward with purpose and motivation.

Contents

Preface ix
Foreword xi

Introduction 1

Part 1: Perception 11
The Ring Walk 15
Evolution I 19
Chapter 1: The Mind 25
Chapter 2: The Monster 46
Chapter 3: The (Dis)Comfort
   Zone 63
Chapter 4: Desire 81
Chapter 5: The Mirage 112

Part 2: Power 133
Evolution II 137
Chapter 6: Victimhood 139
Chapter 7: Control 164
Chapter 8: Authorship 182

Part 3: Play 213
Evolution III 217
Chapter 9: Metaphor 219
Chapter 10: Narrative 235
Chapter 11: The First Drafts 256
Chapter 12: Meetings of
   Minds 269

Part 4: Purpose 295
Chapter 13: Mentors 299
Evolution IV 316
Chapter 14: (Re)Purpose 322

Appendix 1: The Complete Diving
   Down Process 331
Appendix 2: Calibration 335
Appendix 3: Task Index 338
Appendix 4: Evolution Task
   Drawing Pages 342
Appendix 5: Task Forms 351

Acknowledgements 357
Get in Contact 359
Bibiliography 361
Endnotes 365
Index 371

Preface

The human brain is like some kind of hi-tech supercomputer. It is believed to generate around 50,000 thoughts per day and it can move information at speeds of up to 268mph. However, unlike the RAM in an expensive laptop, the storage capacity of the human brain is considered to be illimitable. There are no boundaries to what you could learn if you put your mind to it. What's more, your brain is not only capable of updating the information it stores, but also of physically rebuilding itself to support new ideas. No computer can do that.

It's a wonder, really, that we have any psychological problems, but of course we do. It's estimated that for most people 70 per cent of their 50,000 daily thoughts are negative. People bring destructive habits and limiting self-beliefs to therapy, wondering how they'll ever make a dent in them. However, the beauty of having a regenerative brain is that it means we *can* let go of unhelpful habits and update unrealistic beliefs. We do it all the time. Do you still believe in Father Christmas? No, I thought not. Yet, he did seem real once, didn't he?

Your mind is a self-adapting, intelligence-generating machine of truly awesome power. And this book is about learning how to collaborate with it, rather than battling against it in order to make a difference. Because believe me, there's more to life than just brawling for the win. The real fun comes from learning to love the game and make something meaningful out of it.

Foreword

By Trevor Silvester, founder of
Quest Cognitive Hypnotherapy

I've learned many things from being a therapist, but without doubt the most important is that we are all fellow strugglers. Through the bravery of my clients in sharing their stories with me I've discovered that the one thing that unites us is that, in our heads, we are all fighting battles nobody else knows about. And, so often, these battles cause ripples in the outside world that make our lives harder than they need to be, because no one should be stuck with any version of themselves that isn't happy.

The trouble nowadays is that so much self-help advice is at hand that it's easy to be confused about where to find it. With everyone peddling their version of how to live a fulfilled life, who should you learn from? Who better than a fellow struggler prepared to share the lessons she learned battling herself on the inside as she battled the world on the outside at the highest level? And, most especially, someone like Hazel. To meet her is to be immediately struck by her intelligence, wit and vibrancy. She exudes confidence. She's a world-class athlete, a professional-standard singer and a very talented therapist. So how can she have problems being herself? How dare she?

Because, as I said, we're all fellow strugglers. It's the great equaliser.

I've had clients who are supermodels, Olympic athletes, top business people, multi-millionaires, and that battle in their heads has consumed them just as completely as clients who are cab drivers, sales people, IT support workers and homemakers. What Hazel is about to share with you about her struggle – the journey she embarked on to free herself – and what she will teach you that could free you from your own limitations, deserves a gold medal for personal development. A reward that can be shared with anyone who finds themselves nodding at her story.

Trevor Silvester (Cert. Ed., FNCH) is a pioneer in the world of therapy. In the year 2000, he launched The Quest Institute, the world's first cognitive hypnotherapy training school. Quest used findings from neuroscience and psychology to advance its processes, and turned the notion of hypnotherapy on its head by rethinking the very meaning of 'hypnosis'.

In 2003, Trevor received the National Council of Hypnotherapy's Researcher of the Year award for his book Wordweaving: The Science of Suggestion *and, in 2007, was granted their highest honour, the Heartland Memorial Award, for his contribution to hypnotherapy.*

Trevor has trained under some of the most respected NLP and therapy practitioners such as Tad James and Gill Boyne. He has published six books, as well as contributing to many other publications and journals.

Since the launch of Quest, Trevor has overseen the qualification of thousands of therapists who work all over the world, one of whom is, of course, Hazel Gale.

Introduction

About Quest Cognitive Hypnotherapy

QCH [Quest Cognitive Hypnotherapy] may offer a brief, effective treatment for clients with clinically significant levels of anxiety and/ or depression, widening client choice.

Mental Health Review Journal,
September 2015

Quest Cognitive Hypnotherapy is a modern approach that draws on recent theories and discoveries from evolutionary psychology, positive psychology and cognitive theory, and which utilises practical and technical elements from a broad range of therapeutic styles such as neuro-linguistic programming (NLP), gestalt therapy, cognitive behavioural therapy (CBT) and traditional hypnotherapy.

Scientific backing

In 2011, the Quest Institute of Cognitive Hypnotherapy launched a research project with the aim of demonstrating the efficacy of our particular approach. The study used the same outcome measures as IAPT (Improving Access to Psychological Therapies), which meant that we could compare our practice directly with the leading therapeutic models within the National Health Service such as cognitive behavioural therapy.

In September 2015, the pilot study was published in the *Mental Health Review Journal*. Using 118 cases of people suffering from depression and/ or anxiety symptoms, it recorded that 71 per cent of those included in the study considered themselves recovered after an average of four sessions. This compared to an average of 42 per cent for other approaches like CBT that have used the same measures.

How to Use This Book

My purpose – in both my private practice and in my writing – is to empower people with the knowledge needed to solve their own problems, rather than feel dependent on anyone or anything else. I'm a firm believer that we can all change and that we already have the resources required to do that. All it takes is a little knowhow.

The Mind Monster Solution has been written to guide you through a process that will help you to maximise your potential for success, happiness and harmonious relationships. You'll learn through stories, personal anecdotes and easily digestible theory; by the final chapter, you'll be well-versed in some of the most powerful techniques for claiming control over the way you think, feel and act.

My intention is to take you on the kind of therapeutic journey travelled by my clients when they visit me for one-to-one sessions. I do not work from a set protocol with individuals in my office, so an exact replication is not possible; however, I have outlined the key processes and models that tend to have the most transformative effect for people across a broad spectrum. As a result, you might find that some sections resonate with you more powerfully than others, and that's fine. But I would hope that even the ideas that you don't put to immediate, personal use will provide you with an understanding of how the mind works, and therefore help you relate better to those who think differently to you.

A key aim of this book is to build an understanding of – and then power over – the behaviours and emotional reactions that you might call 'self-sabotages'. Some people will have a specific issue that they want to tackle with a book like this – something like a bad habit, social anxiety, procrastination or stage fright. If that's you, then you can focus exclusively on making that improvement. However, you don't need to have 'a problem' to fix in order to benefit from knowing your mind. The tasks and theories included here can be used to increase your happiness or performance in any area of your life where things could just get a little better too.

Note: parts of this process will involve looking deeply into negative emotions and the memories attached to them. Please bear in mind that if you're dealing with a very serious issue, or if you have experienced some major trauma in your past, then some of the techniques included may not be right for you. If at any stage in this book you feel as though you might be touching on experiences that you feel ill-equipped to deal with on your own, then please consider visiting a therapist to work through your problem under their guidance.

Time

Meaningful, unconscious change does not happen in a flash, so this is probably not a book that you should expect to plough through in just a few days. The most important piece of advice that I can give you before you start reading is to take the process at the pace that feels right for you; it could feel overwhelming to try to steam through it all too quickly. I suggest that whenever you reach saturation point, you should feel free to stop and let your mind chew things over while you do something else. Your unconscious will process the information more effectively if you consume it in smaller chunks.

Choosing your focus

In case you're not sure of what you can work on, this list highlights some of the most common self-sabotaging thoughts, feelings and behaviours. Any of the following could indicate the kind of inner conflict this book will help you to resolve; I'd suggest you circle or make a note of those that you struggle with the most.

* Unwarranted fear, anxiety or phobias
* Harbouring long-term resentment of other people or external circumstances
* Consistently putting the needs of others before your own
* Procrastination, underachieving or anything else that feels like avoidance of a potentially beneficial challenge

* A recurring feeling of fraudulence or failure, no matter how legitimate your achievements might look on paper
* Regular negative or self-defeating thoughts such as 'I can't ...' or 'I won't be able to ...'; these could be specific, like 'I'm no good at maths', or much more general, like, 'I'm just not good enough'
* Over- or under-eating (or any kind of eating disorder)
* Self-harm, self-pity or physical neglect
* Withdrawal from social circles
* Addictions and dependencies like alcoholism, drug addiction, gambling, overspending or work addiction
* Reluctance to seek or accept help
* Doing things that sabotage your relationships
* Dissociation from emotions (as in, not feeling much of anything)
* Frequent, poorly timed injury or illness

Does any of the above sound familiar? Please don't worry if it does. In fact, I think you may have more to worry about if nothing on that list got you nodding. I don't believe that anyone is completely free of a self-destruct button, but I do think some of us try to deal with it by building a facade of strength and denial. In the long run, as we'll discuss later, these kinds of coping mechanisms are almost always counterproductive.

However, just because it's normal to have the odd glitch doesn't mean we have to let these things dominate our lives. You might have a serious block to address, or you may just need to do some fine-tuning in order to excel further, faster. Either way, the approach will be roughly the same and it starts with an understanding of what lies beneath the surface-level symptoms that tend to grab our attention. This is what we'll be exploring in Part 1 of this book.

The tasks

This book is intended to be flexible. There are processes in most of the chapters, and you can, of course, work rigorously through all of them if you like. But please don't feel forced. I'm not a teacher setting home-work assignments. Whenever you find yourself drawn to a particular task, then jump in. There's no need to have done all the others first.

Test the ropes

Most importantly, what you will be learning in the task sections of this book are troubleshooting tools that you can take forward and use for the rest of your life. This means that there's absolutely no reason to 'get them right' the first time. When I was fighting, I used to test the ropes before I competed in a new boxing ring. You can do the same with the processes in this book. Feel free to just read through them the first time you come across them. If you do this, ideas and connections will come to you and you might even make some changes without feeling like you really did any 'work'. Then, if you want to come back with some paper and a pen at a later time, you can always do so. I've included a task index on page 338 to make this easier for you.

Guided meditations

I have recorded some guided meditations for you to listen to as you read this book. These are optional but powerful, and may work as a catalyst for the cognitive-hypnotherapy process, helping you to effect change at a faster rate and improve your results.

There is one audio file for each of the four parts of *Fight*. The aim is for them to encourage your mind to make gradual positive changes to the ways in which you think, feel and behave. You can find the relevant website link on the contents page for each part and I've listed them all here as a quick reference:

http://hazelgale.com/home/mindmonsters-part1-recording
http://hazelgale.com/home/mindmonsters-part2-recording
http://hazelgale.com/home/mindmonsters-part3-recording
http://hazelgale.com/home/mindmonsters-part4-recording

Journaling

The Healing Power of Putting Pen to Paper

To write about what is painful is to begin the work of healing.
Pat Schneider,* *How the Light Gets In*

Putting pen to paper (or perhaps finger to touchscreen) helps us to achieve our goals. Every client who visits my office takes a fresh notebook home to log their experience and document their thought processes between sessions. Over the years, I have noticed that those who use it tend to make the most rapid and pervasive changes. So that you can too, I'd recommend that you find a journal to use as you work through this book. Of course, it will come in handy for the tasks, but you will also benefit from keeping it with you to make notes of relevant thoughts and feelings as you go about your day.

Although it seems counterintuitive, this can be particularly true for the less than positive ideas that run through your mind. When we write uncomfortable thoughts down on paper, they tend to lose their emotional impact. It's hard to explain the difference between the feeling of an idea that lurks in the shadows of your mind and one that gazes meekly up at you from a piece of paper. It's as if forming something like a negative self-belief into a complete sentence – with a capital letter at the beginning and a full stop at the end – both humanises and paralyses it. What's more, a little like getting a politician to answer a question directly, when your beliefs are forced to take off their stealth clothing, they're infinitely easier to counter.

Expressive writing

Over the past few decades, hundreds of studies have been published on the effects of expressive writing, which basically means writing in a fluid

* American author, poet and writing teacher.

and emotional way about the more challenging moments in life, including childhood trauma. The results are impressive and extensive. They indicate that writing about painful memories for as little as twenty minutes a day over a four-day period can improve physical and psychological wellbeing as much as working through the issues with a therapist.

Here are the research highlights taken from *Expressive Writing: Words That Heal* by James W. Pennebaker and John F. Evans.

Physiological improvements

Considerable improvements have been shown in the physiological health of study participants, including a general enhancement of immunological functioning;[1] improvements in lung function and joint mobility in asthma and rheumatoid arthritis patients;[2] higher white-blood-cell counts among AIDS patients;[3] improvements in IBS (irritable bowel syndrome) symptoms;[4] and improvements in cancer symptoms.[5]

Psychological changes

Across multiple studies, people who participated in expressive-writing processes reported feeling happier and less negative after taking part (it should be noted that this is a long-term effect because it's normal to feel slightly down or drained immediately after writing about something emotional). Improvements of overall wellbeing and cognitive functioning have been registered,[6] and depressive symptoms, rumination and anxiety have been shown to decrease.[7]

Behavioural changes

Finally, behavioural changes such as improved grades in college,[8] improved functioning of working memory (the ability to concentrate on complex tasks)[9] and improved social functioning (participants were shown to talk more with others, laugh more easily, use more positive emotional words)[10] have also been documented.

All in all, studies like these have shown journaling about the challenges of life to be a surprisingly effective tool for improving and maintaining a healthy body and mind. You'll have various opportunities to reap the benefits of writing as you progress through this book.

Calibration

Tracking Your Progress

At the beginning of the therapeutic process, it can be remarkably easy to miss the positive changes that you make if you don't take measures to objectively assess your emotional state. Granted, this isn't quite as straightforward as taking your body temperature, but there are ways to get an idea of how you're doing.

You can use the table below to take a reading of your current emotional wellbeing. As you progress through this book (and if you continue using the tools after finishing it), I would hope you'll find that your total score increases. For the most comprehensive results over a period of time, I'd suggest that you return to this form at fortnightly intervals.

Basing your answers on the last two weeks, give each statement a rating from 0 to 4, based on how often you've been thinking in that way.

Emotional Wellbeing Scale	0 None of the time	1 Rarely	2 Some of the time	3 Often	4 All of the time
I've been feeling optimistic about the future.			✓		
I've been feeling useful.		✓			
I've been feeling relaxed.	✓				
I've been dealing with problems well.			✓		
I've been thinking clearly.			✓		
I've been feeling close to other people.			✓		

Emotional Wellbeing Scale	0 None of the time	1 Rarely	2 Some of the time	3 Often	4 All of the time
I've been able to make up my own mind about things.		✓			
I've been able to think creatively.			✓		
I've been able to assert my own views and opinions.		✓			
I've been enjoying the things I do.		✓			
I've been feeling as though I'm learning and developing.			✓		
I've been feeling like I'm contributing to something important.	✓				
Total score:					

Any individual statement that scores a 2 or lower could warrant some attention. But for now, I'd suggest you make a note of the areas in your life to which you could make the biggest improvements. You will have the opportunity to focus on any issues you're facing while completing the tasks in this book. We'll return to this questionnaire after the final chapter, so you can calibrate your progress.

15/05/20

PART 1
PERCEPTION

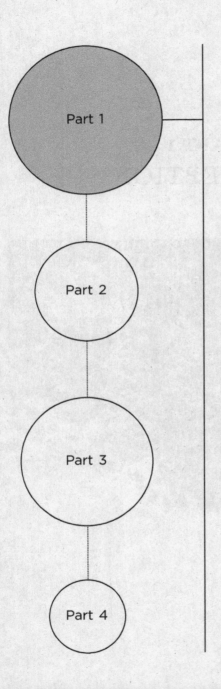

Perception

The most technical section of the book, Part 1 is about analysis and understanding. We need to know why we do what we do in order to make lasting changes. Here, we'll lay the theoretical foundations and shine a light on some of the most fascinating functions of the mind.

Part 1 Contents

The Ring Walk   15

Evolution I
Meet Your Mind Monster   19

Chapter 1: The Mind
Understanding Internal Conflict   25

Chapter 2: The Monster
The Power of Belief and the Making of Monsters   46

Chapter 3: The (Dis)Comfort Zone
Understanding Self-sabotage   63

Chapter 4: Desire
Unconscious Attachments and the Trouble with Wanting   81

Chapter 5: The Mirage
The Disabling Effect of Unmet Needs   112

You can listen to the guided meditation for Part 1 here:
http://hazelgale.com/home/mindmonsters-part1-recording

The Ring Walk

tat
tat, tat
tat, tat, tat ... boom.

   That rhythmic thud of glove on pad never leaves you, and I can hear it now breaking up the barked instructions from coach to fighter: 'Don't get drawn into a war ... keep your head moving ... use your jab!' A heady blend of tiger balm and sweat hangs in the close, warm air as this roomful of boxers prepare to do battle.

   Today is the 15th of December 2013 and I'm here to box for a national title. All the old fears should be here with me. The lead-up to this competition has not been great. I'm still recovering from a torn hamstring and I've got a fractured bone in my wrist. For the last few weeks, I've been unable to hit the bag or do any pad work, so instead I've been training on my own; long, solitary hours of shadow-boxing in the car park behind my flat.

   Making weight has been tough. Although a gruelling seven-day juice fast almost got me down to my category, I still had to be up at six this morning to 'skip off' the final kilogram in sweat before travelling to the competition. By the time of the weigh-in I was dehydrated, hungry and exhausted. I had to miss my best friend's bout just so I could grab some fitful sleep in the van outside before it was my turn.

   Around me now, fighters sit with towels draped over their anxious faces, each one waiting for their moment. Alone. It feels as though time has been suspended, and yet the future – everything I have trained for – is coming at me like a freight train.

   One by one, the boxers' names are called and they disappear into the arena. The victors come back beaming and taking selfies with their coaches and their medals. The losers return bruised, dejected or in tears.

   Normally, by now, I'd be beside myself. I would be questioning everything: my skills, my cardio, my arrogance at even thinking I could do this. We've all felt it: your hands and legs desert you first, your face freezes into a telltale look of horror and your mind locks onto that freight train with a rapidly intensifying sense of doom. Even though I would want to picture myself grinning for photos with the other winners, instead I'd be cycling back on what I'd been told about my opponent. Someone said she was a big hitter. The words 'that girl can bang!' would be echoing around my mind as I'd picture myself laid out on the canvas ... overcome, overwhelmed ... over.

But not this time. This time my feet are dancing expectantly to the song of the skipping rope as it whistles past my ears. I am absorbed in the task.

After eight years of competition something profound has changed. I completely inhabit my body as I make my way out to fight. One purposeful step after another. And as I enter the arena I feel ... at peace. It's as if the crowd has been hushed by a crisp layer of freshly fallen snow. The stillness in my mind interrupted solely by a curious little voice that says: 'I've got this.' Is this the sound of self-belief? It's not something I'm used to hearing at this stage. But there it is. Clear and unerring. For the first time, I know that I deserve the win.

The fight is no walkover; it turns out the girl can 'bang' and I take some good shots. But my focus is unshakable, and as we begin exchanging punches, my belief only grows stronger. There's a deep-felt sense of purpose as I scrutinise her attacks, and it keeps my mind trained on what I need to do to figure things out and make it happen. For two minutes at a time, I'm living in a soft, slow-motion version of reality. Even space is beginning to feel as if it's opening up before me. It's like I can see her shots before they're thrown, and the millimetres by which I ensure they miss provide a comfort equivalent of miles. Even when they land, it's as though the blows have been cushioned.

I feel present and alive. Focused without focusing. My hands do the work for me, and my feet know where to go without a thought. It's as if I can sit back and watch calmly as my body does exactly what I need it to do. I'm relaxed. I'm enjoying myself. I'm in flow.

The real difference between this fight and any other, though, comes at the end. As we stand, side by side, waiting for the judges' verdict, I suspect we both know that I will get the decision. But as my hand is raised, I feel a surge of alien emotion. I'm not sure if it is happiness, or pride, or just a good old-fashioned sense of achievement. But it is new.

With every win before this, when my hand was raised I'd hung my head and averted my eyes. I have never felt that I deserved victory and I have always been ready to write off any achievement as a fluke or chance. Just another lucky day when I got away with it. Looking back, I can tell you that what I had felt upon winning – up until now – had been shame.

This time I own the triumph.

I don't come from a fighting family. I was brought up by scientists who liked politics, art and academia. Combat sports weren't on our radar. Instead, my sister and I took part in gymnastics, horse riding and athletics when we were young. By the time I was in my twenties, however, pretty much any sport was out of the picture. Newly graduated from art school, I got my exercise by stacking barrels and serving bankers their beer from behind a busy London bar.

One evening, having followed my latest crush into the local dojo, I found myself in a kickboxing class almost by accident. I wasn't expecting to enjoy it. Press-ups and punching? No, I was much more interested in smoky nightclubs and drunken, late-night conversations about nothing. Yet, within fifteen minutes of my first session, I was hooked on the thrill of smacking pads and tussling with other sweaty bodies. It was a departure from everything I'd ever known.

My family were wary. My friends thought the idea of me in a gym kit was laughable. But to me, it felt like a rite of passage. It was only when I started training in earnest that I remembered all the fighter fantasies I used to have as a teen. I dreamed of being the fearless warrior woman who could beat down attackers in the streets. I loved any film or TV series with a kick-ass female protagonist who could take all the male villains out with one flying kick. So, when I first learned how to throw a punch it felt like a kind of homecoming. And when I realised that I was good at it, I thought that – just like She-Ra or Buffy – I had found my calling.

As my new hobby became more serious, the drinking and smoky nightclubs faded into the background. I had discovered an even more intoxicating drug; I had found competition. And it changed me.

Fighting made me stronger as a person. There's no doubt about it. But that strength didn't come about in the way that people tend to assume. It wasn't only that I was empowered by the ability to fend for myself or fortified by the stress of the contests. I didn't end up becoming famous or going to the Olympics. Even if I had done those things, they would not have been the focus of this book. Competitive fighting put me on a journey of self-discovery by painfully exposing my weaknesses and making me face up to them. It's this aspect of my story – not the wins or the titles – that I believe to be important enough to share with you here.

Ultimately, what I have learned from the challenges I failed to overcome has improved my life far more than any big, objective achievement ever could. The pressure of competition almost broke me. I dragged myself through periods of depression, eating disorders and years of chronic fatigue, all for the promised glory of the big win; a prize that never seemed to taste as good as it should. Even when I won my world titles in kickboxing before I moved to boxing, a sense of genuine, heartfelt achievement always escaped me somehow.

So, that moment when I first felt joyous in victory was about far more than just winning a boxing title. It symbolised a departure from an anxious, self-defeating mindset – something I hadn't even known I was doing until I was forced to address it. It marked the beginning of better health, energy and relationships. It opened the door to a fulfilling career and a general sense of everyday ease that I had no idea were even possible. Ironically, it meant that I could leave boxing behind peacefully and call a truce on a number of other external conflicts as well.

Of course, not everyone finds themselves literally fighting for a feeling of self-worth. However, as I continue to see therapy clients from so many different walks of life dealing with that same old sense of psychological struggle, I'm convinced that we all know what it's like to be in a brawl. The thing is, though, you can't fight your way to self-acceptance. At least, I don't believe that you can. Self-acceptance requires an altogether different type of valour.

The following chapters will help you ask and answer the same questions that fighting forced upon me. The stories I'll tell you – both my own and those of my clients – are included to give you the motivation and the tools not just to resolve your own battles, but to own the valuable sense of victory that you can take from doing that. And you can have it all without a single bloody nose.

Evolution I

Meet Your Mind Monster

Until you make the unconscious conscious, it will direct your life and you will call it fate.

Carl Jung*

In order to make a meaningful difference to our lives, it's not just the conscious mind that needs to know about the desired changes; we need to talk to the unconscious mind as well. However, these two systems speak in different tongues. While the conscious can respond to pure logic and reasoning, the unconscious works with symbolism, imagery, emotion and metaphor.

To make sure that we're covering all the bases, I have included four small sections, like this one, throughout the book. These are here for you to let go of the need to analyse and freely engage with the metaphors your mind presents to you. In doing this, you can learn perhaps the most important of all languages: the one that helps you 'make the unconscious conscious'.

These sections involve creative visualisation. This should be fun, rather than threatening (although I am aware that it will seem like the latter for many). However, I urge you to take a leap of faith and give yourself full creative licence. There is no right or wrong because absolutely anything goes. And the more curious and expressive you are, the more you stand to learn. Basically, I'm giving you permission to approach this task like a kid with a new set of colouring pencils at Christmas. Feel free to go nuts (just nothing on the walls, please).

---

* These words, very often attributed to Carl Jung, may well be apocryphal. I have yet to find a definite source. However, they match the essence of his philosophy quite beautifully, as well as one of the key themes of this book: to shine a light on the unconscious thoughts that can dictate our emotional reactions and behaviour.

Task: Identifying

People bring all sorts of issues to the therapy room, and although some things come up often – social anxiety, performance anxiety, lack of confidence, lack of capability, incompatibility with others, fear of failure, addictions and destructive habits – I think it's fair to say that no two clients ever describe exactly the same problem. However, nuances aside, there is one thing that appears to be true for everyone: the times when we are at our most uncomfortable are usually moments when we feel somehow 'out of control'.

Whether it manifests as an inability to dictate our own behaviour, a feeling that we're helpless against external forces, or the sense that we're at the mercy of overwhelming emotional reactions, the feeling of powerlessness seems to be universally unwelcome.

Yet, we all have moments when we feel like we've let slip our sense of command. Rather unhelpfully, our instinctive reaction is usually to relinquish even more control by attempting to deny, forget or otherwise disown them. We look back on our most perplexing decisions and say things like, 'I don't know what I was thinking!', 'Something came over me' or 'I wasn't myself!' In order to overcome our self-sabotaging tendencies we need to take responsibility for them, and to do that we must first be able to recognise them for what they are.

This first Evolution task is here to help you start by identifying the aspect of self that can be held responsible for the thoughts, feelings or behaviours that you'd most like to free yourself of. This, as I'm sure you will have guessed, will be your monster. It takes courage to meet these parts of the personality but I promise that you're safe. And, as with so many important challenges, what you stand to gain here far outweighs the discomfort of getting started. So, let's be brave. It's time to meet your monster.

Step 1: Remember

I'd like you to bring to mind a recent moment of self-sabotage; something you'd dearly love to erase from your life. If you have a particular issue that you'd like to tackle with this book, then imagine a time when that was at its worst. If not, pick anything that you have done, said or felt – probably repeatedly – that gets you undesirable results.

Settle on a memory before you read on. Please don't worry about finding the 'perfect example' though. Pretty much anything uncomfortable will do.

Next, I'd like you to reconnect with that experience by doing the following:

Step into the situation, so that you can see what you saw around you (if this is a moment that you can't remember clearly, then just go with what you imagine might have happened). Remember how you behaved and, if relevant, how others responded to your actions. Remember the sounds that you heard and recall the thoughts that ran through your head. Then, take your awareness inside your body to feel the emotions you felt on that day.

Close your eyes for a moment to engage fully with the experience. Then come back to the page and read on.

Step 2: Visualise your monster

Now, I'd like you to imagine that you can visualise the part of your personality responsible for your reactions in that moment. For example, if you're thinking of something like a binge-eating or drinking habit, it would be the part that makes you indulge; if you're thinking of anxiety, it would be the part that makes you feel scared; if you're thinking of procrastination, it would be the part that tempts you to go and watch the TV, rather than do your work.

Imagine that this element of your psychological makeup is an actual physical thing that you can observe, as if it's in the room with you right now – a part that has a mind of its own. Then, to start creating a visualisation, consider this question and just go with whatever comes to mind:

If you could see the part of your personality that takes over when you self-sabotage, what would it look like?

Pay attention to whatever flashes up, bearing in mind that it doesn't have to look like a traditional monster. You might have a clear and defined image, or you might just get a hint of an idea. Either way, go with it. To develop the visualisation, you can ask yourself these questions, but you don't need an answer to all of them:

※ If you could point to this thing, where would you point?
※ Is it large or small?
※ Is it dark or light?
※ Is it humanoid, animal-like or something else?

* Does it move or is it still?
* Does it make any sounds? If so, what kind?

What people see when asked these questions varies widely. Some imagine an amorphous shape like a dark cloud, blob of slime or black void. Others see something anthropomorphic; perhaps a devil, goblin or ghoul-like creature. Others yet will imagine something that resembles a certain person from their life, themselves at a certain stage of their life or an inanimate object.

Step 3: Log it

Your monster may seem like the enemy but it holds the key to a freer, happier and more successful life. The way you imagine it is likely to develop as you read this book, so please don't worry if your visualisation is vague at this stage. Just make sure you have an idea before moving on.

The last step is to log it. You have two options:

a) Drawing: if you are so inclined, I'd love you to draw a representation of what you saw at the front of your notebook or in the space allocated on page 343. Of course, your picture does not need to be 'good'. Some people draw little more than a single line or an angry squiggle here. The idea is simply to explore the way that you currently perceive this part of your psychological makeup.

b) Journaling: if drawing really isn't your thing, then feel free to make a few notes about what you imagine, so you can refer back later.

If you'd like to view some other people's monsters, you can do so here: https://www.mindmonsters.online

———•• ———

The Alchemy of Monsters

A few years ago, I would have told you that this part of my personality was made of a dark, heavy and formless material. It wasn't me, really. It was something else; some kind of shadowy anxiety monster that had assigned itself to me. Yet, no matter how hard I tried, when the pressure was on, I couldn't shake it off.

Most of the time I tried to pretend it wasn't there, but sometimes it could loom too large for me to ignore. In those moments, I'd fear my monster in the same irrational way that I once dreaded the beast I imagined swimming beneath me in the darker parts of the ocean when I was little. If I was distracted and having fun, I could forget about it. But then, with a brush of seaweed against my leg, I'd remember the threat in a flash and the panic would consume me. In the end, choosing to dive in courageously and take a look was the only way to overcome the terror.

As an adult, a similar feeling of dread came connected to the possibility of failing or looking stupid or weak. My fear was good at disguising itself, and it was sometimes subtle, but I felt it whenever I had to step onto a stage, into the ring or even – at times – through the door to a big party. My biggest self-sabotages – the things that left me feeling powerless, lost and out of control – happened in the moments when that fear took over.

Competitive sport was the perfect breeding ground for a fear-of-failure monster. The more opportunities I had to fall short, the more terrifying it would become. In the end, fighting caused me to burn out. In doing so, it forced me to meet the beast that it had nurtured, but only once that beast had dragged me down so deep that I had no choice but to look it in the eye.

Of course, we don't all need to do something as extreme as competitive fighting to start sabotaging our success, happiness or health. I'm sure that no matter what profession I found myself in, I would have had to face the monster at some stage. Fear of failure caused me to withdraw from both music and fine art earlier in my life. Regardless of any 'on-paper' success or potential, I chose not to pursue my passions beyond a certain point because I simply didn't think I was good enough. The physical nature of fighting (in retrospect, I can say 'thankfully') forced a big enough crash for me to have to take notice. Had that not happened, I might have spent my entire life running away from anything and everything that got even remotely challenging.

Your 'monster' may operate differently to mine. Perhaps it's more related to rage, jealousy or guilt than to fear. Or perhaps it doesn't feel emotional at all; maybe it's just a randomly destructive thing that makes you overeat, drink, push people away, procrastinate, bite your nails or engage in other unwanted behaviours for no apparent reason.

Whatever it's made of, it's only when we choose to seek out and understand this part of our personality that we can harness its energy and make it into something better.

Solutions

Consider this question:

If there was something you wish you could do with your monster, what would that be?

Before reading on, note down whatever comes to mind first. Again, do this without overthinking it. What we want here is a gut reaction. There's a space to record your answer on page 342, if you like.

There are two basic types of response that people are most likely to give when asked the above question. They either feel their 'monsters' need some love (or perhaps some positively communicated information) or that they need an eviction notice or a good kick up the backside. Which category do you fall into?

The majority of people tend to err on the angry side when struggling with self-sabotage. However, most of us will recognise that getting annoyed with ourselves after a poor decision or unhelpful reaction rarely achieves the result we hope for. Fortunately, battling is not the only option. There are many different ways for you to effectively (re)train your mental programmes, so you can let go of the futile fight. Over the following pages you'll begin by learning what this part is really up to when it makes you hit the self-destruct button. As you progress through the chapters you'll build an entire repertoire of psychological tools to challenge and re-engineer the thought processes that constitute your 'monster of the mind'.

So, if you're ready, let's begin with a look at how your mind does its thinking.

1

The Mind

Understanding Internal Conflict

Rewind eight years from the day of that peaceful ring walk and I'm getting ready for my first ever title fight. I'm at the National Kickboxing Championships and I'll soon be climbing into the ring to compete in the Full Contact final.

My body doesn't feel as if it belongs to me as I try to warm up on the pads. My punches are inaccurate and weak, and I'm consciously avoiding any kicking because I'm pretty sure my legs have been filled with heavy, wet sand. How am I supposed to fight if I can't even lift my legs? So I stop, opting instead to just stand, unmoving and rooted to the ground, which I wish would open up mercifully to swallow me whole.

As my name is called, I find myself grasping for a can of Red Bull. A last, desperate attempt to feel something – anything – that vaguely resembles energy. My coach snatches it from me in disgust: 'What the fuck do you think you're doing? Give me that. Let's go.'

The journey through the bustle of spectators and other fighters is surreal. It feels more like a spacewalk than a ring walk; as if I'm trapped in a stuffy bubble behind a thin layer of glass that separates me from the hostile world outside. This silence isn't peaceful. I'm forced to listen to the sound of my own breathing and the ear-splitting thud of my rapidly beating heart. Beneath all of that – growing stronger with every step – is an agonising sense of alarm that pulses through my body and implores me to turn and run.

I know I can't get out of fighting. Not now. Quitting is out of the question; but there isn't a single part of me that can remember why I ever signed up for this in the first place. All that promised glory and excitement seem a million miles away. This feels more like willingly walking to my own execution.

Yet, it's not getting bruised or bloodied that I'm worried about. Most people assume that's what will be on fighters' minds before they compete.

In reality, at least for me, that's a relatively minor consideration. What I fear the most here is humiliation. Or, maybe more accurately, I'm scared that I'm not going to be as good as everyone has come to expect. That this will be the point where, in front of all these people, my cover will be blown and the real me exposed: weak, untalented, out of my depth, pathetic.

The Calling

If only I'd known that my fear was actually a call to action, then this fight and many others that followed could have been very different. The things I saw as problematic back then held the key to a freer, calmer, more connected and ultimately more powerful-feeling existence. To enjoy those prizes, I just needed to learn how to dance, rather than do battle with my own mind.

Back then though, I wasn't ready. I didn't consider on that day that I could or even should address the way I was thinking because I had no real awareness of what was going on in my mind. All I knew was fear; the kind of fear that convinced me entirely of my inability.

My monster took control on that day by telling me its favourite story: 'You're not good enough.' Yet, instead of acknowledging my self-doubt and working with it for what it was, I tried to disprove it by fighting it. This meant that every time I climbed through the ropes to compete, rather than battling another human being, I was up against an increasingly fierce psychological shadow. It was a fight that I was destined to lose.

Why monsters?

'Limiting beliefs' is a term that I'll be using often in this book. These are the restrictive and negative ideas that we take on – usually about ourselves – and then file under the damaging heading of 'truth'. Recognising and then working with these thoughts is important because it's our limiting beliefs that tend to lie at the heart of our most mystifying moments of self-sabotage and other painful experiences.

I chose the monster metaphor to talk about this kind of thinking because – just like the creatures that lived under our childhood beds – limiting beliefs are not real. They're just stories that we tell ourselves and then use as scripts to live our lives by. Of course, a sensible, adult part of us usually knows that our most damning self-judgements are imaginary. However, that doesn't stop them from feeling like very real threats whenever they rear their ugly heads.

The irony is that the stories our monsters make us believe — 'I'm not loveable', 'I'm stupid', 'I don't fit in', 'I'll never be able to ...' — are actually the key to our development. Yet, in a misguided attempt to feel good about ourselves, we hide these vital pieces of the puzzle from our conscious awareness and choose to focus — usually ineffectively — on the symptoms that spring from them instead. Rather than dealing with the root cause of our stress, we seek treatment for our inability to sleep; instead of focusing on a fundamental dissatisfaction with who we are, we attempt to get thinner, more muscular or more qualified in order to feel better about ourselves.

Ignoring the deeper reality of our discomfort only makes things worse though, because when those problems continue to surface, we can end up feeling like the victims of our own minds.

Thankfully, there is another way.

If not victim, then ...

The hero's journey is a much-used metaphor in therapy. The idea is that we should be able to look back on the challenges we've faced in life and see ourselves as the hero, rather than the victim of our own story. This is an extremely powerful idea, and one that I have used to great effect in practice. However, although I believe that the theory is sound, I have always felt just a little uneasy about the archetype. Heroes slay their monsters, dragons and evil goblins in order to save the helpless villagers. If we are to buy into this as a metaphor for internal change, then we must be tempted to assume that our personal demons are things that we need to obliterate. This is not only self-destructive; it's impossible. Any demons we may have are a part of us and we simply cannot defeat or detach an aspect of the self. In the same way that amputees may continue to feel pain in missing limbs, even when we think we've managed to successfully sever a part of our personalities, it will retain the capacity to cause us considerable discomfort.

But that's OK because we don't need to slay our monsters; we just have to brave a proper look to discover that they're not what we thought they were. Once we've done that, we can make use of them, rather than waste all our energy fighting them. With a little work, our monsters can help us form deeper and more cooperative relationships; they can improve our work, enhance our creativity and teach us more about the world than any textbook or university degree.

A better metaphor

I think a more appropriate archetypal opposite for the victim is the author. Overcoming life's challenges is not about slaying negative thoughts or feelings; it's about exploring them and ultimately making something wonderful out of them. It's the process that any writer must go through when they create their work.

When we learn to think of ourselves as the authors of our own existence, life can be anything we want it to be. We can edit and rewrite the old beliefs that once determined our sense of self. We can compose new expectations of the future; and perhaps most importantly, by claiming authorship in the now, we can control the self-defining stories that we write for ourselves moment to moment, every time we make a decision, choose a response or speak a word. Authorship is about awakening ourselves into the present and owning our ability to choose.

In order to do this, we must meet our monsters. We have to hear the destructive stories that our minds like to tell us, because those are the rough drafts we need to work with in order to write something more appealing. The solution, in other words, begins with awareness.

No Such Thing as 'Normality'

We go through life feeling the way that we feel. If we're always a little anxious or angry or sad or bored, then we assume that is the norm. But just because things have always been a certain way doesn't necessarily mean they have to remain so.

I received this feedback from a client – let's call him John – who visited me for help with insomnia: 'I feel like I've been untethered from something non-specific; something that I didn't really realise was there before, but that I feel much better equipped to proceed with my life without.'

Before we worked together, John would lie awake each night, staring at the ceiling and fretting over the demands of his fast-paced media job. His relentless inner dialogue could keep him awake for hours and the sleepless nights were starting to take their toll on his performance. He initially came to therapy with the intention of learning some relaxation techniques to help him fall asleep. But instead of simply addressing the symptom (the insomnia), we spent a few sessions working on the anxious self-talk that caused it.

In those meetings, John chose to face his monster. Underneath his racing mind's attempts to pre-plan the following days at work was a sense that 'something bad was going to happen'. This was a feeling that he had been living with for decades, ever since a frightening childhood experience, but his mind was responding to it as if it was a present-day reality. As a result, he'd find himself going on a nightly search for evidence of an upcoming disaster. And, of course, when we really want to find something like that, that's exactly what we do. The monster in John's mind was telling him an old, false and outdated horror story, but it wasn't until he decided to stop and listen to it that he could see it as such.

This is the age of the quick fix. When we hit an obstacle, it's easy to just look for the pill or the supplement or some other kind of miracle product to put things right. Fortunately, John chose to take the psychological route, rather than turn to medication for his insomnia. But it hadn't really occurred to him that stress could be the cause of his problem because he didn't really *feel* stressed. At least, he didn't think he did because that low-level anxiety had become his normality.

The magic pill that John needed was respite from his habitual and unconscious sense of foreboding. Once 'untethered' from this, he was able to enjoy a new perspective on his work and his relationships, as well as better sleep. Ultimately, he grasped the opportunity to tell himself a better story and his world became a calmer place for it.

Awareness

The conscious mind may be compared to a fountain playing in the sun and falling back into the great subterranean pool of subconscious from which it rises.

Sigmund Freud

It's time to lay some theoretical foundations. There are a few key concepts that will put you quite quickly into a more powerful position in relation to your inner world. I'd like to start by clarifying the difference between conscious and unconscious awareness.

Note: there are some very subtle differences between the terms 'unconscious' and 'subconscious'. However, for our purposes, the two words essentially mean the same thing, and I will be using the word 'unconscious' in this book.

The conscious mind is what most people associate with who they are. It's what we call 'me'. Conscious awareness is what you are capable of thinking about (or feeling, hearing, seeing, etc.) right now.

*Un*conscious awareness, basically, is everything else.

Think of your right ear for a moment. Until you read that, you probably weren't consciously aware of that part of your body. Now that you are, your present knowledge of that ear has come to the forefront of your awareness. As soon as you forget about it and move on, however, that information will slip back out of your conscious awareness until it is next deemed to be relevant. Your unconscious mind, on the other hand, will continue to be aware of your right ear, as well as everything else inside and around your body, regardless of what your conscious mind is thinking about.

While all that is going on, the unconscious mind is keeping itself busy with a plethora of other tasks as well. Its primary purpose is your survival, so it is taking care of all your bodily functions like digestion, breathing, blood flow, immunological functioning, etc. It is also storing and organising all your memories, values, abilities, beliefs ... Just like the awareness of your right ear, these units of information will be forwarded to your conscious awareness whenever the unconscious decides that they require your full attention.

Conscious understanding: the captain

We rate thinking highly in the Western world. Probably too highly. We tend to assume that as long as we have reasonable, logical evidence for our conclusion, then we can know it to be true. This kind of rational thinking is a product of the conscious mind and it's what we want to attribute our behaviour to. But it's limited.

On my very first day of training as a therapist, my teacher explained the difference between conscious and unconscious awareness using a metaphor. Of the many others I've heard since, I still believe this to be the most powerful and poetic way to get to grips with the distinction.

Let's think of conscious thought as an arrogant ship's captain, haughty and with delusions of grandeur. He barks orders and takes all the credit when things go right, getting angry and critical when they don't. The captain is the one who shouts, 'Do *not* eat that massive lump of cheese!' right before you tuck in, and then says, 'I told you so, idiot' when you put on weight.

In reality, it's the crew (*un*conscious thought and behaviour) who actually sail the ship. They're the muscle; the first responders to choppy seas and unpredictable winds. They're also the ones who'd have to fight off any Cheddar-smuggling pirates who might try to get on board.

So, does the captain really have the control he prides himself on? No. Our conscious captain does not (cannot) truly sail the ship.

Unconscious understanding: the crew

The unconscious mind handles the way that we feel. It works with hunches and intuition and is largely responsible for the way in which we act. Studies estimate that approximately 90 per cent of our behaviour is governed by the unconscious mind.[1] Let that sink in for a moment ... You are only really choosing one tenth of your actions each day (if that). Everything else is automatic.

Remarkably, conscious awareness has also been shown to function half a second behind reality. It takes us 500 milliseconds to register anything that we see, hear, feel, smell or taste from the outsi world, so it's a good thing that the captain isn't really calling the shots.*

Sports (at least most of them) would be out of the question. It takes less than half a second for a tennis ball to be smashed over the net or for a punch to be thrown. Conversations would ... be ... really ... slow ... And every single thing that has ever fallen from your kitchen cupboard as you opened the door would have smashed to the floor. Not ideal.

So, unlike the captain, the crew can act nigh-on instantaneously. The unconscious mind doesn't have time to listen to logical reasoning and it doesn't wait for commands. It uses beliefs, fears, values, previous experience and the voices of people in our past to determine our feelings and behaviour. And it does so, largely, outside of conscious awareness.

There is a point of interconnection, however. A good captain can communicate, educate and influence his crew members when he needs to, but he has to get to know them first. He needs to speak their language and nurture their trust. Until he can do that, trying singlehandedly to force the ship to turn using willpower or sheer grit alone will usually backfire.

By now, I'm sure you will have realised that the unconscious mind is the monster's domain. As well as all the healthy and useful things that your crew are responsible for, they are also capable of sneaking undesirable cargo past the captain and concealing it carefully in the hull. Your monster is essentially an unwelcome part of your crew. Unless you choose to go down there and take a look, any rebellious deckhand could allow it to run rampant, sending your ship wildly off course while the captain sleeps.

The battle: conscious versus unconscious

Pretty much any issue that people bring to therapy will involve some kind of conflict between conscious and unconscious understanding. What this boils down to is a discrepancy between what we think/know to be true, and what we find ourselves feeling/doing.

---

* First discovered in the 1970s by Benjamin Libet, a pioneering scientist in the field of human consciousness. In a nutshell, Libet used an electroencephalogram (EEG) to time the difference between the unconscious impulses present in the brain to signal the preparation for an action like clicking one's fingers, and the point at which the subject became consciously aware of the 'choice' to click their fingers. Libet's experiment indicated that we unconsciously initiate an action like this 500 milliseconds before we are consciously aware of the idea to do it. Consequently, his research sparked major controversy around the question of free will.

Examples

Conscious says: 'Give up smoking.'
Unconscious says: 'I need a cigarette.'

Conscious says: 'Write your CV and apply for that job.'
Unconscious says: 'Cup of tea.'

Conscious says: 'It's just a harmless little spider.'
Unconscious says: 'ARGHHHHH!!!!'

Conflicts like these can result in seemingly uncontrollable and often pretty undesirable behaviours. These will be the actions (or, more accurately, the *re*actions) that your unconscious mind is choosing for you – a late-night chocolate binge just as the diet was starting to pay off; a crappy decision that ruins any chance of promotion; a mindless splurge on something completely unnecessary when there are important things to save for ...

It may seem counterintuitive, but the mind has its reasons for doing these things. The crew are intentionally keeping your monster on board to protect you from what they think are even bigger and scarier demons. When we sabotage ourselves, it can feel like something inside is simply trying to derail us, but the unconscious mind believes that those behaviours and feelings are solutions rather than problems. Until it learns otherwise, it will continue to cue them up.

Hypnosis

The job of the hypnotherapist was no longer to induce *a trance but rather to* de-hypnotize *the individual out of the trance she was already experiencing.*

Stephen Wolinsky PhD,*
Trances People Live

This is not a book about hypnosis or the trance state per se. At least, I will not be using those particular words often, largely because the things

* Author and psychotherapist.

most commonly associated with hypnosis – animal impressions, orgasm handshakes and the like – are probably not all that helpful. However, seeing as I do have 'hypno' in my job title, I want to make sure I explain the role of hypnosis in my approach to therapy.

In cognitive hypnotherapy we have a different understanding of hypnosis to that of some more traditional hypnotic practices (like stage hypnosis). Trance can be defined as a state of mind in which unconscious rather than conscious thinking determines behaviour, and where a person's thoughts are easily influenced by external input. When hypnosis first appeared on the scene in the eighteenth century, we were under the illusion that the captain was indeed in command. Because of this, the trance state seemed like an otherworldly phenomenon.

These days, we know a lot more about the mind. It's now understood that complete conscious control over our behaviour is a rarity (if possible at all), and that it would be pretty ineffective in most situations. Whenever an experienced driver makes the journey to work in their car, they do not need to consciously think about signalling or changing gear because the crew have got that down to a T. They're in their 'driving trance', and assuming they get safely to where they need to go, this will be an effective and useful hypnotic state.

We also know now that we're all being influenced by external information all the time. Advertising, for example, is quite clearly hypnotic. Walk past enough Gillette advertising hoardings and you'll probably find yourself mindlessly reaching for that brand of razor next time you're in the chemist's. No pocket watches or commands to 'look into my eyes' were necessary for Gillette to make that suggestion.

It therefore makes sense to update our perception of hypnosis. Most now view 'trance' not as an abnormal state into which the subject must be put by someone with special skills, but as a natural phenomenon that occurs more often than not. Some people – those labelled as 'highly suggestible' – make better subjects for stage shows because they respond more readily to direct suggestion, but they're not the only ones who can utilise the trance state for their own advancement. I have never been able to cluck like a chicken on demand (so disappointing), but I have made massive changes thanks to hypnotherapy because trance is something that every mind can achieve just by watching a movie, reading a book or having a deep conversation.

It's absolutely possible, therefore, to get new ideas through to the crew. This is important because it's the unconscious mind that chooses our less than desirable trance states as well as the useful ones like driving a car to work. The comfort eater who automatically makes their way over to the fridge whenever work gets challenging is not consciously making that decision. They're in their 'comfort-eating trance', and if they're eating more than they want or need to eat, then this particular hypnotic state will be seen as a problem by the conscious self. What's important to recognise is that the unconscious mind will be switching the 'comfort-eating trance' on because it sees it as a solution: 'We're feeling uncomfortable right now. How do we get comfortable again? Oh, I know. To the fridge!'

Monster moments (self-sabotages) are nothing more than unwanted trance behaviours. The goal of our work, as we see it in cognitive hypno-therapy, is therefore not to hypnotise people in order to solve their problems, but to help them 'de-hypnotise' (or perhaps *re*-hypnotise) themselves whenever things aren't going exactly as they'd wish.

So, we really don't need a moustachioed, pocket-watch-swinging performer if we want to make a difference to the way that we think. We are our own hypnotists. We just need to learn how to make effective suggestions.

Rebecca's smoking monster

Rebecca came to see me because she had a problem with smoking mari-juana. She smoked at some stage every day, occasionally from first thing in the morning. As a result, she wasn't achieving what she wanted to at work and she had been single for some years. Smoking made her feel like an undesirable failure, yet she was unable to ditch the habit because, on some level, she felt as though she needed it.

In her first session, I asked Rebecca a key question: 'What will change in your life when you stop smoking?' Her response was that she would become a more successful version of herself and that she'd be able to 'meet the right guy and start a family'. The important thing was that, as she said this, she winced.

Rebecca's father was an angry and bitter man who took his frustrations out on his daughter. She was repeatedly told that she was a 'burden' and a 'waste of space' as she grew up, and after a string of dysfunctional relationships in her early twenties, she had even more evidence of this being the 'truth'.

Rebecca's real problem wasn't the smoking habit at all; it was a fear of getting close to people (men in particular). Retreating into a life of zoned-out solitude was her unconscious mind's attempt to avoid the suffering it anticipated if she tried to form a relationship. Her 'smoking trance' was a solution to an old and painful problem. It's just that, in the grand scheme of things, it was a solution that caused more problems than it solved.

Recognising this made an enormous difference for Rebecca. Suddenly, her monster wasn't monstrous at all; it was just a processing mistake made by her young mind in a really tough situation. By working on the messages that came from her father, and by letting go of the other troubling relationships from her past, Rebecca was able to connect with her rightful sense of self-worth. This meant growing it to a far bigger size than it ever had been before. As she did this, the smoking habit gradually tapered off, her career in graphic design blossomed and she eventually found herself back on the dating scene with a newfound awareness of who did and didn't fit the old, abusive blueprint based on her father.

Your Unique Reality

Each of us lives within the universe – the prison – of his own brain. Projecting from it are millions of fragile sensory nerve fibres, in groups uniquely adapted to sample the energetic states of the world around us: heat, light, force, and chemical composition. That is all we ever know of it directly; all else is logical inference.

Vernon B. Mountcastle,[*]
'The View from Within: Pathways to the Study of Perception'

What we think of as the 'real world' and our actual external reality are – in all probability – entirely different things. There is a plethora of angles we could take to explore this concept. I'd like to highlight just a few key

[*] Professor Emeritus of Neuroscience at Johns Hopkins University and widely regarded as the father of modern neuroscience. Deceased.

ideas to conclude this chapter, because for me this information was transformative as well as fascinating when I first learned about it. Of course, if you prefer not to get too technical, then don't worry. It's not imperative that you have a thorough grasp of these ideas in order to get the most out of this book. Your understanding of the key concepts will develop as you progress through the chapters, in any case. What we're aiming for here is just the foundation.

The reality filter

Have you ever had a conversation with someone, say, from a different side of the political fence, or perhaps who believes in something like alien abductions when you do not (or vice versa)? Did you notice how they managed to twist your 'reasonable evidence' out of shape, so that it backs up their idea? Or, did you feel as if they were entirely ignoring – or somehow not even hearing – some of the things you said that would contradict their viewpoint? It's not just conspiracy theorists or particularly stubborn people who do this. We all do it. In fact, you would have been doing it for yourself in that very conversation. The mind automatically deletes, distorts and generalises incoming information to fit with pre-existing belief systems; it warps what we perceive, so that it feels familiar and 'right', and – what's more – it has a lot of info to play with.

While it is estimated that the unconscious mind can be aware of between 2 and 11 million pieces of information at any given moment, many studies suggest that our conscious awareness – the bit that we actually know about – can only include between five and nine units of information at once. That's a massive reduction. To make the cut, the mind uses a personalised stockpile of previous experiences and the connected beliefs and values (among some other variables) to filter the vast amount of raw sensory information coming in. Then it uses its limited selection to create the personalised version of the world that we perceive.

So, when someone disagrees with you wholeheartedly about something, it's not just because they're stubbornly dismissing your input (although sometimes it will be). It could be that their mind is simply incapable of even perceiving the argument you're trying to present because it does not fit with their model of the world.

Monsters are really picky eaters

All of our beliefs will determine the 'reality' in which we (think we) live. Some of them will be very particular to us as individuals and some will be based on general perceived wisdom and the cultural norm.

Whether they come from societal bias or personal circumstances, our most limiting beliefs – our monster stories – are things we might do well to reconsider. If we're used to believing something like 'I'm ugly', then anything corresponding to that idea will be let through our reality filter, whereas contradictory information (like a compliment, for example) is likely to either get rejected outright or warped until it looks familiar enough to be let in.

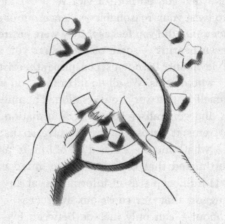

Our monsters are like picky eaters who live inside our heads choosing the kind of information they're willing to consume. If they're used to living on a diet of 'I'm stupid' rectangles, then they'll chow down happily on anything of that shape, but they'll discard all the 'You're so clever' circles without a second thought. Every now and then, the world might try to feed them a 'You did well' square. When this happens, they have two options: they'll either reject it, or they will trim a little off, so that it's a suitable shape. Perhaps they will turn it into a rectangle that says, for example, 'They told me I did well, but they're just being polite.' Mmm ... yummy, familiar oblong things.

Of course, we *can* let go of beliefs and learn novel ideas as we develop. It just takes a bit of work and/or some extraordinary evidence to sway us. In the case of our deepest, most personal fears, it can be extremely difficult getting anything new past the reality filter. Have you ever tried telling someone who is convinced they look horrible that they, in fact, look lovely? Yeah, me too. It doesn't work.

What we add

The reality filter is not the only mental process that goes into making our perceived worlds so bespoke. On top of all the deleting, generalising and distorting, the unconscious mind also adds some extra information before we create our internal virtual-reality replication of the world. In his book, *The User Illusion*,[2] Tor Nørretranders asserts that 90 per cent of what we see, hear, feel, taste and smell is internally generated. This means that the vast majority of what we think we perceive around us could be entirely fabricated. The extra information – which will, of course, also be based on what we already believe – is added by the brain a split second before conscious recognition.

The blind spot

The blind spot in human vision offers a compelling demonstration of the brain's ability to create convincing imagery in lieu of actual information.

We all have two blind spots in our vision: one for each eye. In the back of the eye, there is a sheet of photoreceptors covering the retina. This functions much like the photosensitive film at the back of a traditional camera. It records the information transmitted via rays of light from the outside world. However, at the point where the optic nerve attaches to the retina, there's a hole in this sheet. What this means is that the brain receives zero information from the eye about this particular part of the thing we're looking at. Yet, regardless of these holes, we do not have gaps in our vision. This is partly because the blind spots in each eye are in different places, so one eye sees what the other does not. However, even if you close one eye, you still don't have a big black hole in your sight – because your brain makes up an approximation of what it thinks would be seen in that area, based on what surrounds it, and uses that to plug the gap. So, that part of what you see is an invention; a guess.

To actually see the blind spot being filled in, you can use the image below.

Instructions: close or cover your left eye with your hand, then focus on the cross with your right eye. Slowly and gradually, move your head closer to and further away from the image. There will be a point – probably around five inches from the page – at which the monster disappears. Don't look directly at it to check, just keep looking at the cross and he'll pop in and out of your peripheral vision.

Beliefs

Visual illusions can also be used to demonstrate how the mind will warp and build on the raw information it receives, depending on what it believes to be true and therefore expects. As Nørretranders points out, this next illusion 'shows that we are living on a planet that orbits a star'.[3]

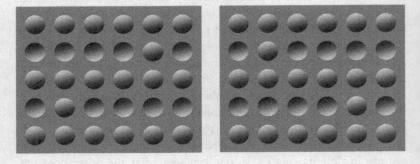

The shapes in this image clearly appear as dimples or pimples, depending on whether the 'shadow' is at the top or the bottom of the circle. But there is no shadow at all. These are two-dimensional circles that have been shaded with a simple gradient. Having lived its entire life on a planet that receives light from the sun (i.e. from above), the brain interprets the gradient as a shadow and consequently sees the circles as 3D protrusions and indentations respectively. Even though you know that it's an illusion, it's very hard to *unsee* the fabricated extra dimension because it's just so ... normal.

The same goes for any other kind of normality. If it's 'normal' for you to be showered in praise, then that's the kind of information you are most likely to notice (or fabricate) when you give a talk at work, even if you're actually pretty mediocre. Conversely, if it's 'normal' for you to bomb completely because you think you're the most boring person in the world, then it would take a pretty mind-blowing reception (probably on a number of occasions) to force your monster to start eating some positive-praise circles instead of its usual diet of rectangular criticism.

The personality construct

Fairly obviously, it is the warped and fabricated inner world that we use to determine our responses – both behavioural and emotional – rather than our actual environment. This is why some people walk into a crowded room and think, 'Party!' whereas others will think, 'Get me the hell out of here.' The desire to either dance or do a runner is likely to be the type of thing we connect to the seemingly rock-solid concept of 'me'. ('I'm a party person. That's just the way I am. Pass the tequila.') However, our personalities, for the most part, are as much a product of our reality filters as our perception of the world.

As we live our lives, we develop particular patterns of response (mental, emotional and behavioural habits), which fire automatically when we perceive certain triggers. These include potentially unusual or problematic reactions, like those caused by a phobia or fetish, but they also include all the other traits that we're less likely to think of as habits that we've learned along the way. Are you an early bird or a night owl? An optimist or pessimist? Are you friendly or standoffish? Do you think of yourself as intellectual, creative, sporty, geeky ...? Our personalities, as definite as they might seem, are really little more than a combination of learned patterns. However, over time we merge these patterns or habits into an inner map for our sense of identity and start to call it 'me'. Parts of that map will be positive and effective, and other parts of it (probably) will not, but if we never question the learned 'truths' that define our sense of self, then our crew will continue to navigate the ocean we're sailing across as if there's only one possible route.

The plus side of this is that it means that we can change a lot more about ourselves than we might have realised. Well, within reason. I'm not suggesting that you can choose to start thinking like Mick Jagger and automatically go triple platinum. But then again, I'm not saying you can't either. So long as you're prepared to put in a serious number of hours (and money), rock stardom could potentially be anyone's. It just won't be easy. (**Note:** if you do go triple platinum as a result of reading this book, then I want a cut.)

New Waters

In summary, reality isn't all it's cracked up to be. What we consciously know about is but a tiny fraction of what's actually out there, and most of that tiny fraction is probably made up, anyway. Great. However, as freaky as this idea can sound when we first hear it, it's not actually a bad thing. If there's anything we don't like about the world as we see it, then it could be the filter, rather than the reality, that we need to adjust. And that's often a far more achievable task.

When I fought that day at the National Kickboxing Championships, I was referring to an old and uncomfortable reality map. In fact, I was trying to fight my way out of it. As a result, it was like there were two versions of me in the ring, neither of which was given the opportunity to do what it wanted. The captain wanted success, of course. I tried to plan my punch combinations, rather than trusting them to my quicker and more accurate unconscious mind, and I focused a large portion of my energy on attempting to ignore the growing sense of alarm I felt inside. But these efforts to control things were usually interrupted (quite rudely) by a smack in the face. The captain, frankly, makes a terrible fighter, and that's especially true when he's up against a beast he had no idea was even on board. It was only my unconscious self — the crew — who stood even the slightest chance of getting the win, but they were too busy trying to flee the sinking ship to really get involved.

I lost the fight that day largely because there was an even bigger battle going on inside my head. But my inner opponent wasn't going to stop when the bell was sounded. Over the years that followed, my monster caused me to binge eat uncontrollably whenever there was a weigh-in on the horizon, which led to shameful purges after meals almost every day. It made me tense, anxious, depressed and antisocial. It made me underperform on numerous occasions (or, at least, it trimmed my good performances into rectangular visions of mediocrity) and, I believe, it was the reason my body developed chronic fatigue: an illness that would perfectly fit the bill for a complete sabotage of any potential athletic success.

Of course I didn't (I wouldn't) consciously choose those things. Consciously, I was desperately trying to *un*think my negative thoughts. I'd try to blame a poor performance on bad luck or illness, and I'd rationalise my eating disorder by telling myself that everyone in a sport with weight categories does that. I yearned for a sense of control, but the harder I tried to get it, the less I felt that I had.

Moving Forward

I don't know what your reality map looks like, but I do know that it's based on your memories and the beliefs that come wrapped up within them. In order for you to either change course or simply do some better sailing, these will be the raw materials that you need to work with. The remainder of Part 1 is about really getting to know what shape of information your mind is willing to consume, what it wants to reject, and why. In doing this, you can begin to shatter the old illusion and start mapping out a preferable journey.

So grab your compass and a magnifying glass. It's time to explore some uncharted waters.

Analytical Questioning

Questions for Understanding a Particular Mind Monster

People can sometimes make quite considerable leaps after doing little more than answering some analytical questions about their unwanted behaviours. To better understand your moments of self-sabotage, you can use the questions below to map out specifically where, when, how and (possibly) why those things occur.

You only need to answer these questions if you have a specific self-sabotaging trait that you'd like to focus on as you read this book. If you do choose to dive in, please know that you don't need to have a response for all of them. Many of these questions will serve as jumping-off points, rather than curative solutions. The aim is to get your mind thinking in the way that will best enable you to fill the gaps as you continue reading.

Start by writing the issue at the top of a clean page in your notebook, and then answer the following questions about that problem.

••

In which context(s) of your life is this reaction most likely to occur?

Around what type of person is this reaction most likely to occur?

Is there a particular day/time when this issue is most likely to manifest (and, if so, what goes on at that time)?

What do you think about yourself while you are doing it?

What do you think about yourself afterwards?

How, specifically, does this problem make you feel?

Are there any other situations in your life now that make you feel a similar way? If so, what are they?

If there was a connection between those different situations, what would that be?

How does your sabotage affect the way the rest of your day, week or month goes?

Does it affect the way you relate to others? If so, how?

Does it affect your expectation of the future? If so, how?

Looking back, for how long has this been going on?

What was different about you before it started?

What was happening in your life around that time?

If there are situations when this issue doesn't affect you (or when you forget about it temporarily), what would those be?

What's different about those situations, and how do you get that to happen?

Monster purpose

All self-sabotaging traits aim to elicit some kind of benefit as well as the (usually more obvious) damaging effect. This can be easier to see in some situations than others because just like the positive intention behind Rebecca's smoking habit (see page 36), the gains are sometimes entirely unconscious. However, I can guarantee there will be something. Answering the following four questions can help you to build an understanding of the purpose behind your unwanted behaviours.

What will you gain if you let go of your sabotaging issue?

What will you lose if you let go of your sabotaging issue?

If there was anything about having this issue that you might like to hold onto, what would it be?

If there was something that your monster could possibly be protecting you from by making you sabotage in this way, what would that be?

2

The Monster

The Power of Belief and the Making of Monsters

I'm sitting on the side of the ring, enjoying a rare moment of stillness in this place of near-constant activity. Sweat drips rhythmically from my forehead to the floor. The little splashy thuds are playing an understated solo part in the percussive orchestra of thumps and cracks going on around me.

The gym is unusually busy tonight; the tight space teeming with a diverse range of people – from city bankers to manual labourers – all stripped of their status and brought together by a shared passion for adrenaline and elbow grease. Large groups of beginners are learning the basics with varying levels of ease: the 'naturals' picking up complex techniques as if they're made for the sport; the less-than-coordinated struggling with even the simplest of drills.

To my left, in the middle of the dojo, my instructor, Stuart, is sparring with one of his best fighters.* The two men switch seamlessly between different states. One minute they're laughing and joking; the next they're locking horns, slamming glove and shin into each other's ribs and temples. Yet, somehow, within their vicious exchanges there's a sense of calm – even beautiful – composure. It's that easy, powerful focus that I aspire to; something that can only come from years of training the body and mind to do what every instinct implores you to run from. To me, it looks as if Stuart is achieving some kind of impossible, psychological perfection, and I yearn to do the same.

As a teen, Stuart would sit for hours on the mats in the north London dojo where he trained, soaking up the subtleties of movement as the more experienced fighters honed their skills. The masters could move with catlike speed, effortlessly leaping into hair-trigger spinning kicks with

---

* Stuart Lawson is a multiple world champion in kickboxing. On the international circuit, he is widely recognised as one of the most talented fighters ever to have come out of this country.

balletic yet ferocious grace. Stuart carefully watched how they could switch their styles for different purposes, how they would taunt and tease in order to arouse and exploit the reactions of their sparring partners. He learned the art of playful combat and created a joker-like fighting alter ego, which he later used to fool his opponents into underestimating him.

Nothing much else ever really interested Stuart before kickboxing. At school, his attention span was always limited. He quickly lost interest in the various short-lived jobs that he started. Even the nightly sessions of computer gaming that all of his friends loved so much failed to satisfy his distracted mind for long. But in the dojo he was consumed. He immersed himself completely into the world of fighting, and on those sweat- and blood-splattered mats, he learned not only what it meant to have purpose, but also what it felt like to belong.

When Stuart fought, he did so with a palpable sense of self-assurance. He could wriggle and dance his way out of almost any attack, and he would fearlessly drop his hands to bait the fighters he came up against. But no matter how confident his style made him appear, Stuart had to deal with all the same doubts as anyone else in the lead-up to a competition. Before every fight he would disappear into the venue toilets just to have a talk with himself. Standing in front of the grubby sports-hall mirrors, Stuart would stare into his own eyes in the hope that he could see the years of training behind them. Even towards the end of his career, after only a handful of losses in well over a hundred fights, Stuart still needed this ritual in order to reassure himself that he was capable of doing what he was about to do.

When he climbed through the ropes, however, any trace of those nerves evaporated. While actually in the act of fighting, his faith was unfaltering because he simply wasn't around to question it. By the moment Stuart's feet touched the canvas of the competition ring, 'he' was gone. Nothing but that beautiful, calm composure remained to do what was needed. The version of the man that won all those trophies and belts was more like an automaton; an unconscious accumulation of years of training representing themselves physically in an often near-perfect display of technique.

How was it that he could do this? He had faith in his body and all its training, and his body had faith in him. It was as if he and his unconscious self had made a pact in those reflective moments before the fight, and each of them knew their role. When the time came for action he said 'goodbye' to the captain and handed things over to the real boss.

But the really fascinating thing about Stu's story is that between rounds, when he sat and listened to those in his corner, the conscious doubting self would switch back on for a brief, incongruous moment. The first words from his mouth were always, 'Am I winning?'

---••---

Unconscious Flow

The relinquishing of (limited) conscious thought that my instructor used to access a state of flow is like the Holy Grail in sports. But flow is not just for athletes. It's what we all need to do most other things well, too. Whether you're getting the kids ready for school in the morning or working as a broker on the trading floor, you can function at a superior level when you give yourself over to an unencumbered unconscious mind (so long as you've been doing what you're attempting long enough for your mind to have access to the right information, that is; you can't just flow in an untrained area).

Mihaly Csikszentmihalyi, author of the seminal book, *Flow*, defined the elusive state as such:

A sense that one's skills are adequate to cope with the challenges at hand, in a goal-oriented, rule-bound action system that provides clear clues as to how well one is performing. Concentration is so intense that there is no attention left over to think about anything irrelevant, or to worry about problems. Self-consciousness disappears, and the sense of time becomes distorted. An activity that produces such experiences is so gratifying that people are willing to do it for its own sake, with little concern for what they will get out of it even when it is difficult, or dangerous.[4]

The key requirements of flow are that the task is challenging and absorbing enough to consume our attention entirely, but not so challenging that we lose confidence. Flow, therefore, exists in the sweet spot between complacency and anxiety. When we tap into it, the crew can take care of multiple things at once, acting instantaneously and accurately, without 'us' needing to give it a second (or even a first) thought.

Flow, in other words, is one of the positive 'hypnotic states' that we'd happily enter into given the choice. It's how we can find ourselves creating things we look back at and wonder where they came from. Perhaps more importantly, it's inherently enjoyable. The more flow moments we can make for ourselves, the happier our lives will be.

When we feel like the unconscious is nothing but the habitat of a meddling monster, though, we will intentionally deny ourselves of flow by striving for complete conscious control. But we already know that doesn't work. What we really want is the kind of magical balance that Stuart demonstrated whenever he climbed through the ropes; to be able to switch off our conscious thinking and flow while we're in action, but to turn it back on at the times when we want to reflect, calculate or make plans.

I'm sure that, just like everyone else, Stuart had his own self-sabotaging problems (I'm also sure that not every fight was as perfect as it looked to the rest of us). However, it seemed to me that he simply didn't let that unruly part of his mind interfere when he was trading blows, and the key was self-belief. Neither the captain nor the monster was at play while he competed because Stuart had developed a contract of trust between the conscious and unconscious mind.

I, on the other hand, experienced something entirely different for the majority of my time fighting. I'd spar for five rounds against a heavier and stronger male fighter at the gym without the faintest hint of doubt or hesitation, but as soon as the judges' eyes were on me, I'd crumble. Sometimes I tried to excuse this by telling myself that people like Stuart simply had experience on their side. At other times, I'd spiral into a pit of 'comparison shame', asking myself why everyone else seemed to find it so much easier than I did. Looking back, I can see that my unconscious self – my reactions, my body and its trained-in technical skill – would have been more than capable of flow, even back then. It was my lack of faith in those things that stood in the way.

What's blocking your flow?

This flow-impeding self-doubt isn't a phenomenon that exists only in the world of combat sports. We can get stage fright in all sorts of situations. You might recognise a similar contrast between the effortless conversation you can have with friends and the rambling nonsense you mutter around people you're attracted to; or the ease with which you can answer questions while studying at home and the mental blank that strikes during an exam.

In any case, a monster belief will likely be playing its part. When a battle between conscious and unconscious is consuming the mind, we will tend to fall short because it means that neither can dedicate itself to the task at hand. Instead, we experience a kind of psychological short circuit that can temporarily disable us at the worst possible moment. All of a sudden, rather than listening attentively to the person interviewing us for a job, we're tuned in to a horribly distracting inner monologue about our own inadequacy that can actually – very frustratingly – make us look a little bit inadequate. Disaster.

This chapter is about how we learn the limiting beliefs that can fuel our feelings of inferiority and prevent us from trusting the crew. To understand what our monsters are really made of, we need to look at the connection between fear, belief, striving and shame.

It starts with perhaps the most common of all human phobias: the fear of failure.

Fear of Being 'Not ... Enough'

The reason the flow state is so alluring is not just that it brings happiness, but also that it tends to come hand in hand with success. People who are capable of getting out of their own way can achieve great things. Some can accomplish the apparently impossible. Flow is behind any of the most spectacular physical performances; from ice skaters and gymnasts who seem to be able to fly to the Rubik's Cube world champion who can solve the puzzle blindfolded in under twenty seconds (*How?*). However, our lust for success is also, ironically, the main reason most of us struggle to get into flow.

This is a world in which we're taught to base our sense of worth largely on what we achieve. As a result, fear of failure has grown into a kind of psychological epidemic. In one form or another, this mental stumbling block tends to be at the heart of most of the problems people bring to therapy. It's not always about professional advancement or sporting accolades. The failure we fear could be personal, romantic, emotional, familial, social, physical, etc. We doubt ourselves when we get the sense that we aren't enough in some way; not good enough, nice enough or pretty enough ... not intelligent enough, strong enough or creative enough. We all have our own versions of 'not ... enough', and we're likely to struggle with more than one. Whatever the nuance, the more a fear of failure threatens to prevent us from achieving our most desired sense of identity, the more painful it will feel.

Of course, we all question ourselves from time to time and that's a good thing. Without a healthy amount of self-doubt, we'd be horribly narcissistic (or possibly dead). A little uncertainty can keep us in check; it preserves our humility and it motivates us to strive. However, it's when a doubt starts to loom too large that we can find ourselves repeatedly doing the things we wish we wouldn't, or avoiding the challenges we really ought to be taking on.

In other words, it's a fear of failure – in one form or another – that tends to cause us to self-sabotage. It has this power because even the most irrational fear has always been based on what we believe to be true.

Fear and belief: lifelong lovers

Here is something that's pretty intuitive, but rarely spelled out: fear necessitates belief. To be afraid of something, we have to believe in it.

Consider arachnophobia. For someone to be afraid of spiders, there has to be a part of them that genuinely believes spiders to be dangerous. Otherwise, their body wouldn't go to such lengths as to produce all that adrenaline in order to get them to a safe distance.

The same goes for a fear of failure. If we fear that we will fail, then a part of us must believe that we will. Or, when we choose not to do something (that really we would like to do) because we fear it might make us look selfish or stupid or weak, then that's because we believe that thing will expose the ugly 'truth'.

But negative self-beliefs are not the truth. This is important: beliefs are not the truth, they just *feel* like the truth. Most of the things we think we know about ourselves are mere ideas – perspectives – that we've picked up somewhere along the way and then filtered through enough 'evidence' for us to buy into them completely.

Belief determines action and action determines identity

*If the way we behave is driven by negative emotions, we end up with
the opposite of what we intend.*

Trevor Silvester,* *How to Click*

The inconvenient truth is that we often manifest what we fear about
ourselves. This means that our limiting beliefs function like self-fulfilling
prophecies because we tend to make real what we least want by keeping
it on our minds.

Have you ever wondered why it can be so much easier to avoid a slice
of chocolate cake in the fridge when you're *not* trying to diet than it is
when you have a beach holiday coming up? This is why: the harder we
try not to do something because it would threaten to verify a fear ('I'm too
fat to look good in my swimwear', or just, 'I'm unattractive'), the more
intensely we think about it. That means it occurs to us more frequently
and therefore has more chance of tempting us into doing what we don't
want to do: 'I shouldn't eat that cake because it'll make me even more fat.
I really shouldn't eat that big slice of chocolate cake. Don't eat the chocolate cake! Leave that juicy, sweet slice of cake alone! Mmmmm ... cake!'

Then, after we finally succumb, we're even more likely to beat ourselves
up about it and do it all over again: 'I knew I'd get even fatter. I *told*
myself not to eat that cake! I deserve every disgusted look I receive on
the beach. Ugh. I need some cake.'

The result is a self-fuelling cycle of fearful belief-strengthening that
goes like this:

1. The belief causes the fear.
2. The fear keeps the believed idea present in the mind.
3. The frequent fear-related thinking leads to corresponding behaviours.
4. Then, the behaviours back up the original fear, making it seem even
   more true and frightful ... And repeat.

I once spent an afternoon with someone I had secretly liked for years.
That day, for absolutely no good reason, I used a horrible swear word

* Founder of Quest Cognitive Hypnotherapy.

about five times over the course of an hour. I just couldn't stop myself from saying it even though, each time I did, I died a little bit on the inside. I'm no angel and I'm not afraid of the odd (well-placed) four-letter word, but this behaviour was pretty out of character and very unbecoming. Why did I choose that particular day to up the potty-mouth stakes? Because it gave me a very real-feeling reason not to bother asking him out. As the word slipped from my self-sabotaging lips for the fifth time, a little voice in my mind piped up and said: 'See? Now, you really aren't good enough for him. There's no point in even trying.' I happily stuck to that excuse for some time, because the very thought of asking for what I wanted was petrifying. And yes, the memory does still make me cringe.

Anxiety: fear in the future

When we project our fear-based beliefs out into our anticipated future we experience even more discomfort. Even though our bodies react to it as if the disaster is happening right now (sweaty palms, racing heart, etc.), anxiety is always fear of something that hasn't yet happened. Even when it's based on things that have already occurred, it's the consequences of those things that we continue to worry about.

Part of the problem is that when we project a negative belief out into the future we cannot challenge it because the future is, by definition, unknowable. In other words, the future makes our monsters even more scary.

But this is how the unconscious is really processing our fear:

'What if they don't like me when I ask them out?' = 'I'm not likeable'

'What if I fail the exam and look stupid?' = 'I'm stupid'

Future fear = Present belief

When we translate our fears into their corresponding present-tense forms, finding at least some evidence to the contrary becomes a far more achievable task. We just don't do that instinctively because we're so used to believing our beliefs, and that's usually because we've been doing it for a very long time.

Childhood Messages: Building Beliefs

We each have our own individual set of beliefs that define the world as we know it, and they are as unique as our fingerprints. Some are negative, others positive, but they are pretty much all a result of learned experience. There are some findings to suggest that memories could be passed down genetically, and even some to suggest that tissue received from organ donation could contain information about the donor's past. But in general, I would say that we don't come into this world believing that we're rubbish at maths, or that we are beautiful or lucky. These ideas develop as we accumulate experiences, especially during our earliest years.

If a parent, teacher, childhood peer, or simply our own interpretation of a certain event communicates that we're falling short in some way, then this message can get learned. Tell a child she can't do algebra enough times and she'll start to believe that it's true.

Limiting beliefs like 'I'm not good enough', 'I don't fit in', 'I'm worthless' or 'I'm stupid/ugly/unlovable' may seem extreme, but somewhat exaggerated conclusions are easy to arrive at when we are young because we think differently as children; the world is binary. Things are either very good or very bad; we're winners or we're losers; we're loved or we're unlovable.

Processing

In his studies on the cognitive development of children, Swiss educationalist Jean Piaget defined four stages through which children must pass before they acquire the rational capabilities of an adult:

Nominal processing: this is the completely binary stage. Put a child into a race at this point in his mental development and he'll only understand two potential outcomes: winning or losing.

Ordinal processing: at this stage, basic gradation becomes possible. Our little racer would now be able to comprehend second and third place, but it's still fairly limited.

Interval processing: here, the degree by which a ranking is achieved can be taken into consideration: 'I came second, Mummy. But it was really close!'

Ratio processing: only at this final stage – potentially as late as age twelve, according to Piaget's study – do children become capable of the type of processing we would expect from an adult. The self-judgements made at this level now take into consideration the individual's value systems: 'I lost the race, but it's not that important. I'd rather be in my drama class.'

Even though the exclusively binary thinking of nominal processing is something we can expect to grow out of relatively early, we're still capable of slipping back into that black-and-white world later in life. This is especially true when we're in the grip of a strong emotion like fear or anger. If you listen to the language of a tantrum-throwing teen (or even adult), you'll likely notice a fair few totalising statements. The daughter of one of my friends famously said, 'I hate *everyone* who doesn't wear DMs' (this was in the 1990s and she was sixteen). There was not a shred of irony in her voice. Unless you were wearing a pair of Doc Marten boots, she'd consider you a fundamentally evil human being and reserve only the bitterest of regard for you. We love to stick to our beliefs. Even when it seems laughable to others, we can be quite happy to delete, distort or generalise any evidence that might prove us wrong.

Piaget's theory could explain why it can be so easy to come to such absolute conclusions about ourselves while we're young. Couple his findings with the fact that as children we are so much more dependent on the love and support of other people (and will therefore want to impress them with an even greater sense of necessity), and it's easy to see how young children can exaggerate the importance of even the most insignificant-seeming occurrences. Just falling over in the playground could come under the heading of 'traumatic' for a five-year-old, given the right (or wrong) set of circumstances.

'It's all about me!'

Additionally, the mental skill of stepping out of the first person perspective and viewing the world through the eyes of another is also something we have to learn as we develop. While we're young, we take everything very personally. If something positive happens, we give ourselves a pat on the back. If something negative goes on, we'll question what we did to cause it. This is why children whose parents divorce relatively early in their lives often carry around a sense of responsibility for it. The message taken from an event like parental divorce could potentially be as damaging as: 'My parents broke up because *I am bad*' or 'My mum/

dad/other significant person left because *I am not enough* for them'.

Please note that I am not condemning anyone who goes through a divorce while their children are little. Equally, I am not blaming parents for seeming disappointed when their kids don't do so well because this is natural when we love and want the best for someone. There is simply no way to prevent a young mind from making damaging decisions. I believe that the most any parent can do is endeavour to make the best decisions with whatever they have at the time, and take care to let their children know that they are loved.

What all this means is that pretty much anything that happens early on in our lives can potentially twist itself into a limiting belief of some kind. Monsters do not only come about as a result of serious trauma; they're just a consequence of being human.

Resistance is Futile

Whatever you fight, you strengthen, and what you resist, persists.
Eckhart Tolle,* *A New Earth*

If someone told you that you're not good enough, what would be your instant reaction? Would you just accept their criticism as the absolute truth, or would you at least conduct an internal search for some evidence to the contrary? I think it's fair to say that we all have a bit of fight in us (although it can certainly wear thin over time). Even when we don't quite have the grit or the energy to battle back, we still wish that we could.

This is why the impoverished or struggling hero is such an archetypal figure. It's why so many people have watched films like *Rocky*, *Chariots of Fire*, *Good Will Hunting* and *The Shawshank Redemption*. We want to see the underdog succeed, and we love to watch a comparable other fighting tooth and nail to prove their worth because it's what we want to do for ourselves.

Alfred Adler, an early psychotherapist and contemporary of Sigmund Freud, theorised that to be a human being means to possess a feeling of inferiority. We acquire a sense of being 'less than' the moment we come

* Author of *The Power of Now*.

into the world and start comparing ourselves to our parents and older siblings in order to learn from them. And so, we're all familiar with the yearning to prove ourselves, and that will to fight is in us right from the beginning. Do we give up on our mission to learn how to walk the first time we fall over and get laughed at by an older brother? No, we climb to our feet and try again – with even more determination – until we get it. The same goes for all the other kinds of negative messages that we're exposed to while we're developing. We resist the damning indictments by striving back: 'No! I'll show you that I'm not a failure/stupid/lazy/unlovable/not good enough. Just look what I can do!'

Making the message into a monster

Although it might seem like the strong approach, continued and dogged resistance of our early negative messages only ends up fuelling the fire of our ongoing struggle. This is because 'what you resist persists'.

The twentieth-century psychiatrist and psychoanalyst, Carl Jung, recognised that patients who denied, hid from or tried to conceal the aspects of their personality that they least wanted to associate with would only ever find that those aspects endured, and often grew increasingly problematic as time went on. What this means is that in trying to overcome a negative belief by either battling with it or attempting to suppress it, we actually make the message feel even more true and painful.

It is resistance, therefore, that makes our childhood messages into monsters of the mind. We may attempt to disinherit our sense of being 'less than' by denying or ignoring the behaviours we least want to admit to (which is how we find ourselves saying 'I wasn't myself' or 'I don't know what came over me'). However, the more energy we put into fighting the part of our personality that believes the limiting messages from our childhood, the bigger and more repellent it will seem to us.

Our monsters, then, are the resisted aspects of our personality that we believe to be 'not … enough' in some way. Many people have an Achilles heel, but most of us will have more than one limiting belief, so our monsters are likely to know how to spin a few different stories to make us feel inadequate. No matter what they're trying to tell us, each time we fight back when they pipe up, we feed them with just what they need in order to grow stronger.

Shame Monsters

Another way of putting this is that our monsters are the aspects of our personalities that we feel ashamed of. We refuse to love, accept or even acknowledge them as a part of us because we've decided they're not fit for exhibition; not good enough for others to accept.

I should mention that shame doesn't need to be a dramatic emotional response, such as we might feel if we woke up next to someone other than our partner, or if we got caught for tax evasion. Shame is more widespread and pervasive than it would be if those were the only examples, and it occurs most commonly at a lower and more insidious level.

Shame is what we experience whenever we feel lesser or unworthy in any way. It's what irresponsible advertising causes us to feel about our bodies in order to encourage us to obtain things like diet pills, protein powders, breast augmentations or a penis extension, and it's what we experience when we're bullied, rejected, belittled or ignored. Shame is the emotional state that causes us to hide our 'dirty secrets' about failure, illness, addiction, earnings, sexual desire, etc.

Psychologist and shame expert, Brené Brown, says that we all experience this destructive emotional state. She describes it like this: 'Shame is the fear of disconnection – it's the fear that something we've done or failed to do, an ideal that we've not lived up to, or a goal that we've not accomplished makes us unworthy of connection.'[5]

'Unworthy of connection'. That's the kicker. We experience shame on some level whenever our most painful self-beliefs are triggered because those are the things that make us feel as though we're somehow unworthy of other people's love, time, respect or admiration. When they fire up, we get drawn into an inner word of hidden anxiety, which makes us feel even more alien, even more 'not ... enough'.

The thing is that it's only painful when our limiting beliefs are made to look true because we reflect them off other people. Would an idea like 'I'm ugly' or 'I'm stupid' be that uncomfortable if the person believing it was the only human being on the planet? No, of course not. We couldn't even entertain those ideas without other people to compare ourselves to. The limiting self-beliefs that hurt us the most do so because the mind adds an invisible extra bit on the end: 'I'm stupid ... *and that means* I'm not worthy of other people's connection'; 'I'm ugly ... *and that means* I'm nothing next to the competition'. It's the last bit – the part that flies under that radar – that stings enough for us to want to fight our monsters' stories with any resource we have available. And there are many options.

In order to block the punch thrown by a shame monster we might start to do things like blame our failings on other people, pretend they didn't happen, drink them away, numb them with 'comfort food' or fight against them with persistent, self-absorbed success-seeking. All of these resistance strategies are things that can quite easily make us feel even less worthy than we already did. No matter how we try to battle the feeling of shame, we never win because you cannot defeat yourself and then emerge victorious. Instead, we end up with ever-growing mental demons; dark and shadowy aspects of the self that we're too afraid to go anywhere near and so feel as if we need to sever and leave for dead ... which makes them even more monstrous.

The alternative is not submission, however. It's not that we just have to get to a certain age and then resign ourselves to the fact that we really aren't good enough, after all (far from it!). The solution to a shame monster is acceptance, rather than submission. We need to learn how to invite these parts back. But that doesn't mean we just have to live with our self-sabotaging behaviours. We don't. When we can integrate our monsters back into the whole, we can control them, rather than the other way around. It's just that before we get to that stage, we have to somehow (re)humanise them.

Jane's eating monster

Jane was a serial yoyo dieter. When we first met, she was approximately 25 kilograms overweight and bit her fingernails mercilessly whenever she was under pressure.

Like many people, Jane sought praise for the things she did in order to feel that she was good enough, but even when she got that praise, she could never truly allow herself to believe in it. In fact, whenever she received external affirmation of her ability – even in the form of a simple compliment – she'd feel awkward and shameful about it.

Jane's preferred weapon of resistance was food. Whenever her shame was triggered, she would find herself mindlessly eating out of an open fridge or wandering into the local shop to buy chocolate. If food wasn't available, she would compulsively bite her nails. When we worked on the memory associated with her lingering sense of 'not good enough', Jane remembered a day from around the age of seven when she was praised at school for a piece of work she wasn't the sole author of. At the time she had felt like a 'con artist' when she got her gold star, and even though this happened when she was so little, decades later she still squirmed at the very thought of it.

Jane's monster believed that she didn't deserve praise and it told her stories about her unworthiness at every given opportunity. Along the way, she had learned to use food as a means to numb the emotional pain she'd been carrying around ever since that time. However, as the weight continued to pile on, her self-loathing only grew stronger.

Awareness of where it all began meant that Jane could let go of both the painful emotion ('not good enough') and the resistance (overeating) by accepting the part of her personality that she had once believed to be unworthy. That little girl who copied someone else's work in order to feel a sense of achievement was far from monstrous. Jane only needed to see the situation through adult eyes to know this to be the reality.

I should mention that there were other contributing factors. It would be unlikely that this kind of reaction would persist had everything else in Jane's childhood been absolutely perfect. However, it did not take that much focus on the surrounding issues before she could make the all-important initial shift, and the result was that she could gradually begin redefining her relationship with food, success and, ultimately, with herself.

Within two months of her first session, Jane had already lost 15 kilograms. When she arrived at my office that day, she looked like a different person – not just because she had lost weight or because she was wearing new clothes, but because she was glowing. Her posture had changed, she was smiling more and she radiated enthusiasm and vibrancy. Jane had been taking loving care of herself and, as a result, she looked altogether more whole.

The Plight of the Overachiever

Numbing or denying shame with things like food, drink, drugs, gambling or procrastination is not the only way we fight our monsters. Someone who too aggressively resists a negative belief like 'I'm not good enough' is likely to become an 'overachiever'. This, of course, is a curious term, because anyone who fits that description would almost certainly tell you that *over*achieving is not a possibility. In this mindset, nothing is ever enough. Let me explain why.

In order to resist a feeling of being 'less than', the overachiever will strive to do anything they can to disprove their limiting beliefs. They may well perform pretty highly as a result of this decision, perhaps getting the best grades in school or winning at sports. They could even grow up to publish a bestseller or win a Nobel Prize. But because the message has already been incorporated as a truth, these attempts fail to do what they are intended to do. In fact, they are destined only to increase the underlying feelings of fraudulence and inferiority because, as the successes get bigger, so does the beast that follows behind them. The result is continual disappointment and a growing sense of shame.

While we're fighting any kind of 'I'm not ... enough' belief with achieve-ment, we'll go through the same pattern over and over again. We hopefully latch onto an endless stream of goals thinking something like this: 'I'm not (...) enough right now, but if I can just do/win/achieve/get that next thing, *then* I will be.' The 'do/win/achieve/get' could be a title, a partner, a bigger friendship group, a thinner or a more muscly body, a qualification, a sports car – anything that we set our sights on as the *one thing* we need before we will feel 'enough'.

However, each goal promises to negate the belief only until it has been achieved, at which point we sadly recognise that the old and painful message still feels true, and so we discount the victory and look for the next big win. It means that while caught in this pattern, no matter what we do, we'll never really feel as if we are where we want to be. So long as the negative message continues to rattle around in our minds, the shame inspired by our sense of lack will persist – and the more we try to fight it, the more monstrous the part that we see as 'not ... enough' will become.

This was what was going on for me when I hung my head each time I won a fight. Although I yearned for the win in order to prove my monster wrong, even when the decision went my way, it still sang the same defeatist little song: 'Nope. Still not good enough.' Regardless of how impressive the titles I won looked on paper, all I would think about afterwards was how I could have done better. My monster made sure that I didn't allow myself a single moment to enjoy my achievement – because getting too close to success is dangerous when you don't believe that you deserve it. So, instead of celebrating happily, the next day I'd be back in the gym grinding my body to the bone and telling myself consciously that I'd get a 'real' win the next time.

Monster Summary

Because the connection between fear, belief, shame and resistance is all a little cyclical, here's a summary of what we've covered in this chapter.

We learn our most painful limiting beliefs during our childhood because at that stage in life we automatically exaggerate the meaning of things (black-and-white processing) and then take it all very personally ('It's all about me!'). Once we've internalised a negative message and adopted it as a belief, we'll want to avoid anything that threatens to make that self-judgement seem any more true. This is when the limiting belief becomes a fear.

What we're calling the monster is the part of our personality that we connect with those painful self-beliefs; it's the part that we see as 'not ... enough'. Because, deep down, we feel as if our perceived limitations make us unfit for connection, we resist that aspect of self by either fighting or denying it. We try to cover it up with falseness, achieve it away, drink it into submission, numb it with drugs, hide it by making everyone else happy or improve it by making ourselves thinner, stronger, more beautiful, better qualified or more cool, etc. We will do anything we can to protect ourselves from the prospect of exposing our shame-inspiring traits, but because 'what you resist persists', this only makes matters worse.

Fighting against our monsters results in self-sabotage because the monster *is* the self. To take control, what we actually need to do is accept the resisted parts of our personality back into the whole. Because acceptance begins with understanding, in the next chapter you're going to get to know your monster a little better by taking a look at the types of self-sabotage it most likes to inspire, and where it may have first learned its limiting beliefs.

3

The (Dis)Comfort Zone

The Siren Song of the Familiar

It's been a long week in this stuffy, Spanish arena. The England team consists of thirty-odd fighters from different disciplines: light-continuous and full-contact kickboxing, MMA and all the non-contact martial arts categories. Everything is taking place in one vast room, which has been decorated with the national flags of all the competing countries, and, if I'm honest, nothing much else. It's cavernous, echoing and intimidating.

Whenever a team member gets called to compete, we're gifted a brief interlude of energy and enthusiasm – a much-needed respite from the nervous tedium of waiting to fight. Today is the final day of this world championship competition. I won my first gold medal in the light-continuous category earlier today, but I put my elation on ice until after the big event. Now it's time for me to step up and into the full-contact ring to see if I can make it a double victory.

Round one is tough. My opponent is strong and I spend more time on the back foot than I would like. In round two, however, I seem to be gaining some ground and, about thirty seconds before the bell is due to sound, I launch forward with a side kick aimed at the Spanish fighter's chin. In the stands behind her I can just make out the red-and-white tracksuits of the England team and, as the shot lands flush, their encouragement crescendos. With my opponent now pinned against the ropes, I move in closer to throw some punches and, peeking out from between my gloves, I think I can see a trace of defeat in her eyes. Yes. I know that look. I've felt that way. 'Just one final push', I think to myself, 'and I'll have done what I need for the glory of the gold.' Sure enough, as my right hand connects, her arms go limp and she turns away, causing the referee to step in and call it. The title is mine.

Afterwards, I grin dutifully for photos and I gratefully receive the hugs, high fives and compliments that come my way, but something is missing. Behind my smile there's nothing much more than a flat sense of relief that

I didn't lose. Later, once the adrenaline has worn off and the Champagne has been opened, I hope that phoning home will trigger my jubilation. Yet, something even feels uncomfortable about making the call. I don't know how to say the words when I'm not relishing the pride that they'll expect, and I don't want to expose my distasteful lack of gratitude. So, I opt to send a text message instead. That way, they won't be able to hear the inglorious lie in my voice when I try to feign a feeling of accomplishment.

At night, I lie staring at the ceiling of the hotel room, while I repeat the two finals over and over in my mind. I'm desperately searching for something to feel proud of. Yet, aside from a couple of shots that I can say were OK, the overriding sense is one of disappointment and deflation. And worse, what's creeping up behind all of that is a familiar old feeling of shame. Two world titles in one day and I still haven't done enough to fight it off. I'm not sure how much more I have in me.

'Live-wire' Memories

In therapy, we call the events that cause children to come to magnified conclusions about themselves 'significant emotional events'. But they don't need to be any more dramatic than tripping over in the school nativity play or getting told off for drawing on the walls, because those things are significant to a child.

As we develop, the unconscious mind carefully holds onto copies of the important moments so that it's able to instantly recognise anything similar in the future. I call these memories 'live-wires'; they're like charged mental bubbles of sounds, sights, tastes, smells, associations and unbearable messages. We hold them true in our unconscious, and we keep them alive, present, accessible and full of all the appropriate emotions, so that we don't forget the important lessons they taught us.

It is the same process that causes any phobic reaction. If a child encounters what they believe to be a dangerous spider, then their unconscious will memorise (immortalise) that spider, along with the belief that 'spiders are dangerous', so that it knows to steer clear of anything else that's even remotely similar ... just in case.

This is how all of our more personal limiting beliefs are formed as well: something uncomfortable happens when we're young, the meaning of which we exaggerate (thanks to our limited processing); the message that we take from it becomes all about us ('I'm bad', 'I'm wrong', 'I'm stupid', 'I'm not safe', 'I'm not ... enough'); and, worst of all, because that message is kept alive by the live-wire memory, it continues to feel true every time anything reminds us of it. Ouch.

Problems are just failing solutions

The reason our live-wire memories are so fiercely protected is that the mind thinks they contain important, life-saving information. If we return to the spider phobia example, whenever our arachnophobe comes across a scarily spider-like thing, their mind will cause them to psychologically regress to the significant moment in order to remember how they survived the threat the first time. This usually goes on outside of conscious awareness, but we all do it. We jump right back inside the frightful bubbles of our live-wire memories whenever they're triggered because the mind thinks that they contain the solution to the problem. Unfortunately, the way we dealt with a seemingly life-threatening spider when we were five is unlikely to be the way we would like to deal with a money spider on our work desk at the age of thirty-five. Yet, the conscientious unconscious mind lumps those two scenarios together nonetheless: 'This looks like a dangerous thing. How did we deal with it before? Oh yes, we yelped and flew into the arms of the nearest adult. Right-oh!'

And so, while consciously we might call our unconscious reaction a 'problem', the unconscious is intentionally choosing that response because it thinks of it as the best way to stay alive. This is pretty easy to understand when we're talking about a spider phobia. It's less so when we consider things like public speaking. But fear is fear to the unconscious. We evolved the 'fight-or-flight' response – the automatic reaction to fear that readies us to either fight or flee – to deal with life-or-death situations. These days, even though the risk of death is not that often on the table when we get nervous, anything that we find scary still gets registered as if it poses such a threat. We see a large audience, an exam hall or someone we fancy, and our heart begins to race, our breathing quickens and our hands sweat. When that happens, the mind triggers an instantaneous memory check to find the relevant live-wire solution. If we dealt with challenge by hiding as a child, then we're likely to retreat as an adult. If we found solace in Granny's cupcakes after being bullied at school, then we might turn to food when we feel threatened as an adult at work.

Of course, there will be positive memories in the mix as well. However, seeing as the good times feel less important to a survival-focused system like the unconscious mind, their effects can be easily overwhelmed by the fearful or angry recollections. Ultimately, even though all of our most important early events define what's normal for us by creating our map of personalised beliefs to live by, the mind will pay more attention to the ones it thinks will keep us alive than those that could make us happy.

Generalisation

The continuing problem is that the more worried we become about triggering our live-wire memories and making true what we least want to be true, the more we look out for things that could spell trouble. If what started as a fear of our primary-school maths class remained a fear of that particular situation, then it wouldn't cause much of a problem after a certain age, but that is not how it works. Failure is an expert shape-shifter. Almost anything can look like a chance to fail if the mind is dead set on seeing it. Furthermore, almost anything we have already done can be interpreted as failure, even when it looked like success to anyone else. So, as if our self-sabotaging behaviours were not disheartening enough, our ultra-cautious unconscious mind starts finding new triggers for our fear all over the place, and the more it finds, the more pain it feels and the harder it searches for even more to avoid. The problem fuels itself.

What's actually going on here is that the stimulus (the thing that triggers the memory of the live-wire) is generalising, and can even jump from one thing to the next. Imagine someone with a phobia of spiders finding one in a dark corner and then beginning to fear any other poorly lit spaces, just in case they too might harbour *dangerous arachnids*. All of a sudden, a spider phobia has grown into a fear of sheds and cupboards as well, which isn't often considered a good look for an adult! It could be pretty demoralising to have to ask your partner to fetch the peanut butter because it's right at the back of the scary kitchen cabinet. And so, over time and with repetition, something that started out fairly contained could feasibly mutate into a full-scale identity complex.

If we apply this to the (probably more common) maths-class example, what starts with 'I'm a failure in maths class' can become, 'I'm a failure when I try to do anything with numbers'. And then later, after struggling with a spreadsheet in front of the boss, just the thought of going to work could trigger fear and a feeling of inadequacy.

This is why we call them 'limiting' beliefs. Even a mild anxiety about going to work could greatly restrict a person's chances of having a successful career and even a happy life. If you ask me, there are better things to do with a Sunday than sit and worry about what's going to happen at the office the next day.

What generalisation can mean is that if you can't think of any memory that could possibly lie at the heart of your self-sabotaging issue(s), it could be because the stimulus has disguised itself. Without being given a means to make the connection, I'm sure that Jane from the previous chapter (see pages 59–60) would have had no idea that her fraudulent gold-star moment could have been the genesis of her binge-eating problem. (In Part 3 of this book, I will walk you through a process designed to help you identify and reframe your live-wire moments, so if nothing seems obvious yet, please don't worry.)

Generalisation can also mean that seeds sown early on can grow into problems that we aren't even aware of until decades later. Most of my clients are in their thirties and forties, and they'll often describe a happy childhood and a confident life up until a few years before our meeting. Monsters can seem to come out of nowhere, when really they've been lying in wait and gathering their destructive power gradually, just outside of our conscious awareness.

Welcome to the (Dis)Comfort Zone

When resisting a live-wire message of any kind, it's as if there's an invisible barrier above us, which determines the maximum amount of success or contentment that we're allowed to have. Transcending that barrier would mean wandering into the previously unknown territory of feeling genuinely, wholeheartedly accomplished or happy or loved, etc. It's like a self-imposed glass ceiling. Break through that glass and we can prove our limiting beliefs wrong, let go of all the shame they generate and fully accept that we are OK as we are.

"(...) enough"

·· GLASS CEILING ···

"Not (...) enough"

Sounds good, right? And it's possible. It's just that we can't simply punch our way through as I tried to do when I started fighting. To breathe the fresh air on the other side, we must first convince the unconscious mind that it is safe to let go of our monsters' stories.

Because the function of the live-wire memories that protect our limiting beliefs is to keep us alive, the unconscious mind is very reluctant to let them go. As a result, it will intentionally sabotage any achievement that might threaten to shatter the glass and burst our old belief bubbles. Then, we can find that we experience what one of my clients once referred to as the 'nearly-there effect': every time we feel as though we might just be getting to where we want to be, we find something to do to screw it all up. If we've always believed that we're stupid, then it will seem safer to fail the exam than to wander into the uncharted territories of 'not stupid'. Or, if we've always seen ourselves as the class clown, then the unconscious could be quite happy to pipe up with a stupid remark mid-meeting, even though we invariably look back on that comment and realise we made ourselves look irresponsible and foolish (again).

Just like landing on a snake in Snakes and Ladders, our moments of self-sabotage cause us to slide right back down into 'failure' territory once more, all because that's where the unconscious mind feels like it knows what to do.

It's not only the obvious, behavioural slip-ups that fall into this category of self-sabotage. The mind can also drag us down just by creating a failure-themed reality map for us to worry about. The night of my world title wins in Spain, my monster found a way of depriving me of any sense of pride – even though I had emerged victorious from two battles that day – just because it felt comfortable when I felt inferior.

(Dis)comfort

What this means is that the unconscious mind's comfort zone can feel decidedly *un*comfortable to the conscious mind. Because the height of the ceiling is defined by the beliefs and behaviours we learn during our formative years, even with zero phobias and the happiest of upbringings, we could be quite seriously limited by having to live in accordance with our childhood rules.

Ultimately, life below the glass is not comfortable because consciously we want growth. We don't just want more of the same; we want to explore novel things and reach new heights. And so, the world carefully preserved by a fearful unconscious mind feels much more like (dis)comfort than happy familiarity. No matter how many times we rally ourselves to fight our way out, we tend only to gravitate back into that zone, over and over again, because our minds think we're better equipped to protect ourselves there. And of course, each time we slide back down into 'not ... enough' territory, we recharge our desire to fight (and therefore fuel) our shameful monsters of the mind all over again.

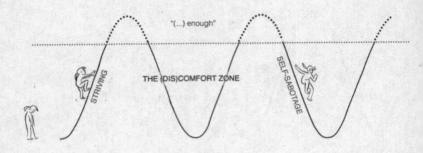

And so it goes on. It is the psychological pattern at work for anyone who yoyo diets, who goes in and out of rehab, who frequently sabotages their relationships or their career, etc. A client of mine put it wonderfully a few years ago. She said that she feels as if she rides the thrill of motivation to succeed as if surfing a wave, but just when the beach is within touching distance, that same wave drags her back out to sea.

Second-place syndrome

Alan is a three-time Olympian from New Zealand. He had been sporty all his life, starting out as a track-and-field athlete and then moving into winter sports to compete at the top level in his twenties. When we connected, he was aiming to get back into competition after retirement to race at a bobsled Masters event in Austria.

We discussed the glass-ceiling concept in session one, and as I explained the 'nearly-there' effect, his eyes widened. Alan had a far greater collection of silver medals than would seem likely to be the result of coincidence. He started reeling off a list of second-place awards that dated back to his teens: 'I was second in the North Island Champs at fifteen. Then I was second at the Auckland Championships in sixth form. Then I went to the nationals and won four different silver medals. As a senior, my best result was a silver medal in triple jump. Then I had a really bad weekend at the Commonwealth Games qualifiers and failed to make it. After that I transferred to bobsled. When we qualified for the Olympics in 2006, we did so by coming second in both qualifying races – to teams that, on paper, we really should have beaten.

Then I either screwed up or crashed uncharacteristically in every Olympic race I had ...'

It seemed that 'nearly there' was the upper limit of Alan's (dis)comfort zone. What he wanted more than anything was to break through the glass and taste the gold. However, when that finally happened, it was not as he expected. Alan and his teammate came first in the two-man bobsled on the North American Cup Circuit in 2005 (which, incidentally, meant that his team finished in second place overall for that event). Rather than the jubilation he had hoped for, as he looked up at the scoreboard and saw that he'd finally come in first, he felt sad to the point of tears. The rare win delivered nothing but a profound feeling of emptiness.

There was another, more subtle, psychological issue that stood in the way of Alan's sense of achievement as well. Throughout his entire career, he had never been able to remember his races until he was back on the track again. As soon as the work was over, his recollection of how he drove the sled (successfully or unsuccessfully) would vanish from his mind. It meant making improvements for second runs a difficult task and his amnesia perplexed his coaches. This is not actually an unusual phenomenon because memory is state specific. When a feeling like fear is very strong, we can sometimes find that we will not remember what we experienced while in that state until the next time we're feeling similarly afraid. However, as normal as it is, Alan grieved for all the races he had forgotten.

With the Masters event coming up, he wanted to make sure his monster didn't sabotage this late opportunity to enjoy his sport. The gold medal was unrealistic this time because he was entering the competition with two friends who were novices in the sport. His real aim was to have fun, and he was determined to hold onto his experience of driving the sled when he walked away afterwards.

In order that he might achieve these aims, we worked on the limiting belief: 'I'm an underachiever.' (That a three-time Olympian should hold this particular belief is a great example of just how untrue our monster stories can be.) The goal here was to reduce the threat level. Driving a bobsled down a tunnel of ice at 70 mph is unlikely to be an entirely calm experience, but the arousal added by his fear of failure was something that could be addressed.

We used techniques similar to those you'll learn in this book to make 'I'm an underachiever' feel less like the absolute truth. Then, before the race, Alan took control by repeating carefully constructed visualisations of the correct way to take a famously difficult corner on the track (a corner that he'd crashed on earlier in his career), and he listened religiously to the recordings that I made for him during his sessions to keep his nerves at the minimum level.

The result was that he performed better than ever before but, perhaps more importantly, he enjoyed and remembered the experience. When he messaged me after the competition, he gave me a detailed description of exactly how well he'd driven. He could recall the individual corners and how he had negotiated the particularly difficult bend that had scuppered the dreams of so many athletes before. The team may not have won the race that day, but they didn't have to for Alan to claim the real prize of finally *feeling* like the skilled and worthy athlete that he so clearly is. Furthermore, thanks to his new and more lucid mental state for competition, he will always be able to remember that feeling.

~~Pride~~ Happiness Comes Before a Fall

It's important to know that the mind will not always pick the most obvious way to self-sabotage. The (dis)comfort zone spans across all the different contexts of our lives: career, relationships, health, hobbies, etc. So, just because we're striving at work does not necessarily mean we will sabotage our professional life in order to sink back down into (dis)comfort. Our monsters can be much more sneaky than that.

When I ask my clients what was going on in their lives just before they tripped themselves up, they'll often think back and realise that things had been going pretty well up until that point. Perhaps they had just found the perfect romantic partner before their health failed; or maybe they had just been given the promotion they wanted before they developed a serious case of the yips to derail their golf game. It's as if the (dis)comfort zone comes with an overall emotional standard that the mind feels it ought to regulate – like a kind of psychological homeostasis. And so, no matter which part of our lives the mind chooses to moderate, the end result tends to be the same: our general sense of happiness is kept at the same (dis)comfortable level that our minds feel to be the safest.

Everyday tickets to the (dis)comfort zone

This means that it is not only the dramatic slip-ups that we need to look out for. Literally every moment of every day, the unconscious mind will strive to keep things (dis)comfortable. For example, to the chronic worrier, anxiety is the norm. You could give them the most perfect day – a picnic in the park with their best friends and ideal weather – and they would still find a way to worry about whether the strawberries they brought are nice enough. This is not just them being difficult; it's the version of reality that their mind feels is safest to navigate.

I'd like to highlight four of the most common ways that our monsters like to keep us in our respective (dis)comfort zones, so you can start catching even the most understated forms of self-sabotage.

Comparison ('compare and despair')

Comparing ourselves to other people is a sure-fire way to limit our sense of worth. If 'less than' is your norm, self-comparison could be one of your mind's go-to ways to self-sabotage. There will always be someone who is doing something better than we are. It's a simple matter of mathematics. Rating ourselves in relation to others only ever leads to unwelcome conclusions about our ability or value. Even when we think we 'win' the comparison game, the fact that we chose to play it in the first place means that we're feeding the part of the mind that questions our worth.

Many of the clients I see who struggle with body-image issues will admit to a destructive social-media addiction. They know full well that scrolling through image after image of glistening fitness selfies is pointlessly painful. Yet, they find it remarkably difficult to quit because the siren song of the (dis)comfort monster is just too strong, and comparing themselves to dehydrated and half-starved effigies of perfection helps them to stay in the agonising position of 'less than'.

Worry and anxiety

Worry, as discussed, can make sour strawberries out of any picnic. This self-sabotage hijacks our awareness, prevents us from seeing real solutions and it gives undue power to the external things we feel to be harmful by depriving us of a feeling of control. Of course, worry is useful on some occasions, but only when it highlights the things we can actually do something about (and when we take action). However, if the object of our anxiety is something that we can do nothing about, then that worry serves no function beyond self-harm.

Anger, blame and complaining

We tend to think that deflecting blame away from ourselves will make us feel better, but in the long run it does nothing of the sort. There are times when anger is justified and even useful but, just as with worry, this is only the case if we are actually going to take responsible (rather than vindictive) action. Otherwise, those emotions can fester and stagnate in the mind, and while they do, they'll block us from feeling anything more positive. Resentment is just another way of souring the strawberries. So, by all means, offer constructive criticism to the person who needs to hear it, but complaining to a third party or stewing over other people's wrong-doings while you lie awake at night will usually only ever drag you back down into (dis)comfort.

People-pleasing

By 'people-pleasing' I don't mean helping others. That's very different. People-pleasing means consistently putting the needs, wants and import-ance of others before our own at times when it is not entirely necessary. When it begins, this trait fools us into thinking we're just 'being nice'. However, if – when we bolster another person's ego, or even help them out in a time of hardship – our efforts to please continually have the opposite effect on us, then we are sabotaging ourselves. I'm not advo-cating selfishness, nor justifying only ever acting out of self-interest. The difference comes down to boundaries. If an act of love, assistance or support is made in a healthy way, then it will inflict minimal burden on the giver and, ultimately, bring them a larger amount of good feeling as a result. People-pleasers don't get this benefit because every bit of self-compromising help they hand out will chip a little more away from their own sense of worth, ultimately causing them to feel resentful of those who profit from their efforts.

The reason I mention the above is that most of us don't think of these things in terms of self-sabotage. We're more inclined to consider them inconvenient facts of life. However, we need to recognise these behaviours as *self*-sabotages in order to remember that we're the ones who have control over them. I sometimes give clients the task of spending two hours of their day with a notepad, tallying up the number of times their mind chooses to dampen their experience for no other reason than to keep them at a familiar level of dissatisfaction. For the most prolific self-saboteurs, this can occasionally mean that they spend more time writing in the pad than doing anything else. Granted, it's not the most enjoyable task, but it can be effective in highlighting the amount of time, energy and potential positivity wasted by giving in to the mind's love affair with sameness.

Lifting the Lid on Your Beliefs

We've covered a lot of theory. It's time for a little practical application. By challenging and updating our limiting beliefs we can expand the (dis) comfort zone into something more exciting, loving, creative, successful, adventurous or whatever it is that we want more of in life. The key is to look objectively at the things that hold us back. In doing this, our personal acts of self-sabotage can be used as the gateways to an improved standard of life because they give us access to the ideas that motivate them. Step one is to know them.

Challenging the norm

You may already have a good idea of what your main monster stories are likely to be. However, it's not only the 'negative' beliefs that deserve some attention. When I ask my clients to make a note of what they notice going through their minds between sessions, some find that obviously destructive thoughts like 'I can't do that because I'm not good enough' hold them back the most. Others, however, find that it's their seemingly positive self-beliefs that tend to stop them taking the risks that could ultimately benefit them: 'I shouldn't do that because I'm an intelligent person and intelligent people don't dance on table tops with all their friends'.

The totality of ideas that we absorb over the course of our lives – beliefs about ourselves and about others; ideas of what women are supposed to be like and how men are supposed to be; beliefs about relationships, about emotions, about what is important, about what's possible and about what we should or shouldn't do – all come together to define the version of reality that we call 'life' and the cluster of habits that we call 'me'.

Task: Taking the Tour

An easy way to begin getting an idea of the beliefs that make up your (dis)comfort zone is to imagine taking a tour of your childhood world. If you bring to mind a mental image of the house you grew up in (preferably between the ages of three and seven), you will find that certain memories float into your awareness. Some will likely be happy memories, others might be sad, lonely or scary – but all the events that you can remember (and probably some that you can't) will play some part in determining your sense of self and what seems comfortable to your unconscious mind.

Here's how to take a tour of your childhood world:

Imagine walking slowly through all the rooms and other areas (indoors and out). In each different space, pause and ask yourself these questions:

'What do I remember happening here?'

'What could these moments have taught me about myself?'

'What did I learn about the world/other people here?'

Write down anything that comes to mind for each location, not forgetting the less obvious places like hallways, bathrooms and outdoor spaces. When you've taken the tour of your home, consider visiting your school(s) and the houses of your friends and other family members as well. Give yourself a couple of minutes to do that. I'll wait.

––––––––●●––––––––

What you find

You're likely to remember moments that could have influenced your feelings of capability; your expectations in terms of physical health; your most familiar emotional states (and those of others); and your values, morals and other ideas about what you should and shouldn't do.

You may notice relationship patterns that have since repeated. Did you have a close, affectionate connection to your parents or other caregivers or were they angry, critical or abusive? How about your siblings, friends or your teachers? Were there any particular situations or activities that were out of bounds while you grew up? Was it OK for you to freely express emotions like sadness or anger? Was it OK for you to ask questions about sexuality? How was conflict dealt with?

The way our adult relationships play out – with life partners, friends, colleagues, bosses, etc. – is often a matter of (dis)comfort zone information. Those who had loving parents are likely to expect, and therefore perceive, more love in relationships when they're older. (This is not an absolute rule, of course; there are always going to be other factors to consider.) Conversely – and again, this is not a given – those who felt detached from their parents are more likely to encounter a similar feeling of disconnection in their adult partnerships. In these cases, it could be that the unconscious has deliberately sought out a partner who feels (dis)comfortably familiar. If their childhood guardians were emotionally unavailable due to alcoholism, for example, then they could find themselves dating someone with a similar dissociative issue, even though, consciously, they strove to seek out the opposite. Even when the partner does not have a substance habit, the disconnection could be repeated by finding someone who works too much or just struggles with commitment.

Making the unconscious conscious

Although all of our memories and beliefs will potentially influence our behaviour, it's the least conscious ones that tend to have the greatest impact. This is because when we are unaware of where an urge comes from, we take it as an objective truth. What the above exercise can do is help you to make conscious the unconscious. When we know that we do or don't want to do something simply because it does or doesn't fit with our original map for 'me', then new possibilities can open up. We can choose a different behaviour just for the sake of change. We can say 'no' to things we'd usually do without thinking and we can say 'yes' to novelty.

This is made easier when we have an idea of where we learned the limiting pattern in the first place.

If, while taking the tour of your childhood home, you remembered a particular moment that could be making your adult life feel like a broken record, then you'll have the chance to rewrite that section of your reality map in Part 3 (see page 319). However, you might not have to leave it any longer before you can effect some change using that information.

When I first started writing this book, I told a number of people that I was most nervous about the anecdotal sections because 'I'm not good at creative writing'. It wasn't until I'd said this about three or four times that I actually heard myself and thought, 'Oh! That's a limiting belief!' With that realisation came the memory of some particularly damning criticism from an early English teacher. I had found a live-wire. However, I didn't need to do any 'work' on it because just linking the belief to the memory made sense of my unwarranted anxiety. From that point forward, I found that the more creative passages in this book became the most enjoyable and rewarding, not least because they gave me an opportunity to learn a new skill.

Task: Rewriting the Future

I'm choosing happiness over suffering, I know I am. I'm making space
for the unknown future to fill up my life with yet-to-come surprises.
Elizabeth Gilbert, *Eat, Pray, Love*

Take a look at what you found while taking your tour and ask yourself whether old messages you recognised might still be playing a (dis)comfortable part in your life now which feel linked to the self-sabotage(s) that you're focusing on — stories that your monster still likes to tell? Pick the most uncomfortable or defining story and answer this question:

If someone came along and removed that belief from your mind while you were sleeping, how would you know as the following days went by that it had happened?

To give your unconscious a new map for the changes you're going to make, I'd like you to put together a list of the differences you'd most like to notice in your life as things improve. There's one rule: be sure to *state all of the details in the positive*, rather than the negative. Remember how much more likely you would be to eat the chocolate cake in the fridge if you kept telling yourself *not* to? The same goes for any other kind of self-sabotage. If you resist the problem by telling yourself *not* to fail, *not* to overeat, *not* to watch an entire season of *Orange Is the New Black* when you should be revising for an exam, then you're just stoking the fires for the impending self-sabotage. It's time to turn your attention away from the problem and onto the solution.

So, instead of saying 'I wouldn't be anxious' or 'I wouldn't be over-eating', what you want to consider is what you *would* be thinking, feeling or doing if those problematic things were not happening. This sounds simple, but it can be quite challenging because we're simply not used to looking beyond the limits of the (dis)comfort zone, and that's precisely why it's so important to make the effort.

Let your list include anything you'd like to see more of in your life as a result of having let go of the old negative belief(s). What would you be able to enjoy more? What would become easier? What might you get better at?

Take a couple of minutes to write down anything that you can think of.

Visualising

Next, I'd like you to visualise this new version of yourself going about your life. Note that this is meant to be the you that you are now, just with a different set of beliefs. It's not about seeing a future version of yourself who has already made everything perfect (the importance of this will become clear over the next two chapters). See yourself as if you're playing the lead role in a film about the gradual improvement of your life. Watch the ways in which you'd begin to behave differently and the new types of interactions you'd be able to enjoy more. Notice your positive body language, your tone of voice and the other things you can start to do that would speak of your growing confidence, calm or happiness.

Close your eyes now and spend a few moments visualising. As you do this, please remember that not everyone sees clear images in their mind, so if all you get is a vague idea or flashes of pictures, that's absolutely fine. It's also fine if you'd like to focus more on the sounds or feelings associated with the scenario.

My challenge for you is to repeat this visualisation – just for a few moments – every day for the next week. So that it's easier to remember, you could make it a pre-bedtime routine or something you do while brushing your teeth in the morning. You might find that it plays out the same each time, or it could be that new details come to mind as you repeat it. Just remember that this is your improving self and not your 'already improved' self. To map the way to somewhere new, you need to provide your mind with information about the steps it can take right now to put you on track.

Taking action

The more time and thought you put into a task like this, the more likely it will be that you're able to make that shift in reality. However, it's not just about visualising and then waiting for the changes to magically manifest. It's going to require a little conscious decision as well. You can encourage your mind to begin rewriting your old beliefs just by behaving more often as if something better is true. So, here's a final question:

What could you sign up for, take part in or say to someone today that would be an unusual (yet welcome) occurrence for you?

––––––––––●●––––––––––

Making a really big difference takes a little time, and it's likely to be challenging. The lure of familiarity will always be there and it can make even the smallest drop of novelty look quite threatening. However, each time you feel reluctant, yet do something to challenge the norm regardless, you will blur the boundaries of the (dis)comfort zone, making future change increasingly easy. All that is required to get things moving is a bit of self-awareness and a moment or two of affirmative action. I think you're ready for that now, so I'm throwing the gauntlet down. Go and do something different for the sake of difference. And when your monster pipes up? Well, you can thank it for its concern, but then kindly remind it that joining a public-speaking group is not the same as having to recite a poem at your primary-school assembly.

4

Desire

Unconscious Attachments and the Trouble with Wanting

My feet pound relentlessly on the treadmill in the dingy basement gym. It's 2 a.m. on a cold December Saturday and I can't tear my eyes away from the flickering display before me. The little red numbers perform obediently for my scrutiny: time, speed, distance, incline – a digital record of my current worth.

The streets outside buzz with the sound of people making their way home after Christmas drinks, but in here it's deserted; silent but for the drum of my running and the tired whir of the old machine beneath my feet.

Nine miles ... Ten miles ... Just a little farther and I'll have done enough.

Inside my mind, I'm fixated on a vision of my next fight. I desperately want to be able to design it – to control it. I plan the shots that I'm most keen to prove I'm capable of. I rehearse the moment when the medal will be hung around my neck. Yet, no matter how hard I try to stay positive, flashes of far less glorious conclusions keep interrupting my fantasy and, before long, my inner dialogue catches on: 'What if I'm not strong enough or fit enough? What if my opponent is bigger than me? What if she's better?'

I have more work to do.

On the opposite wall, surrounded by glistening trophies, there's a proud portrait of all my instructors. They look calm and accomplished and healthy and happy. A reminder of everything I'm striving for right now. It feels as if they are watching me, so I punch in a faster, harder, better set of numbers and feel the burn in my legs as they wearily respond.

I'm conscious of the fact that this is how it has to be: my body driven forward by the force of my will. I won't stop. I can't stop. This is what winners have to do.

The Mission

I cringe to remember that I felt superior walking home after that run. Drenched in sweat and with steam rising off my arms into the winter air, I considered myself different to all the cheerful Londoners on the streets that night. I was on a mission, and nothing – not even a Christmas celebration with old friends – was going to stand in my way.

I had already completed two long sessions that day and I was tired. Yet the urge to train – something too powerful to ignore – had lured me back to the gym. It is obvious to me now that my drive to succeed was, in fact, breaking me, physically and emotionally; but at the time, I was blinded by my goal. Instead of listening to my body (or to reason), I just continued racing towards the inevitable burnout on the horizon.

I never would have said it at the time, but in many respects, my connection to fighting was like an abusive relationship. Training controlled me. It punished me when I failed to live up to expectations; yet, simultaneously, it was the only thing that could possibly satisfy the craving I experienced on a daily basis. I was infatuated with the promise of a sense of achievement that never fully made itself available.

Motivation

The last two chapters have taken a past-focused approach to uncovering psychological stumbling blocks. In this second half of Part 1, we're going to turn our attention to the future, because it's equally about the flipside of the coin: the positive outcomes to which we're so faithfully attached. To fully understand our (dis)comfortable reality maps, we need to take a look at desire as well as doubt.

The downside to desire

One of my biggest blocks while I was fighting was my refusal to think outside the parameters of my most highly valued outcome: I wanted to achieve the standard of 'effortless winner'.

Looking back, it's painfully obvious that I was setting myself impossible targets. The only future I was willing to consider was the fantasy one filled with trophies – trophies lit spectacularly by the glow of effortless perfection. I didn't just want to win. I wanted it to be easy. And so, unless I defeated an opponent by complete annihilation, I was embarrassed to accept the medal. I felt that any struggle was a sign of failure. The real problem, of course, was that even when I did win easily, I'd tell myself that the victory didn't count. Ultimately, although I strived for it ceaselessly, 'effortless winner' was too far from the (dis)comfortable norm for my monster to let me achieve it.

As unreasonable as it was, this goal was at play in the back of my mind at all times and it influenced all of my choices. It was the shame of consistently failing to hit my impossible target that caused my anxiety and eventual burnout, not just the undeniably frightening context of the boxing ring or the simple exertion of a gruelling training regime.

Task: Understanding Your Motivation

It's time to begin the next task. We're going to start by creating a list of the most motivational things in a particular context of your life, and we'll be referring back to it over the next two chapters (so, if you want something to work with, it's a great idea to get these down on paper).

Because this sequence of tasks has such a definite structure, I have included a series of forms for you to use as guides in Appendix 5. I'll prompt you with the relevant page number when you will need them.

Choosing your focal context

In which area of your life does your monster create the biggest problems? It could be a sport, a hobby, work, a particular friendship or partnership, relationships in general, family, etc.

When you have chosen a context, write it down at the top of the form on page 351 (or on a blank piece of paper if you're allergic to writing in books).

Now answer this question:

What's important to you about (your chosen context)?

For example, if someone was looking at the context of 'having an intimate relationship', they would ask, 'What's important to me about having an intimate relationship?' Their answers might include things like, 'Being with someone who enjoys the same things as me', 'Sexual attraction', 'Long conversations', 'Having someone in my life who's prepared to take the cat litter out', etc.

Write down all the answers that come to you. If you're using the form on page 351, then write your answers in the numbered rows.

When you have everything, read your answers out loud using this format:

> **'If I had item 1, item 2, item 3 (list all the things you just wrote down), what *else* would be important to me about (the chosen context)?'**

I'm fairly certain you won't have found all there is to find in your first attempt. So, ask yourself the above question and then sit with the blank for a moment. Then, write down whatever else pops up.

Then, when you're sure that you have found all the answers, do it one more time. (I know. Sorry. But it's highly likely there's even more to squeeze out.) Read the question again, listing all of the items you have so far, and then notice what else crops up after you have sat with the blank for a bit:

> **'If I had item 1, item 2, item 3, etc., what *else* would be important about (the chosen context)?'**

That really was the last time I'll ask you to do that, so make sure you've given yourself the space to think of absolutely everything you can before reading on.

––––––•●•––––––

What you will now have is a list of things that you place value on in that context. Some are likely to feel practical, some aspirational. Some might feel like 'needs', others more like 'wants'.

When I was asked for my list of boxing/kickboxing motivators before I'd worked on my emotional connection to fighting, I came up with this:

* Winning
* Achieving
* Proving myself
* Being fit
* Being strong
* A sense of community
* Doing something challenging
* Doing something not many women do
* Doing something people think women can't do
* Pushing myself to do something I haven't done before
* Learning

These were my driving motivators; the things that inspired me to run on a treadmill at 2 o'clock in the morning and take fights even when I wasn't feeling well. Your list will include the things your mind uses to motivate you in whatever context you're addressing.

Values

In NLP (neuro-linguistic programming), the term given to these personal motivators is 'values', because they not only motivate us to act, but also help us to evaluate the actions and decisions that we (and other people) make. For example, my 'winning' value both inspired me to train hard and judge myself harshly whenever I skipped a session. It wasn't just a nice thing that I aimed for while I was fighting; it was a value that I strove to uphold at all costs.

'Values' is a tricky word because it's often used differently in everyday life (which is why I went with the term 'motivator' for the process above). Commonly, when we talk about values, we think of big, abstract and seemingly universal principles like 'honesty', 'equality' and perhaps things like 'environmental responsibility'. These standards most certainly are values, and if they are ones that you uphold, then they may have cropped up in some form on your list. However, they are not the only things that come under the heading.

Put most simply, our values are the things we believe to be important. They are the things that drive us to take action, get things done and know when we've done it right. They can be quite specific, like 'doing something that people think women can't do', and they can be more broad, like 'learning'. When they're being met, we will feel good about ourselves and our endeavours. When they are not, we can experience considerable unease.

However, not all values are equal. Each item on the list you created earlier will have its own place in a hierarchy of unconsciously determined importance.

Task: The Hierarchy of Importance

Take a look at your list of values from the 'Understanding your motivation' task again. Which would you say was the most important? What we're going to look at here is whether the captain and crew agree on the answer to that question.

Unconsciously motivated behaviours (i.e. 90 per cent of our actions) will be selected by the crew based on our list of values as well as our beliefs.*

Values at the top of the unconscious hierarchy will take precedence and have the most sway. Furthermore, until the mind believes that our most important goals are being satisfied it will devote far less time or energy to those in the runner-up positions.

Often, however, what we consciously think to be of greatest consequence will differ from what the unconscious mind would put at the top of the list, so we need to know what that is. To identify which of those things your crew deems the most valuable, you can play a game of Winner Stays On with your values. Here's how:

Consider the first two items and then ask yourself this question:

'If I could have (value 1) but *not* (value 2), would that be OK?'

Of course, it wouldn't be completely OK because all those things are important to you, but if you absolutely *had* to get rid of one, which would you keep?

Note: please bear in mind that sometimes the question will seem

---

* Technically, values are beliefs anyway; they are beliefs about the importance of things, but in practice it makes sense to set the two concepts apart because value-beliefs have such a specific function.

illogical. You may have to play 'Growth' off against 'Learning', for example. Clearly, you can't really have one without the other, but you will need to still answer the question as if you *can* choose. Or, if you think the two values are exactly the same, you can amalgamate them, but make sure they really do feel equal before you do that.

To get the crew's response, it's important to go with your gut instinct and not the thing you think probably *ought* to be the most important. Follow the sense of yearning that says, 'Aww ... Yeah, I really want *that* the most.' Be honest. Nobody needs to know your answers.

Let's say you kept value 1. Next, ask the question again to play value 1 off against value 3:

'If I could have (value 1) but *not* (value 3), would *that* be OK?'

Again, go with your gut. Then, keep the winner of that round on to play against value 4, and so on. If you go through the entire list – and you need to go through all of the items to get the correct answer – you'll end up with your number-one unconscious value in that context.

———————•••———————

And the winner is...

Was the winner what you thought it would be? More importantly, was it one of the things you mentioned right at the beginning? Of course I don't know what you've written, but the majority of the time, in practice, a client's number-one unconscious value will be one of the things they only thought of after pushing through a blank or two. What this means is that the motivations that really drive us to act are often not the things we consciously consider while making our decisions. This is how we can end up in jobs and relationships that were never really right for us. Our gut instinct may try to steer us in a different direction, but if we choose to go with our conscious and practical checklist instead, we could be on the road to disappointment.

If I were completing a process like this with you in my office, we would go through all of the items a number of times to get a comprehensive hierarchical list of values for your problematic context. So, after working out what the number-one unconscious value is, we'd cross it off the list and then start at the beginning again to work out what number two is, and so on. This information can be extremely useful when it comes to identifying things like inner conflict, the reason for a lack of enthusiasm, the reason for unexplained failures and, of course, the reason for repeated self-sabotage.

There's another form on page 352 for you to list your values in order of their hierarchy. I'd suggest you use the Winner Stays On game for at least the top three. After that, if you don't have time to go through the whole lot, you can just organise the remaining answers into whichever order feels right.

Changing for the sake of difference

Luckily, just as with other beliefs, neither our values nor their hierarchy are set in stone. Simple awareness can give us enough control to make new and better decisions when an unwanted motivation is trying to sway our choices, because the connection between our unconscious drives and the behaviours they generate is a two-way street. Our beliefs and values determine our actions, but if we act in a different way for long enough, the mind will helpfully readjust its idea of what's true and/or important in order to remain congruent.

This works for both the positive and the negative. If you decided to tell a lie every day, your mind would (probably) let honesty slip down the ranks over time. However, if you decided to do something challenging and new every day, then your mind would likely start to place more emphasis on things like learning and novelty. Then, as the desirable motivators move up the rungs of the ladder, it will become more and more natural to live in a way that fulfils those values. Making a change like this takes a little determination, but the 'fake-it-until-you-make-it' approach is a viable strategy nonetheless. Again, it all starts with action.

Consider these questions:

If you could move one value from the bottom of the hierarchy towards the top, which would you pick?

If there was a value that you would like to add to the list, what would that be?

Finally, if there was something you could do today that would fulfil either of those desirable values (and therefore encourage your mind to place more emphasis on them), what would that be?

Again, if you have an answer to that final question, I'd say it would be an excellent idea to do that thing right away. Remember that if it's different enough to your (dis)comfortable norm, then your monster won't like the idea. It may already have started to try to talk you out of it, but that doesn't mean you can't do it anyway. Go on. Here's another gauntlet. I challenge you.

Amy's corporate conflict

Amy works in investment. Having displayed unusual skill with numbers and a developed business acumen from an early age, she was plucked from high school and introduced to the world of banking far younger than most. When we met, Amy was in her thirties and working in an executive position. She was, of course, paid well for her work and she had a life that, on the surface, many of her old high-school friends would envy deeply. However, Amy wasn't happy. For years now she had been on the move, shifting from company to company and country to country, trying to find an environment within which she could enjoy the work she was so good at without the horrible restless sense that something wasn't right.

Our first session focused exclusively on values analysis. Amy spoke passionately about her list of work values, which included things like integrity, mutual respect, problem-solving, teamwork, ideas, vulnerability, courage, freedom and flexibility. The problem for Amy was that the reality of work in her chosen field – a place of hierarchy, superiority and, ultimately, exploitation – consistently failed to live up to the principles she wanted to live by.

Amy had tried to fit into the standard corporate structure all of her adult life, but she was unable to shake the sense of dissatisfaction that it inspired in her because a key requirement was missing. Right at the top of her values hierarchy sat the words 'true value exchange'. She wanted to work in a way that meant people would come together as equals to solve the bigger problems. This was important to her because she wanted to contribute to something greater than herself, rather than feel as though she was just taking from others, and she wanted to be able to do that without feeling patronised or pushed around by people who saw themselves as superior. These conditions were not being met and the result was that she was left in a chronic state of slightly anxious dissatisfaction.

Bringing her unmet values to light meant that Amy could seek ways to change her working environment. Initially, this meant addressing her professional relationships to sidestep the uncomfortable corporate power struggles. There were certain kinds of interaction that could cause Amy to freeze and fall silent. This self-sabotage needed to be dealt with for her to feel as though she could meet the more authoritative types on a level playing field. But better than that, once her self-confidence had started to fortify, Amy began working towards integrating a brand-new system for corporate consulting that aligns with her values. Rather than feeling as though she needs to bend to the (dis)comfortable shape expected of her, Amy is taking matters into her own hands and finding a way to ensure that she can 'give back' in the way she'll feel the most proud to.

Needs

Values are not quite the be-all and end-all of wellbeing. There's another consideration; something that takes precedence in the unconscious mind and will pull rank in order to sway our behavioural choices when necessary. That thing is our list of needs.

Needs trump values. Human beings will scrap a value if they are required to do so in order to fulfil a need. I can (honestly) say that I value honesty. Like most people, I think being truthful is very important. But would I tell a white lie in order to eat if I was starving? You're damn right I would.

Stress levels tend to depend on how well our needs are being met and how effectively we are able to deal with the situations in which they are likely to be jeopardised. Analysing our needs fulfilment can therefore provide useful information about how to increase wellbeing, reduce anxiety and take control in moments when our monsters might otherwise revolt.

Individual therapists and therapy approaches will define human needs using different words, but they all tend to come down to similar principles. The model that I find the most useful in practice outlines six main categories of human need:

1. Certainty
2. Variety
3. Significance
4. Love and connection
5. Growth
6. Contribution*

Although fulfilment of all these six needs is required in order for a person to enjoy a balanced sense of wellbeing, most people will find that they consistently prioritise one (or some) over the rest. In many cases, this imbalance can mean that they experience a deficit in the needs that are overlooked. The problem with this is that when a need is not being met healthily, the unconscious mind will rise up and attempt to satisfy that need in whatever way it knows best, which is likely to be decidedly (dis) comfortable.

Let's look into the six needs in a little more detail so you can start to get a sense of where your priorities may lie:

1. Certainty

This need is essentially a survival mechanism. It will cover all of the most basic human needs like access to air, water, food, shelter and privacy, but also a feeling of security, familiarity and of being in control. This need is what the monster is concerning itself with when it heads back into the (dis)comfort zone for a safety sandwich.

As with all the needs, there are both healthy and unhealthy ways of trying to satisfy the need for certainty. Some will do this by making autonomous choices and taking responsibility for themselves. That's

---

* This model was originally outlined by NLP Master Tony Robbins. It is based on (although different to) the most frequently referenced theory regarding human needs developed by Abraham Maslow in the 1940s: 'Maslow's Hierarchy of Needs'.

healthy. Others may attempt to feel in control by micromanaging situations, dictating the actions of others or going into lock-down and never doing anything they're not entirely sure about. These strategies would be less healthy, and the fallout could well end up depriving the certainty-seeker of the feeling of safety they were looking for.

At the times when we prioritise this need over the others, we will take fewer risks in order to plan safely for the future. Someone who makes a habit of focusing on this need may have a super-healthy savings account and feel reluctant to change jobs or move house, etc. They may also get defensive when asked to change their plans or act spontaneously. It all comes down to the (dis)comfort zone again. An unhealthy focus on the need for certainty amounts to an unconscious addiction to the predictability of safe misery over the uncertainty of novelty (and therefore growth).

2. Variety

This is the need for change, surprise, excitement and difference; it's about fun and stimulation. If we place a high level of importance on this need, we will likely come across as dynamic to others. The downfall is that we may, at times, act irresponsibly or take too many risks. A stereotype of the kind of person who makes a habit of prioritising this need would be an adrenaline junkie or someone who hops from job to job or partner to partner, never settling down. A more healthy and balanced way of meeting this basic requirement, however, may involve careful time management to ensure that work stops at a certain time and therefore that hobbies and fun have their place. It could mean actively choosing – forcing oneself – to take a little risk every now and then. Or, perhaps planning separate social engagements to those of your partner, so that not all of your time is spent with the same person.

3. Significance

This is the need to feel important, respected and valued. If met healthily, it will involve sharing equal and respectful relationships with others, perhaps pursuing our career to the fullest (without sabotaging the fulfilment of all the other needs) or ensuring that we're doing work that feels valuable.

If approached unhealthily, significance may be processed as the need to be considered 'unique' or 'special'. We might strive to be the best, to be admired, to lead or to win because we will evaluate our own sense of worth using these kinds of measures. As a result, we may feel the need to accumulate status symbols like the latest gadgets, a fast car, an impressive title or a beautiful partner. Prioritising this need will likely come at the cost of fulfilling the need for love and connection – because those who do will often jeopardise their relationships in order to stay on top in their career (or other important pastime).

4. Love and Connection

This is the need to love, be loved and to enjoy meaningful connections. Those things are all good. However, placing an unhealthy amount of emphasis on these needs can come at the cost of our own sense of significance (and/or the other needs on the list) because we may fall into the trap of 'people-pleasing' and chronically put the requirements of others before our own.

If human love or connection are not available to us, or simply imperceptible due to a limiting belief, we may attempt to satisfy this need by connecting with other things like pets, teddy bears or our homes. More problematically, we might find that we develop a bond to harmful substances like cigarettes, alcohol or drugs in lieu of interpersonal connection. This is particularly easy to do when we discover these substances as young people who are learning for the first time how to socialise and fit in.

Frighteningly, research shows that people who start drinking before the age of fifteen are four times more likely to meet the criteria for alcohol dependency at some point in their adult lives. When working with those who want to give up a smoking, drinking or drug habit, addressing the early associations their minds have made between the problematic substance and a feeling of connection often plays an essential role in the process.

5. Growth

This is the need to feel as though we are developing, learning and improving. It can be satisfied physically, emotionally, intellectually or spiritually. When we place a healthy and balanced focus on this need, we will be able to feel excited about getting involved in new challenges and we may not be dependent on others (or on results) in order to enjoy our own learning processes. Those who prioritise this need may achieve highly because they recognise that failure is an inevitable part of the learning process and therefore fear it less. They may also have a weaker desire for material possessions than others because life becomes more about process, and less about attainment of any kind.

The downfall here is that those who place too high a preference on this need may experience stress when they don't (always) beat their personal bests, and they may neglect their interpersonal relationships and become quite isolated while striving for their own improvement.

6. Contribution

This is the need to feel as though we're playing our part. It's the desire to feel connected to something that is bigger than ourselves, and to give back to the world in a meaningful way (this was the unmet need that stood in the way of Amy's workplace wellbeing – see pages 89–90). The contribution that we make could be to individual people, large groups of people, to a movement, to society or to a non-human-focused cause like animal rights or the environment (of course, it'll be different for everyone). Much like love and connection, this need could be met unhealthily if we try to achieve our sense of contribution by going down the people-pleasing route.

This need is most frequently neglected because it's so easy to get swamped by the other five. However, a need it is, nonetheless, and a deficit in its fulfilment may cause us to feel stressed, empty or to experience the feeling that life is meaningless or hopeless.

Completing an Overall Needs Audit

To get a feel for which needs are and are not being adequately satisfied in your life, you can answer the following questions using a scale of 1 to 7 (a score of 1 meaning 'not at all', and a score of 7 meaning 'very much so').*

* These questions are based on the Human Givens 'Needs Audit' but some have been modified, and some are my own additions. Human Givens is a therapeutic approach that places emphasis on achieving the healthy fulfillment of one's needs.

Certainty:

Do you feel secure in all major areas of your life (such as your home, work, environment)?

Do you feel in control of your life most of the time?

Can you obtain privacy when you need to?

Variety:

Do you feel that there is sufficient variety in your life?

Are there things in your life that make you feel excited?

Can you find something that feels fun in all the major areas of your life?

Significance:

Do you feel that you have status that is acknowledged?

Are you achieving things and competent in at least one major area of your life?

Love and affection:

Do you feel as if you receive enough attention?

Do you think you give other people enough attention?

Do you feel part of a wider community?

Do you have an intimate relationship in your life – one where you are fully accepted for who you are (this could be a close friend)?

Growth:

Are you mentally and/or physically challenged on a regular basis?

Do you feel that you are developing and learning in at least one area of your life?

Contribution:

Do you feel as though you are contributing to something bigger than yourself?

Do you feel as though at least one area of your life has meaningful purpose?

A score of 3 or lower is likely to require some attention. For those answers, ask yourself this question:

'What actions do I need to take before this score will increase to a 4 or higher?'

Don't forget that your monster is likely to kick up a fuss when you consider making these kinds of changes because fulfilling your needs in a new (and healthier) way will move you out of the (dis)comfort zone. But, once again, that doesn't mean you can't do it anyway. (Honestly, I have a never-ending supply of gauntlets.)

Values as Strategies for Needs Fulfilment

The values that drive us to take part in a certain activity (like those on the list you created on page 351) have their motivational effect because they enable us to fulfil our needs. Put simply, our values act as needs-fulfilment strategies. And just like everything else we've discussed, we will learn these strategies as we accumulate experiences in life. If those people we learned from during our formative years achieved their feelings of significance through academic achievement, then we're likely to follow suit and value things like getting top grades or excelling in our profession. Or, if we learned to feel loved when we were given a lot of hugs, then physical contact might crop up near the top of our list of relationship values.

When we only have one strategy for fulfilling a need, then we may develop an addiction to whatever that thing is. For someone who only feels significant when they get praise at the office, for example, work-aholism could become a problem.

Look at the motivators you listed for your problematic context earlier (use the list that is arranged in its hierarchical order). The specific needs that your values are intended to satisfy will become apparent by taking the items one by one and assigning the need(s) that feel most relevant to each of them.

Take a moment to do that before reading on. Here are the six needs categories again, so you don't have to refer back, followed by an example.

1. Certainty
2. Variety
3. Significance
4. Love and connection
5. Growth
6. Contribution

My list of (early) fighting values would look like this:

* Winning (significance)
* Achieving (significance)
* Proving myself (significance)
* Being fit (significance and certainty)
* Being strong (significance and certainty)
* A sense of community (love and connection)
* Doing something challenging (growth)
* Doing something not many women do (significance and contribution)
* Doing something people think women can't do (significance and contribution)
* Pushing myself to do something I haven't done before (variety and growth)
* Learning (growth)

Clearly, when I started fighting, my mind was geared up to try to satisfy the need for significance above the others. My training also had the potential to fulfil all the other needs, but my primary focus was on being 'better than the rest'. That's embarrassing to say, but it was true, and the reason I felt that particular need so strongly at the beginning of my fight journey was because my monster was telling me a story that negated my efforts to fulfil it.

Deficiency needs

People who place their focus primarily on any of the first four needs (certainty, variety, significance or love and connection) tend to feel more limited than those whose energy gets channelled into feeling as if they're either growing or contributing. This is partly because the first four categories work as two opposing pairs: certainty versus variety and significance versus love and connection. As a rule, those who focus on certainty will be likely to jeopardise their need for variety (and vice versa); and those who focus on significance will be likely to jeopardise their need for love and connection (and vice versa). A primary focus on any of the first four needs could cause an imbalance in the whole.

Perhaps more importantly, what the first four needs all have in common is that they are felt most strongly when left unmet. These kinds of needs are called 'deficiency needs' because we will only be aware of them when they are left at a deficit. The longer a deficiency need remains unsatisfied, the more powerfully it will be felt and the more of an influence it will have over our behaviour. The easiest way to understand this is to think of something like hunger. The longer we go without food, the hungrier we will feel and the more energy we will devote to our search for a meal.

What this means is that if we are striving to fulfil these needs, then we must be sensing some kind of lack. But that doesn't necessarily mean that there's a practical, objective lack of those things in our life. Sometimes it just feels that way. The problem with this is that, very often, the more we strive, the more urgent the deficit will seem, meaning that our efforts only make the void feel greater. I have worked with clients who had unstable upbringings and therefore put the vast majority of their energy into trying to satisfy the need for certainty. This unconscious decision bears a hefty price tag because absolute certainty (beyond death and taxes, of course) is rarely possible. As a result, people who strive for certainty above all else can be left feeling as if none of their needs are being met. In my experience, those who focus primarily on this need will be the people who feel the most stuck, disconnected and lost.

However, it's not only striving for certainty that can limit our sense of fulfilment. Deficits in variety, importance and love/connection all have the potential to hijack our awareness, dominate our unconscious motivation and potentially trigger some monster reactions.

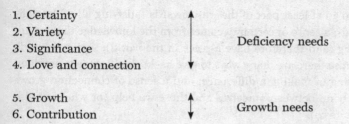

1. Certainty
2. Variety
3. Significance   Deficiency needs
4. Love and connection

5. Growth   Growth needs
6. Contribution

Growth needs

Growth needs – sometimes referred to as 'growth and being needs' – function differently to deficiency needs. Rather than being felt when left unmet, these will continue to be felt and may even grow stronger as they are satisfied. However, because they are not processed as a feeling of lack, but as a positive drive for more, their presence in our awareness is not painful or desperate, but inspiring.

The idea is that once our deficiency needs have been sufficiently fulfilled, our attention will move away from the pain of 'not ... enough' and on to the things that help us to feel as though we are expanding our sense of self. Growth needs make themselves available as we move into a state of self-development. They generate a momentum and energy of their own, which inspires us to bring more and more of the things that fulfil them – like creativity, inspiration, a sense of purpose, spirituality and continued learning – into our lives.

What's important is that growth needs fulfil us 'in-process', rather than bringing us relief at the point at which we have 'enough' of them. They mean that life feels less like a chase and more like an enjoyable ride.

As a client improves, therefore, I expect their focus to ascend up and out of the deficiency needs and into the higher category of the growth needs. Once someone's energy is devoted largely to the satisfaction of the need for either personal development or purposeful contribution, that person will tend to feel freer to change, grow, develop and to enjoy the process of doing that. It doesn't mean that all self-doubt will be completely eradicated, just that it can be overwhelmed by a more positive and fulfilling kind of drive.

The need for contribution is particularly powerful because it has the

potential to go at least part of the way towards satisfying all of the deficiency needs: a sense of certainty comes from the knowledge that we are
contributing (and therefore have a place in the world); variety is made
easier because there are many ways to give back; significance is provided
by the feeling of making a difference; and a sense of connection grows
out of the bond between ourselves and those we help (or whatever else
we contribute to).

However, in order to get to that place, we first need to clear the way
by ensuring that there are no unconscious programmes blocking the
healthy satisfaction of our deficiency needs. It's our monsters and their
limiting stories that stand in the way of our ascension.

Monster Beliefs and Missed Opportunities

Limiting beliefs have the potential to chronically impair our needs fulfilment. For example, if someone has a limiting belief like, 'I'm not lovable',
'I don't fit in' or, 'I'm a horrible person', then they're likely to feel a deficit
in terms of their need for love and connection. This doesn't necessarily
mean that they will not be loved, liked or important to others, just that
their reality filters could fail to let any evidence of their connectedness
through, and so they'll feel at a perpetual loss in that area. The result may
be that they will strive for love and connection to the detriment of all the
other categories. It could also mean that they're more likely to find themselves having an extra-marital affair in search of a feeling of love, even
when they have a technically good relationship with their partner. (I am
not excusing infidelity here, just offering an explanation as to why people
who really don't want to do that kind of thing can sometimes slip and fall.)

Alternatively, while the need for love is hampered by a limiting belief,
some people will find themselves turning to other, less healthy bonds, like
drugs, alcohol, gambling, sports addiction or smoking, in order to feel
connected. Any of these behaviours would be likely to add even more fuel
to the original limiting belief fire. Once again, the monster feeds itself.

Without work to make the unconscious conscious, our needs, values
and limiting beliefs alike will – for the most part – elude our mindful
awareness. Because they are not rational considerations, these things
present themselves as urges, rather than logical thoughts, which means

we're infinitely more likely to follow the impulse and find ourselves doing something we might later regret. We will, of course, attempt to explain our undesirable behaviours using logic after the fact: 'I slept with my colleague because I was drunk'; 'I had to smoke a cigarette because Manchester United lost'; 'I gambled because I thought it was a sure-fire way to pay off my debt'. But those rationalisations are nothing more than the misguided ramblings of the conscious captain. Only the crew really know why the ship has run aground.

Bringing our unconscious motivators to light helps us develop a deeper and more realistic understanding of why we do what we do. Only when we know the real reason why – for example, we're lusting after an extra-marital affair or lying to others in order to seem more important – can we start to look for alternative strategies to help us fulfil those unmet needs in a healthier way.

Task: Considering Better Strategies

To begin implementing some positive changes right away, you can make some conscious decisions about your needs fulfilment and values strategies.

Let's start with the direct connection between needs and self-sabotage. There are three steps for this mini task:

Step 1

Write down a self-sabotaging trait (e.g. 'procrastination' or 'drinking on a work night').

Step 2

Consider which need (s) that behaviour could be attempting to fulfil.

Step 3

Ask yourself this question:

'If there was something I could do differently to ensure that need (or those needs) get met in a healthier way, what would that be?'

For example, if someone can't resist going to the pub when they should be studying for an exam, then (as well as avoiding the stress of the exam) they might be fulfilling the need for either love and connection or variety. Both those needs could be met in ways that don't leave them with a raging hangover the following day if they budget and plan for their fulfilment. Maybe this person would benefit from a scheduled game of football with friends to break up the day, or an allowance for something fun like playing a game or a musical instrument at set intervals in their timetable. Our brains work better when they switch from task to task, rather than being forced to do the same thing for twelve hours straight. So, approached in this way, the breaks we take can be seen as a productive part of the process – because that's what they are when we have control over the way we take them.

Take a moment to complete the three steps above if you haven't already done so.

Task: Values Strategies

Next, take another look at the full list of values ('motivators') that you wrote for a specific context earlier (use the one with the connected needs stated next to each of the values – see page 351).

To get an idea of any needs that could be at a chronic deficit in this area, and how you could rectify that problem, answer these two questions:

Which deficiency need occurs most frequently on your list (or, if relevant, which one dominates the top of the hierarchy)?

Remembering that if you feel a deficiency need strongly, then it must mean that it is not being fully met: what kinds of practical changes could you make in this context to better satisfy that need?

Make a note of any ideas that come to mind.

Then, to encourage your mind to shift up and away from a focus on the deficiency needs, you can turn your attention to the growth needs. Answer these questions:

If you were to place more emphasis on the need for growth, what would become more important to you in this context? And, what might you find yourself devoting more time to?

If there was a way for you to contribute to something other and greater than yourself in this context, how could you do that?

If you have answers to any of these questions, then you know what to do ... Gauntlet.

——————●●——————

Fiona's value trap

Fiona is a writer and artist. She came to see me because she could sense the moments when her head was crashing up against the glass ceiling above her, and the resulting limitation was affecting her work, her health and her relationships.

Fiona had produced books of poetry and most of a novel, but these things had not been sent out into the world, regardless of the fact that numerous publishers had expressed an interest. Over the last thirty years, however, her financial success had been considerable. Fiona had worked as the chief editor and media manager for a national political organisation, set up her own landscaping business and worked in various other corporate roles. Yet, none of those types of work satisfied her completely. She felt trapped by having to comply with a system or answer to a boss and, over time, her stifling working environments had triggered an emotional and physical burnout (not unlike the one I experienced).

When we discussed the context of 'work', her language exposed a 'damned-if-I-do, damned-if-I-don't' type of conflict. Her mind was unable to perceive creative work as a feasible means to make money, but the prospect of returning to the corporate world threatened a spiritual death that she was not prepared to face ever again. She was stuck between the rock of impossible ideals and the hard place of what she considered to be financially viable employment.

In these kinds of situations, when people express their desires among a mess of contradictions like, 'I really want to do X but I can't because ...', or, 'I know it sounds crazy but I'd really like to ...', I'll always take a look at the structure of values and other beliefs connected to the problematic context. It's within those systems of thought that we're most likely to find the psychological glitch at the heart of the issue.

When I asked Fiona what the word 'work' meant to her, she seemed to regress instantaneously to the age of a small child and said: *Yurghhhhh!* I just don't *like* it! It feels ... Well, it feels like when I had to polish my father's boots to earn 25p as a kid.'

Growing up in 1970s Yorkshire, Fiona learned the value of hard graft from a family who championed the importance of putting in effort to the point of pain. Her grandmother had single-handedly dragged the family out of poverty after the war by working her fingers to the bone in multiple jobs at once, and her father was intent on impressing on Fiona the importance of 'earning her keep', rather than being given pocket money like many of her friends. Furthermore, she was also the only girl of four siblings and, thanks to the traditional views on gender in the family, she was always given the most subservient of tasks.

Each week, the young Fiona was told to get to her knees and shine her father's shoes in order to be paid her allowance. When she recalled the experience, she could remember enjoying the task itself. She liked the satisfaction of applying the polish, working it into the cracks and making something beautiful. However, the overwhelming feeling attached to the duty was one of subordination. The values Fiona's young mind had attached to the context of 'work' were things like conformity, compliance, hard effort and servitude. These strategies, while she was young, had helped her to fulfil her need for certainty, significance and connection, because they earned her praise and enabled her to feel like a secure member of the family unit. Overall, however, she felt demeaned by the work, and this association had endured into her adult life, making any type of paid employment feel somehow inglorious and shameful.

On the flipside, the associations she had attached to the 'not-work' areas of her young life – the things she really enjoyed like painting, outdoors games and storytelling – included the values of imagination, discovery and creativity. Fiona's need for growth was best met by pursuing her creative goals, but during her formative years these kinds of activities were deemed inappropriate. The end result was a psychological double-bind: work for money and feel demeaned, or express your creative self (without financial gain) and feel shamefully Other.

Values analysis exposed the all-important unconscious glitch for Fiona and me to work on in our sessions. She needed to accept and reintegrate the creative little girl part of her personality as valuable in and of herself. The result of doing so meant that she could get back into writing after a long lull, and ultimately begin to feel OK with the prospect of expressing her creative self to the world. She's currently finishing the final chapters of the novel she started and then ran away from years ago and, having read what she's written, I can tell you it is well worth the wait.

Drivers

Finally, a great way to recognise how beliefs and values influence our behaviour is to consider the Transactional Analysis model of Drivers. In 1975, psychologist Taibi Kahler defined five distinct unconscious programmes that automatically motivate certain types of behaviour.* Kahler's drivers can be understood as clusters of key values that represent themselves as conditional, unconscious beliefs like so:

'I'm *only* OK if/when I ...'

Drivers are pre-programmed defence mechanisms that tend to activate in times of stress. The level of stress needn't be high, though; most of us will recognise driver activity on any standard workday.

We acquire our drivers by observing and learning the behaviours we are given recognition for during our childhood (i.e. those that during our formative years successfully fulfilled our needs). Later, as adults, our minds go searching for known methods to boost our sense of wellbeing whenever we're under pressure, and find our old, known strategies for feeling safe, special, loved, etc. As a result, we repeat the strategies that would have won us a gold star or pat on the back while we were little, regardless of whether they're actually likely to yield the same result now.

---

* Just as a point of interest, Kahler was also Bill Clinton's Communications Advisor. Transactional Analysis quickly became known as an effective model for use in business and politics, as well as in the therapy context.

For example, someone who is brought up in an environment where praise is handed out for achieving good exam results, excelling in sports or the arts or even keeping a tidy bedroom will be likely to develop a 'Be Perfect' driver ('I'm only OK if I get it right'). Or, someone who is raised in a family where a high level of importance is placed on remaining calm under pressure and resisting overt displays of emotion may well develop a Be Strong driver ('I'm only OK if I don't show my emotions').

We're all likely to identify strongly with at least one driver, but it's not uncommon to recognise a few (if not all) of these at play from time to time in your behaviour. Kahler's five drivers are:

1. Be Perfect ('I'm only OK if I get it right')
2. Hurry Up ('I'm only OK if I'm doing things quickly')
3. Please Others ('I'm only OK if everyone else is happy')
4. Try Hard ('I'm only OK if I'm working hard')
5. Be Strong ('I'm only OK if I don't show my emotions')

The profiles below summarise the common effects that each driver, when activated, is likely to have on a person's behaviour. These are not a means for pigeonholing people because they are not independent personality types. Having said that, you may recognise people in these descriptions if you know any with strong leanings towards a certain driver.

1. Be Perfect

The values associated with a Be Perfect driver will be things like achievement, success, winning, being right, doing things well/properly and autonomy.

Even though most people will agree that perfection is an impossible goal (at least once we're beyond the stage at school where 100 per cent is achievable in the likes of spelling and maths tests), a person with this driver activated will hold the unconscious belief that perfection is a realistic outcome and they'll strive hard to achieve it. As a result, if Be Perfect fires up, we will set very high standards for ourselves. This driver can also cause us to resist appearing naïve or acting in a childish way, and we'll be likely to avoid taking risks for fear of making errors.

2. Hurry Up

The values associated with a Hurry Up driver will include things like speed, efficiency, responsiveness and the ability to multitask. Someone with this driver will have grown up in an environment where things had to be done quickly, or where dawdling was a punishable offence.

Unsurprisingly, this driver causes us to rush. We might speak quickly and come across as impatient. We may even develop a habit of finishing other people's sentences. Those with a propensity for this driver will be more likely to enjoy great enthusiasm at the beginning of a project but may lack the ability to see things through to the end. They're also likely to thrive in times of crisis and change but may trip themselves up by overlooking details in favour of expediency.

3. Please Others

The values associated with a Please Others driver will include things like consideration, kindness and amenability. People with this driver will often have taken the role of peacekeeper in their family while growing up.

Fairly obviously, the Please Others driver is just another way of talking about 'people-pleasing'. With an active Please Others driver, we will automatically put the needs of everyone else before our own. We'll some-times find that we take too much on in times of stress because we fear saying 'no'. We may also resist standing out or speaking our minds and we'll often attempt to second-guess what others are thinking, so we can act in a way that will keep them happy. Someone with an active Please Others driver will be likely to avoid criticism and conflict at all costs.

4. Be Strong

The values associated with a Be Strong driver will include things like courage, cool-headedness, strength and dependability. This driver is often the result of an upbringing where displays of emotion were frowned upon in favour of the 'stiff-upper-lip' or 'toughen-up' attitude.

Someone with this driver is likely to endeavour to be the one who can shoulder the burden, rather than ask for help. Emotions are seen as weakness and, as a result, people with this driver can appear as guarded and inaccessible. When in the grip of Be Strong, we may overload ourselves in times of pressure and might lack tolerance for those who ask for help or appear to be 'needy'.

5. Try Hard

The values associated with a Try Hard driver include effort, persistence, patience and determination.

This is the 'no-pain-no-gain' attitude. Someone with an active Try Hard driver will tend to put large amounts of effort in, even when it does not necessarily yield better results. 'Easy' achievement is considered less valuable than something that has to be worked for. With an active Try Hard driver, we will tend to resist being satisfied, relaxing, 'giving up' or taking a break. We may be tempted to overcomplicate a process, just so we can throw more resources at the task, and we may pride ourselves on having large amounts of 'willpower'.

Drivers as needs fulfilment

Drivers, like values, are programmed-in strategies for our needs fulfilment. At first glance, we may struggle to recognise how a value like persistence (Try Hard) or speed (Hurry Up) could possibly fulfil one of the six categories of human needs listed earlier. When we look into our personal history and recognise that those qualities brought us security, love and praise during our formative years, however, the link becomes much clearer. Yet, as we already know, what fulfilled our needs while we were young is not necessarily going to do the trick in our adult lives. What becomes important, then, is to run conscious checks on our driver urges to determine whether those strategies will actually fulfil our present-day requirements for emotional wellbeing. Again, once the unconscious has been made conscious, we can increase our sense of choice and control tenfold.

Driver Awareness

Drivers are not all negative. Upholding the values associated with each of them will come with its own set of benefits. The pitfalls come when we lack awareness. Our drivers taint the version of reality that we perceive and can present as an objective truth, rather than a personal preference. This means that the driver will feel like a threat.

For example, someone with an active Hurry Up driver will feel that it's absolutely imperative that whatever they are doing is completed quickly. They'll find ways to justify their need for speed: 'If I don't get this done by tomorrow, people will lose interest', or 'If we don't finish this by the end of today, the boss will think we're slacking'. However, these rationalisations are not necessarily based in reality; they're just the captain's attempts to makes sense of something that *feels* important. Blindly following the driver urge could mean that the task at hand is not completed to the standard it might be otherwise.

Drivers as the monster's tools

When we're not feeling entirely OK about who we are, our drivers highlight some of the most painful nuances of 'not ... enough' for us. They encapsulate the specific ways in which we learned that falling short would deprive us of love, support and safety while we were young. Whether we fear that we're not good enough, not fast enough, not pleasing enough, not industrious enough or not strong enough in the moments when a driver is triggered, we will feel as if we are less than we need to be for other people to love, respect or value us as human beings.

This means that drivers are like a workman's tools to our monsters. When the mind is intent on finding something to feel ashamed of, then falling short of a driver standard can provide the perfect means to hammer the (dis)comfortable message home: we are 'not ... enough'.

Task: Creating a Driver Symbol

I include drivers here because they provide an excellent way of challenging our internal representation of the world and the self. When we can learn to identify the specific urge associated with our main driver(s), then we can take a step back whenever we sense it and question whether we're responding to the reality of the situation or just our pre-programmed pattern for stress management.

A good way to encourage your mind to recognise a particular feeling is to create a symbolic representation for it. The process of doing so – although it can seem a little abstract the first time you do it – allows you to explore the unconscious information more deeply than you might otherwise. This helps when it comes to identifying the feeling in the future. Start with this question:

Which do you think could be your primary driver?

When you have your answer, think back to a time when you've felt that urge and imagine you're in that situation again. Step right into the remembered moment, so you can see, hear and feel what was going on at the time. Take a moment to get fully immersed in the memory.

Now, to create your symbol, ask yourself these questions:

* If you could point to the position in your body where you feel the urge associated with your driver firing up, where would that be?
* If that feeling had a shape, what would it be?
* Is it large or small?
* Is it heavy or light?
* Is it stationary or does it move?
* Is there anything else that stands out about that feeling?

You might find it helpful to create a visualisation of your driver urge. Have a think about how you might see it. If it had a colour, what would it be? Is it light or dark in shade? Does it look similar to anything else that you can think of? Or, you might find that the feeling comes with some kind of sound. My Hurry Up driver sounds like screeching tyres and rapid internal chatter.

Spend a moment getting in touch with the urge and linking it to its symbol by imagining the visualisation, sound or feeling in the part of your body where you experience it.

Once you have done this, keep an eye out for the times when you find yourself feeling that way over the next few days and challenge the driver urge to see if it's actually a real consideration. Simply pause and say to yourself: 'This could be driver activity. Is it really important that I Hurry Up (or whatever) right now, or could my mind just be making it appear that way?'

When you think that a driver could be tainting your perception, you can counter it with a converse mental command. This can function as an internal mantra: a 'reality check' in times of stress. You can choose your own words, of course, but here are the standard Transactional Analysis suggestions:

1. Be Perfect counter: 'Good enough'
2. Hurry Up counter: 'Slow down'
3. Please Others counter: 'Please yourself'
4. Try Hard counter: 'Do enough'
5. Be Strong counter: 'It's OK'

Summary

We've now covered all the major perceptual components of the reality filter: unconscious processing, memories, beliefs, values, needs and drivers. These things all play interconnecting roles in determining the version of the world in which we each live and how we react to it. Our memories provide the raw information that our minds turn into beliefs (including values, which are beliefs about the importance of things; and drivers, which are like unconscious rules on how to boost self-esteem). As we grow, we hold onto these units of information and use them as strategies for the fulfilment of our needs, which we can do either healthily or unhealthily.

All the concepts we've covered so far form the foundation for the changes you're going to make with this book. You don't have to memorise all of this though. I'll prompt you whenever you need to remember something specific.

There's one final way of considering these ideas to shed light on your most destructive monster thinking before we look into taking control in Part 2. Everything comes together when we consider the concept of what I call mental 'mirages'.

5

The Mirage

The Disabling Effect of Unmet Needs

'All that matters is the goal.' I tell myself this over and over. Sometimes it feels like that shimmering vision of success ahead of me is the only thing that keeps me moving.

It's almost 6 p.m. and this will be my first training session of the day. I notice that the old spark of enthusiasm is missing as I climb onto the treadmill like some kind of gym zombie. I enter in my usual warm-up pace, but my legs feel heavy and very reluctant. I don't think this is going to be a good session, but then again, not many are at the moment. Rather than being drawn forward, it's started to feel as though I'm being pushed or forced. These days, I more often do what I think I should rather than what I really want to. That's OK, though, because all that matters is the goal.

Recently, people have been telling me to take a break, but the idea seems preposterous. It's true that I'm tired, but time off doesn't help. My body isn't as strong as it used to be. More importantly, it isn't as strong as I need it to be to compete in the way that I want.

Up until a few months ago, I had been on a long winning streak. Now I'm looking back on two loathsome losses and I can't shake the feeling of betrayal. On both occasions it was like my body just gave up after a few minutes of fighting. By the end of each competition, I found myself standing motionless in the middle of the arena, unable to duck or step out of the way, let alone throw any kicks or punches.

My friends, family and coaches can see that I'm not right. When they suggest that I rest, I want to be thankful for their well-meant advice, but it hurts when they tell me to slow down because it feels as if they're trying to take something absolutely vital away from me. Rest isn't an option. If I want to get back to winning form, I'm just going to have to train harder. It's as simple as that.

It's not only fighting that feels like a strain these days though. It's *everything. My running times are slower, I'm having to lift lighter weights, I'm getting really tired and irritable after my sessions, my digestive system isn't playing ball and every time I shower I leave handfuls of hair in the drain. A part of me knows that I should take stock of these things, but I don't. The one thing that I am having great success with is ignoring that annoying little voice of reason. I've become an expert in denial.*

———••———

Task: Monsters and Mirages

We're going to pick up where we left off with the last task because you can get more out of analysing your values than just an understanding of your needs. This information can give you a direct line to your monster's most influential stories, and you could be surprised by how much more powerful you can feel when you know exactly how your mind is using those ideas.

As you answer the following questions, you will need to record the exact wording that you use. You might find this easiest if you respond out loud using a Dictaphone or smartphone. If you're writing on paper, directly, be sure not to edit your responses in order to be concise. Just let the chain of thoughts flow onto the paper as they occur to you.

I've included another form for you to use in Appendix 5 (see page 353).

If you're ready to begin, grab your list of values and write the item that sits at the top of your unconscious hierarchy in the second row of the form, where it says 'Value 1'. We're going to start by looking into the specific purpose behind that motivator.

Considering your number-one value, answer this question:

What's important about (that value)?

Note down the answer that first comes to mind. Then, ask that same question about the answer you just wrote down:

What's important about (answer 1)?

Again, be sure to record your exact wording, and then ask the question a third and final time about *that* answer:

What's important about (answer 2)?

Example

If we take my value of 'A sense of community' and apply these questions, I might say something like this:

Q1: What's important about 'a sense of community'?
A1: Being with people who are interested in the same things as I am.

Q2: What's important about 'being with people who are interested in the same things as I am'?
A2: Feeling like I'm part of a team.

Q3: What's important about 'feeling like I'm part of a team'?
A3: The camaraderie and support that it provides.

Your answers might include some negative responses. For example, when I answered these questions about my value of 'winning' during my therapy journey, I said this:

Q1: What's important about 'winning'?
A1: Knowing that I can beat the opposition.

Q2: What's important about 'knowing that I can beat the opposition'?
A2: So I <u>don't</u> feel like I'm incapable.

Note: if you hit a negative response like that, you do not need to answer any more questions about that value.

If we were working together in my office, I'd ask you these questions about every value on your list. Please feel free to do the same. It will give you the most accurate understanding of the unconscious reasoning behind your motivation. However, I'm aware that it's a bit of an arduous task. The top three values in the hierarchy will be sufficient if you're low on time.

When you've done that you can put your answers to one side for a moment. We'll come back to this a little later in the chapter.

———————•———————

Types of Motivation

The process you just completed is called 'chunking up' in NLP – possibly the worst term anyone ever came up with. I don't know what it was like where you grew up, but in Norwich 'chunking up' is what happens to teenagers after a few too many alcopops. In NLP, however, this term refers to the process of moving up through increasing levels of abstraction. What we're doing here is asking for the purpose of each item on your list.

Carrot or stick?

Some values present as positive ideals, towards which we automatically gravitate because they bring us something that we want. In NLP, these are called 'towards values' and they signify the healthy fulfilment of a need. The values that tend to cause us the most problems, however, are the negative motivators that move us away from something we fear, don't want or don't believe that we can have. These are known as 'away-from values'. In some cases, they are just as important and healthy as the towards values because there are things in this world that we should all avoid. However, when a value like this moves us away from something other than a genuinely abusive person or a raging fire, it can become problematic because it means we're spending more time than necessary in a state of defensiveness.

The Pleasure Principle

The movement towards something positive and away from something negative is instinctive. We're programmed to seek pleasure and avoid pain. Picture someone smelling something wonderful like freshly baked bread. Can you imagine them leaning into the smell? Now imagine someone smelling something absolutely vile (I'll let you come up with an example for that one). I'm assuming the reaction you imagined in the second scenario was different to the first.

Freud called this the 'Pleasure Principle', and it can be observed in any living organism on the planet. If you put an amoeba in a Petri dish with water and add a drop of something nutritious, it'll move towards it. If you add a drop of something poisonous, it will move away.

The Pleasure Principle describes our most basic of survival mechanisms: when we feel safe and there's pleasure or nourishment up for grabs, we'll enter into a state of **growth** and flow comfortably in the direction of what we want (reacting to a towards value). When in this state, we're free to expand, develop and change. When we sense a threat, however, we'll go into an automatic state of **protection** and retreat (reacting to an away-from value). While in this state, we'll shut our development right down. We'll avoid challenge and change in favour of staying small and safe.

When the threat causes a significant amount of anxiety, we'll go into 'fight-or-flight' mode, and then we'll shut down physically too. Our digestive system is put on hold because blood gets sent to the extremities instead of the gut (so that we're equipped to either fight or flee), and our cognitive abilities will be impaired because, when under threat, the crew take full control (the captain needs no say when we're running from an avalanche). Being able to enter into a state of protection is obviously essential, but if it happens too often or goes on for too long, we can find ourselves shrinking away completely. We may suffer from physiological issues related to stress like irritable-bowel syndrome or chronic fatigue. We could start having panic attacks or heart palpitations. We could find ourselves in a depressive state where we struggle even to get out of bed. Or, we could find that the anxiety causes such a strong need for certainty that we jeopardise the fulfilment of all the other needs. Needless to say, having too many unessential away-from motivators at play is not enormously desirable.

How motivation affects performance

For many people, the result of an away-from value will not be as dramatic as all that. However, whether we're unconsciously opting for the carrot or the stick can still affect both our choices and our performance.

To understand the difference between towards and away-from motivation in a more contained context, imagine that two conscientious public speakers are preparing for an event, and that they are both responding to the value of 'giving a great talk'.

Speaker 1 – Towards motivation (a state of growth)

Speaker number one has towards values in connection with public speaking. If you asked her what was important about giving a great talk, she might say, 'The feeling that I'm communicating effectively'. She gravitates *towards* the opportunity to speak because it excites her and gives her a sense of purpose. That's not to say she feels no trace of nerves before going on stage (she almost certainly would do). However, because the positives occupy more space in her awareness than any fear, she's able to feel excited rather than frightened by the prospect of presenting; and she's able to remember that she wants to do what she is doing.

Speaker 2 – Away-from motivation (a state of protection)

Public speaker number two is also intent on fastidious preparation, but in her case this is because she's determined *not* to stand up in front of people and appear unknowledgeable or foolish. If you asked her what was important about giving a great talk, she might say something like, 'I really can't bear the thought of getting up on stage and looking like an idiot'. The positive aspects of presenting are not paramount in her mind; she's more concerned with the risks than the rewards.

Fear will be occupying the second speaker's awareness for a reason. Perhaps she's had a terrible prior experience on stage, or perhaps she has always been afraid of speaking publicly because deep down she doesn't believe that she's articulate enough to do it well. Either way, the fact that she is fearing failure means there must be a part of her mind that believes it to be a real (and dangerous) potentiality. That part, of course, will be the monster, and it will tell her stories that make her feel like she's 'not good/intelligent/funny/clever enough' to give the great talk she wants to give. As a result, her mind will create a state of protection in an attempt to move her *away from* the threat of failure. This might manifest as standard 'stage-fright' symptoms: anxiety, mental distraction, poor sleep, procrastination, etc. It could also crop up as something like a hoarse voice or even sleeping late on the day of the performance (both great ways for the unconscious to try to keep her from getting on stage at all). Alternatively, her fear could inspire her to over-rehearse until the presentation becomes lifeless and dull, or to pick an easy or boring subject just because it's 'safer'.

Ultimately, self-sabotage of some kind is far more likely to crop up when we're in a state of protection than it is when we're in a state of growth.

That said, I'm not suggesting that away-from motivation will always result in an objectively poor performance (I fought from a place of fear for years, but still won the vast majority of my fights during that time. I just didn't find it very fun.) It would be entirely possible that both our towards- and away-from-motivated speakers could end up giving equally good performances. But who do you think would be most likely to enjoy their time on stage and have a long and fruitful career in public speaking?

Growth and protection: a summary

Ultimately, if you perceive something as a thing that you want, your mind will remind you how to walk towards it and get as much out of it as possible. If your reality filter processes it as a dangerous threat, however, the only thing your mind will tell you is to get the hell out of there. This worked perfectly at the stage in our evolution when what we needed to run away from was the fabled sabre-toothed tiger, but these days, we can find something like a bad haircut threatening (there are some things you simply cannot run from). What we have to do is retrain our minds to see those fake threats differently, and the way to do that is to address the beliefs that can turn the safe into a source of dread.

Tracing the Limiting Belief

When they crop up in a problematic context, away-from values expose our monsters' limiting beliefs. Identifying them during a process of values analysis (like the one that you've been completing in this chapter) simply comes down to spotting negative language – because when the mind is unconsciously focused on some kind of threat, we will usually end up saying something about it.

Of course, both the carrot and the stick will normally be relevant and logical for all values. Anything that brings us something positive will almost certainly simultaneously move us away from something negative. The point here is to discern what the mind is giving the most attention to.

If we return to my example from above, when my therapist, Trevor, asked me about the importance of beating the opposition, instead of saying something like, 'A sense of achievement and the feeling that I'm good at what I do', I said, 'So I *don't* feel like I'm incapable'. I was thinking about protecting myself from the threat of 'not good enough' far more than I was enjoying the growth opportunities inherent in the challenge. This type of away-from value cropped up as I chunked up through almost all my boxing values. It did so because it was the story my monster most liked to spin.

Task: Identifying Your Monster's Favourite Stories

So let's see if we can catch your monster in the act. Grab your answers to the questions from the beginning of this chapter ('What's important about value 1?', etc.). Then, go through all your responses and circle anything that has been expressed as a negative; 'So I don't ...', 'So I won't ...', 'So I'm not ...', etc. Any statements written like that are likely to point towards a relevant limiting belief in that context. For example, 'So I don't look ugly' is likely to signal a fear that ugliness is the reality. Or, 'Not being selfish' would likely indicate a limiting belief along the lines of 'I'm selfish'.

I should mention that I have found that people tend to identify away-from motivators less often when they complete this task in writing than they do when speaking freely in a session. However, if you've chosen a problematic context, I'd wager a good amount of money on there being at least one away-from in the mix. If you have not actually written down any obviously negative statements, you'll be able to tell the difference between your towards and away-from values by how they feel. The positive motivators lure you in gently ('Mmm ... Juicy, juicy carrots'), whereas the negative ones tend to feel more urgent or even desperate ('Stick!!!').

To boil it down, make a note of all your away-from statements.

Example

'So I don't feel as if I'm unworthy of other people's attention.'
'So I don't feel left out.'
'So I'm not excluded.'

Then, look at them together and answer this question:

If there was a statement – beginning with the word 'I ...' – that seems to link all those fears together, what would it be?

Here are two potential limiting beliefs that may trigger the above away-from values:

Example

'I don't fit in.'

'I don't belong.'

Take a moment to come up with some ideas for potential limiting beliefs in your chosen context. It's normal not to wholeheartedly agree with these statements as you write them down. Usually the captain will have some objections. However, we're not interested in what he thinks here, so look past any of his rationalisations and focus on your gut instinct. For some, that will be a sinking feeling as they read the limiting belief back to them-selves. Others might get flashes of uncomfortable memories, or hear a sighing little voice that says, 'Yeah. That's me.' Any statement that provokes those kinds of reaction is likely to be an important monster story for you.

Finally, to link everything together, draw a little picture of your monster (in whatever way you would envisage it right now) and write your limiting belief(s) in a speech bubble next to it. Please don't worry if it looks silly. That will be nothing but helpful. There's a section in Appendix 5 (see page 356) for you to complete this final step of the values analysis process.

<hr />

Mirage Fantasies

Identifying our monster stories is important because we're often completely unaware of the times when the unconscious is reaching for the stick to beat us with. All too easily, we can find ourselves hypnotised by the sparkly success stories that we spin in response to our fears.

If you'd told me about these types of motivation while I was still overtraining, I would probably have sworn that I had positivity nailed. After all, I thought about success all the time! Retrospectively, I can see that my zombie-like training mindset, lack of enthusiasm and rapidly deteriorating physical condition were quite clearly a state of protection. What's more, my attempt to counter it with that shimmering image of my perfect future was only making it worse because it was based almost entirely on a collection of fearsome away-from values. However, while it was all going on, I had very little awareness of my sense of 'not ... enough' or my fear of failure (aside from just before a bout), because I had become a master of denial. We really do get so very good at hiding ourselves from ourselves.

The perfect picture

Ambition is (or at least can be) a wonderful thing. Equally, goals are really important. However, there are some highly ineffective ways of using these things, and unfortunately, they're the ones we tend to go for.

Because we're so used to idolising the inspirational experts who have already made it – the athlete on TV who's already number one, the musician who has already gone platinum – we get used to thinking of that 'finished product' as the goal. What we don't see so often are the years (decades, probably) of hard graft behind these visions of perfection. Yes, on some level, we know that they must have worked for it, and if we push ourselves, we'll probably concede that they must have had some failures along the way, but the process of growth is largely invisible. As a result, we tend to omit it from our own fantasies of personal success. Instead of visualising ourselves on a journey, we are more likely to imagine ourselves at the destination – the point at which we're already 'good enough'.

We can easily fool ourselves into thinking of this as positive motivation. We tell ourselves that we have a goal – a mission – and that we're *going to* get there. But our incomplete maps for success are inherently flawed.

Studies have shown that fantasies about our completed goals can actually demotivate us.[6] What this means is that visualising ourselves on top of the podium, acing the interview or slipping into a size ten dress could make it less likely for us to ever experience those things for real. There are a couple of reasons why this is likely to be the case. One theory is that over-rehearsing a future success satisfies our lust for achievement just enough to prevent us from actually putting in the hours needed to attain it. The other issue is that these kinds of outcome-focused visualisations accentuate our sense of longing to be better. By focusing on what we would like to be in the future, rather than what we can feel satisfied with right now, they consistently remind us that we're not quite where we want to be. This means that they cause us to feel 'not enough' in the present moment – not enough *yet* – which is disempowering and usually quite counterproductive because it locks us into a state of protection.

And still we do this all the time, either in an intentional, premeditated way or just by drifting off into a 'happy' little daydream. We indulge in fanciful visions about the very best version of ourselves who can wow the crowd, get the girl or guy, achieve critical acclaim, raise the perfect family or show off their perfect abs ... *because* we feel incapable of doing those things right now.

I like to think of these glorified future projections as mirages. They are the glimmering illusions that our success-thirsty minds like to thrust out ahead of us to keep us staggering forward. They promise to solve the 'not ... enough' problem, but they actually enforce it because they're just our monsters masquerading as friends.

Mirages as faulty needs-fulfilment

This doesn't mean that we can't achieve the objective content of the fantasy as we see it; just that we fail to experience what it tempts us with emotionally. There's a missing link in our reasoning. If we wanted washboard abs just for the sake of having washboard abs, then we would feel satisfied when we got them. But it rarely stops at that. When the goal is a mirage, we will have unconsciously connected it to a bigger prize: 'If I could only have those perfect abs, then I would be attractive to others'.

Mirages make the false promise that they'll fulfil a need that's currently at a deficit: 'If I win that competition, then I'll feel significant', 'If I lose more weight, then I'll be lovable', 'If I make a few more sales, then I'll feel financially secure'. But if we have a limiting belief that stands in the way of those needs being fulfilled, then no matter how many things we achieve in an attempt to counter it, nothing will ever truly quench our thirst. We may win the competition, but then we want the title. We may lose weight or get the washboard abs, but then we want a facelift.

It's easily done. Our monsters tell us that we're 'not ... enough' so we assume that what we need to feel is '... enough'. But this is a problematic word. 'Enough' sounds as though it's quantifiable, as if you can accumulate your way to it, which is almost certainly not the case. 'Enough', as a goal, seriously lacks definition. How much is enough? Enough of what exactly? Good enough for whom? These important qualifiers were missing from my little self-esteem mirage while I was fighting, so how could I ever hope to realise it? I know now that what I actually wanted was to feel 'OK'. Not as in, 'Meh ... I'm OK, I suppose', but as in a full, resounding: 'I'm OK! In my body. In myself. Right now.'

The kind of OK that I really needed was the type that meant I didn't have to achieve anything else before I felt it. The reality is that no matter how much we like to think they will, external things, like status, qualifications, accolade, beauty, possessions and all the other things we like to strive for, don't really bring us that feeling (at least, not beyond a fleeting glimpse). OK has to come from within.

And so, we never really get to drink from the oasis when it's a mirage. And what's worse is that the more we look at it, the thirstier we become. Each time we have a little win, the mirage will transform into something bigger, better and farther away, so that we remain in the same old state of anxious longing, with our monsters hot on our heels.

When is Enough Ever Enough?

Multiple Olympic swimming champion Michael Phelps (the most decorated Olympian of all time) is famous for saying, 'I hate losing more than I enjoy winning'. So let's just be clear, I'm definitely not saying that away-from motivation will necessarily stand in the way of objective success. However, when Phelps was arrested for drunk-driving in 2014, he hit an all-time low and was forced to address the depression and substance-abuse issues he'd been battling quietly up until that point. When he spoke out about his mental-health issues, he said this: 'I was lost, pushing a lot of people out of my life – people that I wanted and needed in my life. I was running and escaping from whatever it was I was running from.'[7]

Thankfully, this isn't the story of every top athlete, but it will ring true for many. The sense of futility that can grow out of ceaseless striving against a negative belief, even at the highest level, is something I frequently discuss with sportspeople in my practice. Addressing a blocked competitor's fear of failure, more often than not, forms a substantial part of their treatment.

Six weeks spent in a rehab centre in Arizona turned things around for Phelps. After announcing his retirement at the 2012 London Olympic Games he returned to form for Rio 2016 and claimed another six Olympic medals (taking his total tally to a staggering twenty-eight). Perhaps more importantly, in this, his fourth Olympic Games, Phelps looked as if he could even be enjoying himself. 'Before I would have my headphones on and not talk to anybody,' he said. 'I'm a lot more open and relaxed now.' [8]

It sounds as though Phelps met his monster in rehab and learned that he no longer had to run from it. Successful people often resist the relinquishing of their fear because they believe it's the only reason they're as good as they are. Yes, the stick might have been the thing that drove them to the top, but that doesn't mean the carrot can't do the same (or better). A happier and healthier mind did not prevent Phelps from blowing his opposition out of the water. It just meant that he could smile while doing it.

Drinking From the Oasis

By working on our limiting beliefs and shifting focus away from the stick and onto the carrot, we can learn to let go of the impossible future and enjoy the journey instead. Doing this means that we can open up the possibility of a more varied and rewarding life, whereby we can accept our (whole) selves regardless of the results we achieve. Ironically, desperation for success makes us far less likely to achieve it. Training ourselves to let go of that desperation, on the other hand, makes us more likely to find success and infinitely more capable of enjoying it when we do.

Here's the thing: we've got something very important the wrong way round. We tend to think that finding success will bring us happiness, but the reality is that it's getting happy that makes real success – the kind that we can feel for ourselves, as well as being obvious to others – possible.

So, rather than trying to achieve our way to happiness, we need to turn our attention inwards and spend some time working on creating a bit more harmony in there first. This is why it's important that we stop to listen to our monsters' stories; only when we know what we're really fighting will we be able to resolve the battle.

Turning it towards

When a value is not being hampered by the threat of away-from motivation (a limiting belief), the question, 'What's important about ...?' will simply lead up through a chain of increasingly abstract positive concepts that help us to fulfil our needs.

Example
Q1: What's important to you about public speaking?
A1: Relating purposeful information to others.

Q2: What's important about relating purposeful information to others?
A2: Feeling like I'm making a difference.

Q3: What's important about feeling like you're making a difference?
A3: The sense that my *contribution* is of genuine value.

Most frequently, if you push someone right to the top of the ladder (even beyond the needs-like concepts), you'll hear words like, 'peace', 'freedom', 'love', 'joy', 'wholehearted satisfaction' or perhaps something like 'contentment', 'acceptance' or 'flow'. These are the core states that can be achieved when our values align and our needs are being met. I believe that these states are the ultimate aim for all of us – what we truly yearn for deep down. But rather than only manifesting after some external goal has been achieved, these things are available right from the point at which we begin applying ourselves. Feeling them is simply a matter of perspective.

'Not thin enough'

I received an enthusiastic phone call from a friend a few nights ago. He was in the process of reading the first draft of this book and felt that this particular chapter could have provided him with the shift he'd been looking for.

Having been heavier than he'd like for some years now, Bernie's focus while reading (other than correcting all my typos) was on his self-sabotaging food choices. The reason he was so excited when he phoned me was that he'd just made it through his first ever juice fast without cheating.* The way he had done this, he said, was by redesigning his 'Don't-eat-that!' thinking. Up until now, Bernie's strategy for overcoming a craving for fish and chips was either to berate himself with angry self-criticism ('Don't eat that! You're too fat!') or to try to mirage his way out of the chippy by imagining himself looking thin and gorgeous. Neither of these approaches worked when the desire was even half as powerful as it could be because they made him feel a little depressed. What did work, however, was a reminder of the current and process-focused enjoyment he was already experiencing having lost a few kilos. Improvements in his agility were evident on the tennis court and bringing to mind the feeling of moving swiftly and playing increasingly well had inspired him to forgo the deep-fat fryer a number of times. Enjoyment of the game of tennis became his measure of progress. It was no longer about 'not being fat' in the future. Instead, it was about capitalising on his day-to-day enjoyment of developing his skills. In other words, he had switched his focus from the sense of lack inspired by a deficiency need to the love of learning provided by a growth need. And the more he fed that need (both mentally and practically), the more he was able to enjoy it and live by it.

Task: Challenge It

You can start changing your focus right away by challenging the fantasy. Broaden your horizons in the name of growth by asking, 'If my mirage was really a towards value, what would I enjoy most about the pursuit of that thing?' Or, 'If I was in a state of growth rather than protection, what would be more exciting about my life right now?'

Start by having a think about the fantasies your mind is most likely to entertain. What kind of mirage do you find yourself chasing? Make a list.

When you've done that, consider what their present-moment and growth-focused alternatives might be, and write those things next to the mirage. Then emphasise them in some way.

---

* I should mention that I am not an advocate of juice fasting (and also that I am not a nutritionist, so my opinions mean nothing when it comes to diet, anyway). If you're considering practical methods for weight loss, please consult an expert.

Example

Looking 'ripped' >>> **Enjoying my weight-training programme**

Rock stardom >>> **Enjoying the process of writing songs, practising with the band and performing at Wednesday's open-mic session**

Finding 'The One' >>> **Enjoying the experience of meeting people on the dating scene**

It's the things that you emphasised that stand the best chance of bringing you both enjoyment and success together, not the glimmer and gleam of the inner fantasy. And, as always, the more attention you give to those things, the more space they'll occupy in your awareness. This can make it much easier for you to travel the more effective path, smiling as you do.

———— •• ————

The mirage trap is why I was so insistent on you visualising yourself in the process of improving rather than having 'already improved' at the end of Chapter 3. But don't worry if there was still a touch of shimmer and sheen in your future visualisation. It's just as important to get to know our mirages as it is our monsters, and once you're acquainted, you can even put them to some positive use.

Tracking back

I doubt it's possible to de-mirage our thinking entirely, and I don't think that it would be a good idea either. The point of this is not just to wander aimlessly through life whistling a present-moment happy tune. So long as we remember not to invest too much into our visions of the future, knowing what we'd like to happen there can help us to move in that direction. What's important is that we remember that if the goal is a mirage, then it will promise something that it cannot provide. Instead of chasing after it, when we catch a glimpse of the glimmer, we can use it as a prompt to track back into the now and choose a better strategy. Then we can focus on the genuine resolution of the needs deficiency that the mirage drew our attention to. Let me give you an example.

While writing this book, I have noticed various fantasy outcomes floating through my mind. What I find interesting is that as soon as the image of a five-star review hits me, I can actually feel the faint pang of anxiety that comes with it. A few years ago I would have given in to the monster inherent within the mirage, and I probably would have found myself trying to procrastinate the nerves away. Now that I'm aware of the trap, I use that anxiety as a cue to come back to the now, because that's the only place where happiness is actually possible: I'm loving sitting in my office, grappling with metaphors and churning up ideas. I'm not willing to miss out on that just because a little, fearful part of my mind is tempted to believe that I can only feel significant if this book achieves critical acclaim.

Summary: Mirages as Resistance

The upshot is that it all comes down to resistance again. Mirages are simply flawed attempts to fight the shameful parts of our own self-image; but in entertaining them, we'll only ever strengthen our monsters' negative stories and push any genuine satisfaction farther into the distance. When we bring our attention into the present moment and allow some love for the version of ourselves that we find there, however, we might just realise that we've been knee-deep in the warm waters of the oasis all along. It's just that we forgot to look down.

It's only by learning to accept our whole selves – monsters and all – that we can free ourselves from the failure loop created by away-from values and mendacious mirages. I am aware of how impossible this can sound. If someone had told my anxious, striving self, 'Hey! Don't worry about it! Just learn to love your fear and everything will be all right', I probably would have laughed (a slightly unconvincing laugh) right in their face. I wasn't ready to take the challenge while I was doing my midnight sprint sessions and grinding myself to the bone. I wasn't ready because I was being driven forward by a fear that still felt real and powerful. We need to alter our perspective on the monster – to shrink it down to a manageable size and remember that we are more than it. Only then will we be able to even consider accepting it. In Part 2 we'll look at how to start doing this by learning about control.

Round-up of Part 1 – Perception

In Part 1, we've looked at the ways in which the mind can warp, delete and even add to the raw information it receives from the outside before we perceive it consciously. The result is that we each respond to our own unique maps of the world, based on the beliefs, values and old coping mechanisms learned over the course of our lives. Regardless of how much we may consciously desire change, without a means to address this map, the reality the unconscious mind will strive to maintain can feel decidedly (dis)comfortable.

For your reference, here are the key points:

The captain and the crew (page 31)
Compared to the unconscious, the conscious mind is like an arrogant ship's captain. He thinks he has control but it's the crew who really do the sailing.

Subjective reality (page 36)
In order to reduce the vast amount of information available at any given moment into digestible chunks, the unconscious filters all that we perceive through our pre-existing belief systems. What this means is that we tend to get what we expect, for better or worse.

Limiting beliefs (pages 50–8)
The beliefs that are likely to cause us the most problems are those that limit our sense of self or negatively affect our anticipation of the future. These are usually formed early on in our lives, while we're prone to both black-and-white thinking and taking things very personally.

Monsters (page 46)

The monster is the part of the personality that believes our limiting beliefs. Our natural instinct is to battle this aspect of self because of the pain it causes us to feel. However, because 'what you resist persists', the more we try to fight, deny or otherwise overcome our monsters, the more monstrous they will become.

Shame (page 58)

Shame is the fear of disconnection, and it's what our monsters cause us to feel when they tell us their limiting stories. Because we fear that our various nuances of 'not ... enough' make us unworthy of the love, respect or time of other people, we attempt to conceal our monsters by either achieving them away or numbing the feelings that they trigger. However, the resistant strategies we employ — drinking or taking drugs, procrastination or avoidance, angry outbursts, etc. — tend only to exacerbate the problem. In many cases, it's the things we do to try resist the feeling of shame that we'll look back on afterwards and consider to be self-sabotages.

Live-wires (page 64)

Live-wires are the traumatic memories that the mind carefully preserves in order to keep us safe from anything similar that might crop up in the future. They represent the birth of our monsters; the moments when we first learned to believe our limiting beliefs.

The (dis)comfort zone (page 63)

The unconscious mind is reluctant to let go of our limiting beliefs and live-wire memories because it thinks those things are keeping us alive. As a result, it'll repeat negative behaviours and distort our perception of the world so that it stays safely familiar. However, because we consciously want to grow and prosper, the unconscious mind's comfort zone feels more like (dis)comfort to the captain.

Motivators/values (page 85)

Our values are the things that we believe to be important. The unconscious uses these qualifiers to both determine and judge our choices of behaviour. When our actions successfully fulfil our values we will feel content. When they do not, we will feel as though something is not right.

Needs (page 90)
Needs trump values and they come in six basic flavours:

1. Certainty
2. Variety
3. Significance
4. Love and connection
5. Growth
6. Contribution

The deficiency needs (needs 1–4) are felt when left at a deficit. We'll only be aware of them when we don't have enough of them. The growth needs (needs 5–6), however, are felt positively — like a lust for life — and they can grow stronger the more they are fulfilled. Because a deficit in any of the first four needs can so easily hijack our awareness, the two growth needs are the most likely to get neglected. However, they are needs nonetheless, and because it can be so much more fulfilling to focus on them rather than the others, it's a very good idea to train our minds to start giving them some more attention.

Drivers (page 105)
Drivers are conditional beliefs that utilise the values that we learned during our formative years. There are five drivers and we're all likely to relate to at least one of them:

1. Be Perfect ('I'm only OK if I get it right')
2. Hurry Up ('I'm only OK if I'm doing things quickly')
3. Please Others ('I'm only OK if everyone else is happy')
4. Try Hard ('I'm only OK if I'm working hard')
5. Be Strong ('I'm only OK if I don't show my emotions')

The Pleasure Principle (page 115)
Freud's Pleasure Principle describes the instinctive movement away from pain and threat (a state of protection), or towards pleasure and nourishment (a state of growth).

Towards and away-from values (page 116)

Any value has the potential to either put us into either growth or protection depending on whether the mind sees it primarily as a means to get what we want (towards) or to move us away from a threat (away-from). The latter, when they come up in therapy at least, usually have a limiting belief at their heart.

Mirages (page 122)

Mirages are the simmering visions of success that we like to throw out ahead of us. We work towards them because we think they'll solve our 'not … enough' issues. However, when they promise to help us meet needs that are in a chronic state of deficit, we never get to drink the water we're thirsting after. Mirages are nothing more than our monsters masquerading as friends. The more we chase after them, the greater a sense of lack we will feel.

● ●

The remainder of this book is going to focus on the various ways in which we can redraw our reality map and transcend the (dis)comfort zone.

PART 2
POWER

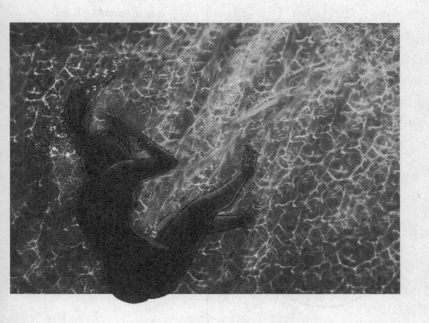

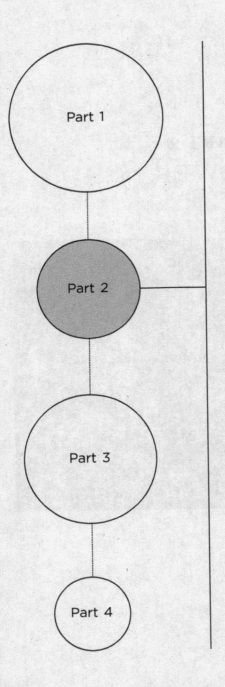

Power

What tends to make our monster stories so painful is the feeling of defencelessness that comes with them. To rise up and autonomously overcome our moments of self-sabotage, therefore, we need to learn how to take effective control. Part 2 is all about reclaiming your right to both internal and external command.

Part 2 Contents

Evolution II
Facing the Monster   137

Chapter 6: Victimhood
How and Why We Keep Ourselves (One-)Down   139

Chapter 7: Control
Paving the Way to Authorship   164

Chapter 8: Authorship
Making Magic Out of Monsters   182

You can listen to the guided meditation for Part 2 here:
http://hazelgale.com/home/mindmonsters-part2-recording

Evolution II

Facing the Monster

Truth does not lie in thought alone. It lies in how various thoughts relate to experience ...'

Eugene T. Gendlin,* Focusing

Part 2 of this book is about taking control. It is at this stage of the process that facing the fought, lost or otherwise resisted part(s) of the personality becomes the most important. Over the next three chapters, we will explore the ways in which you can do this by getting in touch with a deeper understanding of your moment-to-moment experience. By the end of Part 2, you will have learned how to make this a simple, everyday practice. Before that though, I'd like you to check in on your monster visualisation.

Task: Meeting the Monster Eye to Eye

To give yourself the best chance of meeting your monster on a level playing field, I'd like you to follow these instructions:

Step 1

Knowing that it's only while we continue to run from them that our monsters will feel like monsters, I'd like you to stop and take a fresh look. To do this, start by deciding where your monster feels as if it could be in relation to yourself (as always, just go with your gut instinct). Answer this question:

If you could point to your monster, where would you point?

* American philosopher and developer of the Focusing technique ('Felt Sense').

Many people feel as if they are being chased by their fear and so imagine it living behind them. Some feel as if their problem 'gets on top of them' or lurks below, like some kind of subterranean beast. Others feel as though this part is something very distant and out of reach, or simply as if it lives on the inside. There's no right or wrong, so just go with whatever first comes to mind.

Step 2

Once you have located your monster, answer this question:

If there was a way for you to move either yourself or your monster so that you can face one another, how would you do that?

For many, this simply means standing up and turning around. If that makes sense for you, then I recommend you literally stand to face it so you get a physical sense of the act. If not, then just imagine doing whatever you need to do to comfortably face your monster. Then, take a relaxing breath, close your eyes if you need to and calmly observe the way you see this part of you right now.

How does it look?

Step 3

Write a short description of what you imagine in your notepad. If you drew your monster at the beginning of this book, then draw a new picture of whatever you see now (there's an allocated space for this on page 345 at the back of the book).

Many people see their monster differently when they choose to look it in the face. Sometimes we'll see something that looks softer, smaller or more friendly. But it doesn't need to go that way. Some people, at this stage, see something that looks more threatening, more urgent and necessary to deal with.

No matter how you picture it, only when you can see your monster can you confront it. The beauty of this is that when you can do that, you can start to look past it to something different; something better.

6

Victimhood

How and Why We Keep Ourselves (One-)Down

A fog has descended behind my eyes. It functions like a protective wall of white noise, but I'm no longer sure if it's there to stop the bad getting in or out. It changes from day to day. Right now it's thick and heavy and it hurts to think through it, so I've stopped trying.

I don't know how long I've been lying here. Hours? Days? It doesn't matter. Time is all muddled up and I can't see the point in trying to separate things out any more. If I look for it, the future stretches away from me like a long, dark tunnel of nothing; just more and more of the same.

I'm motionless, but my pulse is racing; a quick, erratic heaviness in my chest. There's a weighty sickness deep in my stomach and a dull ache surging through my bones. Every movement sends an excruciating, creeping feeling like a slow electric shock through the fibres of my body.

Underneath all that, I can hear the murmurs of a dark and sinister presence. A knowing that rises up from the depths like the promise of death. But less welcome than that. It tirelessly follows my every thought in the way that a slow-moving beast in a horror movie might do. My shadow monster has breached the boundaries of my body and has taken up residence under my skin. I used to be fast enough to outrun it. I used to be strong enough to fight it. But now that my speed and power have left me, the wall of white noise is my only salvation. Without thought, I drift back into the meaningless drone of the TV that I'm not watching.

Becoming the Problem

Chronic fatigue is a strange sickness. There are no obvious external symptoms. To anyone else, you seem perfectly normal, but inside everything is wrong. For me, it was a world of paradoxes: I was exhausted, yet anxiously alert; utterly uninterested, yet furious with everything and everyone around me for not being able to help. The turbulence – both emotional and physical – was so disorientating that it frequently left me feeling desperate and hopeless. Even when I was making headway, the troughs I plummeted into would obscure all progress from view.

It seems that this is what happens when any kind of discomfort goes on for too long. With a broken leg, the pain is unbearable, but you know it will come to an end, so you can grit your teeth and plan for its resolution – it is just a thing that's happening. You don't *become* the pain. A chronic disorder is far harder to contend with psychologically because there seem to be no boundaries. The symptoms consume you and, over time, the condition fuses with your identity. Rather than being a person with a problem to solve, you start to feel as though you are the problem.

Things get even more damaging when the problem – that you see as yourself – starts to affect other people. In feeling like a burden to friends and family, the shameful fear of disconnection aggravates further until asking for help starts to look like an impossible task. The more detached you become, the easier it is to feel completely flooded by the helplessness of it all.

Fighting the Flow

I was in Nicaragua when I first learned to respect the awesome power of the ocean. One moment I was standing with my feet on the sandy bed, happily diving through the soft, white foam and looking out at the beautiful vastness of the sea. Then, without any warning, I was in the midst of the main break and it was too deep for me to stand. As I looked up, an enormous wall of water began to arc, readying itself to crash down from six feet above my head. The only thing I knew to do was what I had learned as a child: you have to dive through the waves to withstand their power. Over and over again, that water rose up in front of me and I hurled my body into it with all the energy I had. But these waves were bigger than the ones I was used to and I could only dive halfway through before they'd pull me up and back down into the churning, directionless torrent beneath.

Between each bombardment there were a frenzied few seconds when I could see the sky. In those moments, I'd frantically try to touch a toe to the ground, but it was always just out of reach. With every wave I grew weaker and more hopeless, and as I gasped desperately for air, through a mouth filled with salty water, I learned what it was like to feel as if all was lost.

A surfer saved me that day. He untied his board from his ankle, hauled me up onto it and then pointed me in the direction of the beach. 'You have to go with the water,' he shouted, and pushed me towards the shore as the next wave approached. The sheer force of it threw me up in the air and once again I crashed down into the confusion, but this time the sand was there to meet me. When I scrambled to my feet, the water stopped at my chest and, almost immediately, the waves seemed beautiful again.

When I look back on my years of anxiety and then burnout, I remember an experience much like that day in Nicaragua. The initial waves of discomfort seemed manageable, and I discounted the warning signs as the sickness and fatigue symptoms started to mount up. Then, before I knew it, I was in too deep to just push on through, and my repeated, futile attempts to regain a sense of control did nothing but carry me farther out into the alarming, bewildering territory that I had driven myself into.

I was stuck in that holding pattern for years. Every time I got even the vaguest hint of energy, like a relapsing addict just out of rehab, I would ignore all the good advice I had been given and head straight to the gym. Sometimes I would manage fifteen minutes of attempted exercise before that slow electric shock returned to crush any sense of hope. On other occasions I wouldn't even make it out of the flat before I knew that my body was shutting down again. Still, I persisted. Time after time I'd sabotage any chance of recovery by doing more of the very thing that was making me ill. And with every denial-fuelled attempt to dive back into training, my body would shout even louder to make itself heard: enduring headaches, chronic muscle pain and weakness, sickness, allergies, food intolerances, water retention, insomnia, heart palpitations, blurred vision, light-headedness, brain fog, difficulty forming sentences and that horrible, heavy, all-encompassing fatigue that only someone who has pushed themselves to the brink will ever understand. Finally, when all the will to fight had left me, I found myself in front of that droning TV with nothing but the dissociation of my exhaustion-induced depression to keep me afloat.

Seeking the magic pill

As most of us would, I looked for external solutions first. I felt sure that someone or something would be able to 'fix' me. However, every route I ventured down ended with yet another hope-crushing wave of defeat. None of the Western doctors, the nutritional plans or any of the Eastern practices I tried made more than a small dent in my symptoms.* I visited a number of doctors, who ran tests for things like glandular fever, but then shrugged their shoulders and told me that the only way to deal with chronic fatigue was to get some rest. But rest didn't work. At least, the amount of it that I could tolerate didn't change things and no one offered me a solution for the permanent state of anxiety that seemed to be causing the problem. There simply was no magic pill.

I learned later that *I* was the missing ingredient. Perhaps any one of those treatments could have improved my condition had I actually been present and active for the process, rather than just receiving help like a passive object and hoping it would 'work'.

When I finally plucked up the courage to look inside for the solution, cognitive hypnotherapy provided me with what I needed to recover. But this wasn't the airlift to shore that I thought I wanted. Instead, I was pointed in the right direction and given a crash course in how to trust the fear I'd been trying to fight my way through. It was a challenging and sometimes difficult journey. Therapy was tough at times and it took patience to retrain my old thought processes. I'd have days when things seemed to be taking effect, and then there would be moments when the pain and nothingness would return in full force. Even after the months it took for me to get to grips with the reality of my problem, I needed many more for my body to catch up with the progress my mind was

---

* I am not suggesting that these methods of treatment are necessarily ineffective, just that they were for me at that time. If you are struggling with any physical symptoms, then the first thing you should do is consult a medical professional.

making. But I got there. And it was probably the most important battle I'll ever fight.*

Now, I have a newfound respect for my unconscious mind, much like the respect any surfer must have for the ocean. If I push myself too hard, my body will still let me know about it. However, I no longer see those messages as a defeat because I've learned how to work with myself, rather than against. I can both accept and utilise the emotions and (now infrequent) physical symptoms that used to terrify me. They are all part of a language that I would never have understood had I not gone through what I did.

Getting sick turned out to be the beginning of an upgrade and not the death of the life that I wanted. It wasn't that I had to quit boxing to get better, as I feared might be the case at the time. Boxing wasn't the real issue, so quitting wasn't the solution. It was my internal fighting that was causing me problems. I had to resolve my psychological battles before I could begin claiming back my physical health and start enjoying the fights I actually wanted to be in. Ultimately, learning to cooperate with my unconscious mind meant that I could get back into competition – albeit at a lower level of fitness – and then conclude my time fighting in a way that I felt proud of a number of years later.

Neuroplasticity

The brain is an astonishing thing (which is satisfyingly ironic). It's capable of continually updating itself in order to do its job more efficiently. This is called neuroplasticity and it's a physical process. Whenever you have a thought, say a word or perform an action, electrical impulses fire throughout your nervous system. These pass between neurological structures called synapses, which are separated by an empty space called the synaptic cleft. Any thought causes the synapses associated with it to

---

* Psychological causes for physiological illness is a sketchy and sensitive subject. I want to be clear that I'm not blaming anyone who gets ill for their condition. I don't believe that all illness has a psychological cause, and even when it does, blaming ourselves would be an entirely unproductive way to think about an unconscious reaction. However, I do believe that many illnesses can be improved by reducing stress and retraining negative thought process, and that it's both important and empowering to take control of anything we can do to make things better.

bridge the gap between them by releasing a chemical that functions as a neurotransmitter, enabling the electricity to travel to where it needs to go for the thought to manifest.

The importance of this is that every time a particular electrical charge is triggered, the relevant synapses helpfully grow closer together, so that thought will be more efficient in the future. In many situations, this is very useful. When I worked behind a bar in my twenties, my mental arithmetic was really quick (at least, it was when it came to adding up the price of three lagers, a double G&T and a glass of Chardonnay). Now that I don't work behind a bar, it would take me considerably longer to do that sum because those synaptic paths are no longer so well-trodden.

Unfortunately, this process is not reserved exclusively for healthy and productive thinking. We pattern in the negative ideas too. For example, if you chose to start telling yourself that 'life sucks' every time something challenging crops up, then your 'life sucks' thought would get increasingly easy to think. Before long, anything with even the slightest chance of triggering it could lead you to that conclusion, and 'life sucks' would start to feel like the absolute truth. In other words, 'life sucks' would become a belief, and your mind would therefore filter your reality through it, unless you made a concerted effort to change it.

This is why an awareness of our thinking is so important. The thoughts you have about your future, for better or worse, will literally reshape your brain and, therefore, the reality it creates for you. For me, it meant that every time I collapsed in front of the TV and thought about how terrible my life had become – every time I thought, 'Poor me', or 'I'm unlucky', or 'I'm weak' – I was physically making my continued discomfort more and more of a probability. Ouch.

Mirror, mirror, in my mind

There is one other important bit of neural circuitry that it's worth getting your head around here. Mirror neurons are nerve cells that fire when we observe an action performed by another. They mirror external behaviours, so we can understand them. For example, if we watch someone taking a sip of coffee, these brain cells will cause us to create a mental replication of ourselves doing the same. This is why someone who hates coffee might grimace a little when their friend knocks back his espresso.

It's this part of our neurology that makes empathy possible. (As with all relatively recent scientific discoveries, not all scientists are completely convinced that mirror neurons are what make empathy possible, but the theory is widely accepted.) So, we cry when we see people suffering because our brains automatically run a first-person simulation of their situation in order for us to comprehend it. As a result, we feel what they must be feeling (or as close to it as our experience and assumptions will allow). As we do this, the synapses associated with the corresponding mental processes fire up and grow closer together, even though we haven't actually been through whatever it is we're witnessing. It means that we quite literally grow to be like the people we spend time with. Or, as the old adage goes: 'You are the company you keep.' So, choose your friends carefully.

Mirror neurons are how we adopt the beliefs, values, drivers and personality traits of the people we spend time with. We observe their behaviours (including the things they say), replicate them internally and programme the corresponding thought processes for ourselves. It means that just hearing someone saying, 'life sucks' will cause your mind to run that belief as if you're the one who believes it. Then your brain will strengthen the synaptic paths accordingly. For this reason, I'm going to stop writing it. And here are five counters for the times you've read that health risk of a statement so far in this chapter:

Life is awesome.
Life is awesome.
Life is awesome.
Life is awesome.
Life is awesome.

And it can be, if you physically put your mind to it.

Playing the Victim

The problem with having 'hypno' in your job title is that no matter how you frame it, people will always be a little bit hopeful that something is going to magically resolve their issue without the need for them to do any work. This is exactly what I hoped for when I booked my first session.

Even though I knew that it wasn't that likely, deep down I was longing for a little miracle. And, as a therapist, I'm aware that most people who walk through my door will be entertaining a similar wish. Even when we don't completely buy into the idea, if there's a part of us that thinks we need someone with magical powers to save us, then that part at least has cast itself in the role of 'helpless victim'.

I felt horribly victimised when I got ill. I was angry at the world and about my terrible luck. I was angry with my pathetic body because it couldn't keep up with my 'strength of mind'. Up until the point where everything came tumbling down, I saw myself as the warrior in my own little narrative. I literally went out and battled every day. How could I be anything but the hero? However, looking back, I can see that I had been living life from the position of victim for a long time before the final straw broke the camel's back. It's just that, like most people, I had no idea that this was a matter of choice.

The context of competitive sport, at the beginning, was one big shame trigger for me. Everywhere I turned, there was an opportunity for my 'I'm-not-good-enough' monster to pipe up and make me feel worthless. The sense of victimhood that this generated was the primary cause of all my initial anxiety. Later, it was the reason I completely failed to heed the years of (frankly obvious) messages from my body to do something differently. I made no effort to change anything because I didn't really believe that I *could* change anything.

The Victim Culture

I wasn't alone in this. The victim mentality is everywhere and it's not just the weak, ill or anxious who fall prey to it. As I write this chapter, I'm acutely aware that most people really dislike being called a victim because they tend to find this trait frustrating in others. However, regardless of how much we may hate the idea, the victim mentality is far more common than its counterpart, and there's almost certainly going to be some kind of trigger for each of us that will provoke the thought, 'Why me?'

It is rarely a conscious decision when we each tumble into our respective 'victim traps'. Victimhood is a slippery beast that is skilled in pretending to be something it is not. Until we understand it, we can remain completely unaware of the various ways in which we could be ensnaring ourselves.

In the developed world, at least, we're actively encouraged to feel dependent. We're taught to believe in magic remedies like fat-burning pills and antidepressants, and we learn to desire possessions, titles, beautiful partners, Facebook 'likes' and many other forms of accolade in order to feel good about who we are. (**Note**: I am not condemning the use of antidepressants. Many people clearly need medical help to deal with their depression and other psychological disorders. However, I'm convinced that at least some of those who go down this route would be able to recover without the need for pharmaceuticals. The victim preference of the world in which we live, though, makes this option seem like less and less of a possibility, so our knee-jerk reaction tends to be to look for the quick fix instead.)

Consumerism knows that it can get the most out of us when we feel reliant on our various 'fixes', so it feeds our monsters to keep us needing the latest age-defying skin product, smartphone or fast car.

When we're not trying to accumulate our way out of a sense of 'not ... enough', we may attempt to deflect it instead. Looking outside for reasons as to why we fail to overcome our own challenges provides us with a little hit of pleasure, which can hook us — like addicts — into the victim game. It may be the relief of, 'It's not my fault' – the moral vindication that comes from blaming another or the sympathy we receive when we're the ones who got the shitty end of the stick. However we do it, to relinquish responsibility feels good (temporarily) because it allows the mind to breathe a sigh of (dis)comfortable relief.

If you take a look around you, you'll see even the strongest of people battling for their right to the 'defenceless bystander' position. The majority of everyday arguments are good examples of our willingness to play the victim. It feels like an expression of power to exclaim, 'I'm right and you're wrong!' However, in the long run power is the last thing we get from this behaviour. In passing the buck and absolving ourselves of any accountability for whatever is going on around us, we voluntarily step into the wounded-sufferer role: 'You did this to me. You're making me angry/upset. It's all your fault. I am powerless against you.'

The same goes for griping with friends about an evil boss or some other villain in our world. Unless we take our complaints to the source, those conversations rarely achieve anything except to confirm that we are the victims.

Once we've fallen into the pattern, we will look for something to blame for absolutely anything we don't like. And, just as saying 'life sucks'* repeatedly will convince our brains that life really does suck, each time we do this, we fortify the synaptic paths for all our disempowering self-beliefs.

The language of victimhood

When I started looking objectively at the connection between my mental processes and my physical state, I realised that my victim mindset was evidenced and reinforced by the way I spoke almost every day. I had a long list of mini self-sabotaging stories that my mind was using to keep me where I didn't want to be. I'd frequently refer to my less-than-good days as 'ill days', as if I needed to make it concrete: I was not well. My stock-standard answer to the question, 'How are you?' had become: 'Meh … not *too* bad', regardless of how I actually felt. Worst of all, I'd automatically look for an excuse whenever I fell short of perfect. Even if I didn't mention it out loud, I'd search internally for something to pin the blame on, so I could lessen my feeling of inadequacy.

At the time, these things were subtle. My victim addiction only really made itself clear when I first attempted to let it go. Then, I found myself experiencing weird little pangs of loss whenever I tried out a more positive turn of phrase. I was craving the opportunity to prove my monster right. I wanted to say: 'See! I *am* sick/cursed/unlucky. Not my fault. Now please give me a hug and make me feel better.' But feeling better was something that would only happen once I finally found the strength to kick the habit.

Having said that, I'm not suggesting we should avoid negativity entirely and choose instead to make arrogant, self-aggrandising or overly positive statements to cover up our sense of inferiority. People who do that are just living the flipside of the same insecure coin. There's nothing wrong with an honest expression of doubt. This is healthy, and it can even be empowering when done in the correct way. However, there's a big difference between saying, 'I'm feeling uncomfortable right now because I'm questioning my capability' and saying, 'I'm incapable'. The former recognises that you are separate to – and more than – the doubt that you're experiencing, and it creates the opportunity to both question the veracity of the fear and take action to rectify the problem. The latter just tells your mind and everyone else around you that you're a lost cause.

* Life is awesome.

Fortifying helplessness

Our victim synapses grow more and more efficient every time we take our eye off the ball and slip into the trap of defencelessness, blame or unnecessary self-criticism. If what we really want is autonomy, strength, growth, happiness, freedom or all of the above, then this perspective is something we have to make an effort to ditch.

I'm extremely passionate about this aspect of mental wellbeing because I know that it's only once we step away from a sense of victimhood that we're likely to experience what we really want in life. The truth is that however uncomfortable it might be, to rise up out of the (dis)comfort zone we must first be aware of all the things we do to entrap ourselves within it. The people who make the biggest and most rapid changes in therapy are those who take it upon themselves to make as much of a conscious effort as possible to shake off the shadows of victimhood between sessions. It's not effortless, but then again, nothing really worth doing ever tends to be easy.

The Drama Triangle

In the 1960s, psychiatrist, Stephen Karpman, developed the Drama Triangle as a model for understanding the interplay between responsibility and power in conflicted relationships (of any kind). It's immensely helpful for understanding the types of co-dependent interactions that cause us to feel blocked or limited (AKA victimised), and it's a powerful means of identifying the various different nuances of victimhood.

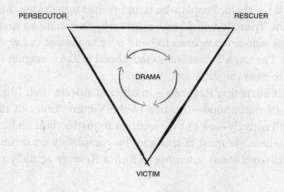

The Drama Triangle involves three interdependent roles: the Persecutor and the Rescuer are in the higher, one-up positions ('I'm OK. You're not OK'); then there's Victim, which is in the one-down position ('I'm not OK. You're OK'). The Persecutor punishes the Victim and the Rescuer attempts to save the Victim, but the catch is that once on the Drama Triangle, we will automatically rotate through all three positions and we always wind up feeling victimised in one way or another. The truth is that all three of these roles are just different styles of victimhood. Whether we are rescuing, persecuting or just feeling victimised by somebody or something else, we are actively (albeit unconsciously) choosing to play the victim.

Entering drama

The three corners of the Drama Triangle are the entryways into conflict as well as the roles we play once we're in. Most people will have a preferred gateway. That is, we will each tend to enter into a conflicted or blocked situation as either the Persecutor, Rescuer or Victim before we begin cycling through the other positions. Let's look into each preference in a little more detail.

The 'Victim' victim

The Victim's perspective is, 'Poor me!' While we are in this role, we feel oppressed, powerless, hopeless, not good enough or otherwise limited by circumstance or other people's actions. People who tend to approach life from the Victim position will hold the belief that they cannot help or take care of themselves and therefore that they require a saviour of some kind to do it for them. People who tend to enter into drama through this corner of the Triangle will often wonder why they have so many people in their lives who are prepared to bend over backward to help them out (Rescuers). The truth is that their victimhood is like a magnet for people who want to save the day.

As well as attracting Rescuers – in order to sustain their (dis)comfortable sense of victimhood – anyone in the Victim corner of the Drama Triangle will actively seek out Persecutors to justify their enduring sense of powerlessness. As most of this goes on completely unconsciously, the Victim's futile conscious attempts to find a Rescuer actually capable of solving their problems will leave them feeling ever more helpless, and therefore even more in need of yet another saviour ... and so it goes on.

As the Victim rotates through the three roles, they will rescue and persecute from the one-down position. To rescue, they may say something like, 'You're the only one who can help me' to those who attempt to save them (which is exactly what a Rescuer wants to hear). In doing this, the Victim can enjoy a deceptive sense of power by successfully manipulating others into taking care of them.

In relationships with a strong Victim–Rescuer dynamic, the Victim can sometimes find themselves intentionally staying down (perhaps financially or in terms of their health or confidence) just so their Rescuer continues to have something to try to remedy. Ultimately, the Victim would rather coerce someone into saving them than risk an attempt at an equal relationship because they don't feel that they're enough on their own ('If you need to save me, then you won't abandon me'). This leads to the Victim's primary means of persecution, which is the guilt trip: 'If you loved me, you'd help me' or, 'How dare you leave me like this?'

All of these manoeuvres, again, are likely to elude the conscious aware-ness of the Victim, who only really knows that they need someone or something to help, and can't quite work out why nothing ever manages to do the trick.

The 'Rescuer' victim

The Rescuer position is, 'Let me help you!' This role is very similar to the Please Others driver that we discussed in Chapter 4.

Rescuers see themselves as helpers, carers or guardians, and they achieve a sense of self-worth by assisting others. In fact, they are dependent on someone to rescue in order to feel good about themselves, which is how they get addicted to the drama of the Triangle, and part of the reason why their attempts to help consistently fail to elevate the Victim out of their victimhood.

Although it is consciously well meant, rescuing is not actually helpful. Because the Rescuer is reliant on having a Victim to save, they unwittingly keep the people they support in the one-down position. This co-dependent dynamic grows out of the Rescuer's unconscious belief: 'If you need me to save you, then you won't leave me', which exemplifies how the Rescuer position is really only victimhood in disguise (or, more accurately, in denial).

Primarily, the Rescuer is the victim of their own sense of guilt and duty. Often, they may have no idea that saying 'no' to someone is even a possibility, and because of their own sense of 'not ... enough', even if they can see the option, they're likely to fear the ramifications of taking it. As a result, they feel bound to the drama of others and so chronically fail to attend to their own needs. Over time, because the help they offer is not born out of complete, autonomous choice, and because it fails to make any lasting difference, the Rescuer's sense of obligation makes way for bitter resentment, which is one of the most debilitating of all the emotional states involved in victimhood. When the resentment grows too powerful for them to stomach, they may attempt to exit the drama by retracting their help, which is their primary form of persecution.

'Yes, but ...'

'Yes, but ...' is a conversational game shared between Victim and Rescuer (although it's also possible to play it non-verbally). It's worth looking out for because it signposts our slip into either one of those roles. Consider this conversation:

Victim: I feel really fat and unattractive. I hate my body and I won't feel better about myself until I get fitter but I just can't do it!

Rescuer: Why don't you come with me on my morning runs? That'll shift a few kilograms in no time!

Victim: Yes, but ... I can't because I have bad knees.

Rescuer: Oh, well, in that case we can do yoga at lunchtime. That's low-impact.

Victim: Yes, but ... I can't do yoga because it always damages my back.

Rescuer: Okaaay ... Why don't you go swimming then?

Victim: Yes, but ... it takes so long to get to the pool and the chlorine makes my eyes go red ... Yes, but ... Yes, but ... Yes, but ... Yes, but ...

At some point, the Rescuer in this little dance will throw their hands up in the air and say, 'That's it! I've had enough. Solve your own bloody problems,' which signals their move over into the Persecutor corner (and then quickly back down into Victim – because withdrawing their help makes them feel guilty). This can happen over the course of a single conversation or it could take place over years of co-dependent activity.

From the outset, playing 'Yes, but ...' is a passive-aggressive form of persecution available to anyone in the Victim position. Its function is to prove that the problem is unsolvable: 'You can't help me. I'm the victim here'.

When we want to play the Victim, there will always be a 'Yes, but ...' No matter what help we are offered, we can never truly benefit while we are psychologically wedded to the role of Victim because all our decisions are influenced by the unconscious desire to remain in that place. In fact, the more help we're given, the more we'll want to prove ourselves to be fundamentally 'unhelpable'.

'Yes, but ...' is a game that people will play with their therapists. Occasionally, clients who feel particularly victimised by life will actively resist recovery for fear of conceding power, as if they're in a competition and the therapist will win if they get better. Alternatively, they may return after a successful few weeks claiming that some kind of magic has happened and that they 'hope it won't wear off'. Or worse, they'll say that everything has been going really well, but that they think it's just because the weather has been good or that some other plausible yet entirely disempowering external factor has (temporarily) rescued them. Awareness of the Drama Triangle and this particular dynamic can help these clients to recognise the part they themselves play in both their issue and their recovery. Although it's a very sensitive conversation to have, it can be an absolutely crucial stage in the process.

I mention this because I am sure that no matter what your situation, if you put the tools and theories in this book to practical use, you will be able to make a positive change to your life. However, if your mind is hell-bent on playing the victim, it may well try to 'Yes, but ...' you out of claiming the successes: 'I've been feeling more confident at work recently. Ah ... yes, but that's just because my line manager is being nicer,' etc. Please don't let the (dis)comfort monster talk you out of enjoying either the little wins or the big ones that could follow them. They belong to you – not your boss, partner or the postman.

The 'Persecutor' victim

Persecutors are bullies. People who enter into drama through this role will tend to be controlling, critical, authoritative, superior and oppressive. Their primary position is to blame others: 'It's all your fault!'

Unlike Rescuers, people with a Persecutor preference will readily identify with a sense of victimhood because, to them, the world is a bad, wrong and evil place where they have to fight for survival. Because of this, Persecutors will blame others for their discomfort and resort to bullying tactics in order to feel OK about themselves. However, they fail to acknowledge this because they feel entirely justified in their persecutory behaviour on the grounds of self-defence.

The Persecutor role is the one that people are probably the least likely to see in themselves. From my practice (and from personal experience), I know that virtually everyone recognises the Drama Triangle as something they've experienced in at least one relationship, and that pretty much all of them will identify straight away with either the Rescuer or the Victim role. But if we've played those other parts, then we must also have played the Persecutor, because one style of victimhood does not come without the rest. Some people just do it more obviously than others.

Persecutors are dependent on Victims because they garner a sense of self-worth by putting others down or feeling as if they're 'winning'. Persecutors will also engage in rescuing, but they'll do it in a way that is (sometimes consciously) planned as a form of punishment. They'll likely blame the Victim for being so demanding and then offer intentionally unhelpful or complicated help to 'get them back' for the inconvenience. They may be the type of person to give backhanded compliments or do the task requested of them poorly on purpose (or with overt grudgingness). Or, they may do something like buy an extravagant gift for someone, only to take it away at the last minute just to show that they meant well but that the Victim, in the end, did not deserve their effort.

The victimhood whirlpool

The Drama Triangle can be easiest to understand by imagining three people engaged in conflict at once. The Rescuer will usually enter the fray after witnessing the Persecutor meting out their punishment. Then, all involved can cycle quite rapidly through the different roles, generating more and more shame as they drive themselves deeper into their various versions of 'not ... enough'.

Imagine a Persecutor parent punishing their child (the Victim) for failing to do his homework: 'You'll never amount to anything because you're lazy and good-for-nothing.' The other parent may jump in as Rescuer and say something like, 'Leave him alone. He's been trying hard, but he's just not quite getting it. Give him a break!' In saying this, the Rescuer may feel like they are the one saving their son from the torment of the angry parent, but they are also inadvertently compounding the child's sense of inadequacy and giving him an excuse not to do the thing that would actually advance him (the homework). Simultaneously, the Rescuer is persecuting their partner by undermining them, and therefore forcing both partner and child to feel the shame of 'not enough'. If the child runs over to stand with the 'good-cop' parent, they will have moved into the position of one-down Rescuer. Here they can keep the Rescuing parent in the game by appealing to their hero-ego ('You're the only one who's ever nice to me. Only you can save me.') Then, to climb back out of their 'bad-parent' shame, the original Persecutor may turn on the original Rescuer by blaming their child's inadequacy on the other parent's lack of discipline, which would put the original Rescuer into Victim ... Hence the whirlpool; around and around and down and down they all go. At the end of the argument, all parties are left feeling as though they can't do anything right and that everyone else is out to get them.

Opting Out of Drama

The gravity of the Drama Triangle makes us feel that we have no option but to play the game once we're in it. If we're rescuing at that particular moment, we will believe we have to help; if we're persecuting, we believe we have to get our own back; and if we're in the Victim position, we will simply feel we aren't capable of taking action. However, there is always a way off the Drama Triangle; it's just that our sense of victimhood makes it difficult (and often frightening).

The way to exit is via the path of honesty. Dishonesty – either with ourselves or with others – keeps us locked in.

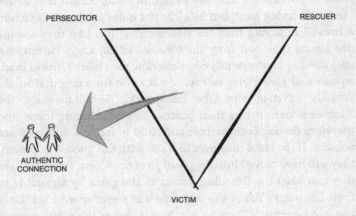

Honesty

When on the Drama Triangle with other people, if we choose to do the courageous thing and (calmly) voice our authentic feelings, we can often step away from the discomfort of the drama in a way that strengthens our sense of self-respect and therefore minimises the feeling of defence-lessness. It doesn't always happen instantly, it isn't always pretty and it certainly isn't always easy, but when we choose to ignore this option, continued drama is most frequently the result.

If we catch it early enough, we can often opt out just by recognising the drama and choosing not to get sucked in. This is why awareness of the model can be so powerful. It means that we can remind ourselves that we don't actually *have* to either punish, be the saviour or feel helpless, so long as we stay true to ourselves.

'Say the awkward thing'

When it comes to personal disputes and painful feelings, 'Say the awkward thing' has become a mantra for me. When whatever I've communicated has come from a place of emotional honesty, I don't recall it ever ending badly. (This, I should point out, is not the same thing as saying it has always ended the way I originally wanted it to.) I'm not suggesting that honesty will necessarily resolve the conflict for all involved. After all, it's often an 'awkward thing' purely because the other person doesn't really want to hear it. However – even if the difficulty continues after we've said our bit – when we know that we been emotionally honest throughout, it can be a lot easier to let go and move forward.

For each of the positions on the triangle, there are some key truths that need to be confronted if we are going to aim for honesty.

Home truths for the Rescuer

Typical Rescuers often have the hardest time with this step because rescuing is the most socially acceptable position on the triangle and looks like the honourable thing to do. However, to get honest about our rescuing tendencies, we must acknowledge that when we're rescuing, we're issuing out our 'help' from the one-up position. We need to recognise the moments when we achieve a feeling of worth, confidence or even love because we feel as though others are dependent on us. Of course, some people really are dependent on us (like our kids, elderly parents and friends in times of need), and we will be dependent on others sometimes too. Love and connection are basic human requirements, after all. What we have to be able to see are the things we do to either keep those people reliant on us, or to make them need us even more. Until we let go of the belief that those we are 'helping' are either incapable of helping themselves or that they will abandon us if they learn how, we will not be able to exit their drama.

The other thing that we need to recognise when we're rescuing is that we do self-damaging things just to avoid letting others down or looking like the bad guy, and that when we fail to make the strong and healthy decision (which often means saying 'no'), it's not their fault but ours.

I worked with a client recently who was worried that he was drinking too much. Pub culture was a staple in his line of work, and he recognised a clear, pivotal event in any evening that determined how his next few days would go. That moment was when he was offered the drink that he knew would be the 'point of no return'. Saying 'no' meant that he'd head home and wake up feeling OK in the morning. Saying 'yes' meant that he would likely still be out the following lunchtime, probably having spent hundreds of pounds and having done things he wasn't entirely happy to have done. The problem for him was that – in that moment – he was habitually going into Rescuer. He didn't want to say the awkward thing (something like, 'Actually guys, I feel like I've been drinking too much lately, so I'm going home'). Instead, he felt as though the only option was to either succumb to the peer pressure and drink more (rescuing) or to reject them by leaving abruptly and without explanation (persecuting). Understanding the Drama Triangle dynamic at play meant that a third and far healthier option became possible: he could say 'no', explain himself authentically and leave respectfully.

Rather than being the victim of an alcohol-loving profession or dictatorial drinking buddies, he was only ever the victim of his own decision to walk onto the triangle. This didn't mean that he instantly made the healthy choice every time, but it did mean that he knew it was an option and, when he managed to take that route, he would wake up the following morning with neither a physical nor emotional hangover.

Helping vs rescuing

Remember that rescuing and helping are not the same thing. If the help we give has been intentionally designed to empower others up and out of their victimhood, then that's a good thing (and we will not feel obligated or resentful, but inspired and energised to see their change).

To understand the difference, we need look no further than this well-known proverb: 'Give a man a fish and you feed him for a day; teach a man to fish and you feed him for a lifetime.' Rescuers would opt to do the former and they'd achieve a sense of self-righteousness from the fact that this 'poor man' relies on their daily offering. Then, at some point, they'd reach the end of their tether and decide that they've given out enough fish, actually. In fact, they're getting pretty hungry themselves. So, they stop rescuing and move guiltily over into the Persecutor position to eat their fishy just deserts.

Home truths for the Persecutor

When we persecute, the home truth for us to accept is that our criticism or punishment also comes from the one-up position and reinforces our sense of self-worth. Honesty when we're persecuting means letting go of the idea that we are the innocent party ('I tried my hardest, but he just kept wanting more and more of my bloody fish!'). This doesn't mean that all Persecutors are to blame. When we do this, we really feel as though we're in the right, so blame is not a good way to look at it, and it would also mean that we'd be persecuting the Persecutor. In order to exit the triangle from the Persecutor position, we must remember that if we're in the drama, then we will definitely have played a part. Then, we need to take full responsibility for that.

Home truths for the Victim

Finally, when we're in the Victim position, we need to recognise our desire to be seen as helpless, small or in need. Then we must face up to the fact that, from that position, we refuse to properly utilise the help offered by others in order to keep them around. The other thing we need to keep an eye out for is the subtler blaming that happens from the one-down position; the type that seeks out and exaggerates the wrong-doing of others in order to validate our own sense of victimhood.

Task: Drama Spotting

Those who find themselves the least impaired by the three different styles of victimhood on the triangle achieve that because they can recognise drama as it arises and deal with it appropriately. It's almost certainly not because they've managed to dispel all conflict from their lives. To better identify any drama-tainted relationships or situations that you're likely to encounter, you can answer the following questions.

Note: I have written these questions as if we're talking about inter-personal relationships. However, all of them could apply to other things like habits, situations, contexts, objects or substances as well as people.

Identifying where you might be playing the Rescuer-victim

* Of all the people you know, whose needs are you most likely to put before your own?
* Do you enjoy being needed? If so, by whom?
* Do you find it hard to say 'no' to some people? If so, to whom?
* Who are you most likely to play 'Yes, but ...' with from the Rescuer side of the game?
* Finally, what do you imagine would happen if you chose to stop doing any of that?

If you fear that the relationship in question would break down if you withdrew your rescuing, then this is a potential drama hotspot for you. That doesn't necessarily mean the relationship is doomed, but it may be headed for trouble if you don't do something to change the dynamic. The questions to ask yourself are these: 'What are my needs in this relationship, and what needs to happen for them to be met?' And, to turn your rescuing into helping, you could ask yourself this: 'What do the people I'm most likely to try to rescue really need in order to take responsibility for themselves?'

Where you might be playing the Persecutor-victim

* Around whom do you find yourself becoming your most aggressive?
* Around whom do you get the most competitive?
* Who are you most likely to insult, put down or snap at?
* Who makes you feel like you need to 'get your own back'?

For anyone that came up in response to these questions, consider what you might be doing to keep them in the one-down position. How do you compound their sense of victimhood? Those will be the Persecutor behaviours that you need to take responsibility for first. If these are people you would like to have in your life, then what would an equal and respectful relationship with them look like?

Where you might be playing the Victim-victim

* Around whom do you find yourself becoming your most passive?
* Do you find yourself caring too much about others' opinions and judgements? If so, whose?
* Do you worry a lot? If so, about what/whom?
* Do you ever complain about people behind their backs? If so, about whom?
* Who are you most likely to play 'Yes, but ...' with from the Victim side?
* About what are you most likely to play the 'Yes, but...' game?
* Who might you expect to automatically come to the rescue whenever you're struggling?

Clearly, it's a good thing to have people you can depend upon. What we're looking for here is those you might expect to show up in moments when even the smallest thing goes wrong. These may be people on whom you rely, but to whom you feel inferior. It's incredibly easy to get 'addicted' to the people we cast as the Rescuer, but the key thing to remember is that the Rescuer will always move over to the Persecutor corner at some point, and they might even start to prefer that role. If you want a relationship like this to continue, you may need to shift the dynamic and take back a little of the control.

When it comes to those we see as our Persecutors, then choosing to stand up for ourselves is the most important step. What could you do to bring yourself onto a level playing field with the people you see as bullies? Also, do you really want those people in your life? If not, then do you really have to keep them around?

The Triangular Mind

The Drama Triangle does not only play out between separate individuals. We can all too get easily sucked into our own inner whirlpools as well. When we condemn ourselves for some kind of observed lack or failure, we are taking on the role of Inner Persecutor. Then, when we get the resulting sinking (or shrinking) feeling as we fret over the veracity of our own self-criticism, we have identified with the Inner Victim. At some point, we'll try to relieve ourselves by either justifying our actions inwardly or engaging in some kind of escapism or striving pattern, which is how we attempt to be the Rescuer for ourselves.

Any self-sabotaging issue will have its own Drama Triangle dynamic. The obvious ones would be sabotages of our relationships. Maybe we struggle with the shame of angry outbursts or the simple inability to hold down a partnership because our connection to others is always tainted by manipulative unconscious power plays. Maybe we just feel like the victims of our own emotions, or we depend on destructive habits like alcoholism, drug use, binge eating, gambling, sex addiction, or any number of other dissociative pastimes like procrastination or playing computer games to rescue us from those emotions.

Drama as resistance

Both rescuing and persecuting are forms of resistance; we learn to either overpower or save other people in an attempt to resist our own feeling of shame (victimhood). What this means is that our external Drama Triangles are mechanisms by which we attempt to fight or deny the Inner Victim: the part we see as weak, flawed, or 'not enough' in some other way. This Inner Victim, of course, is what we've been calling the monster. It starts out as a belief about our own inadequacy that we learn at the hands of past Persecutors (whether they intended this or not). As we try to resist the fear it generates by either denying or fighting it, we allow it to evolve into something that feels like an omnipresent Inner Persecutor, but it's nothing more than our own sense of inadequacy.

What happens on the outside, therefore, can be understood as a projection of our internal resistance to victimhood. For me, the winner identity

I so desired was a rotating character in my little drama. Kickboxing and boxing were initially my Rescuers. They promised to help me beat the shame of 'not good enough' by offering all the glory, strength and success that I felt I lacked. But the Rescuer always becomes the Persecutor with time, and that's exactly what happened as I continued to 'Yes, but...' my way into burnout. My Inner Victim-monster had a 'Yes, but ...' for every victory: 'Yes, but the best opponents weren't there'; 'Yes, but I got really tired in the last round'; 'Yes, but I could have done better'. 'Yes, but ... Yes, but ... Yes, but ... I'm still not good enough'.

When we release ourselves from resistant thinking and choose to step off the Drama Triangle (both internally and externally), our monsters – just like those waves in Nicaragua – can transform into things of incredible and natural beauty. They can teach us about ourselves and help us connect more authentically with others. They afford us access to a higher level of understanding, which involves increased creativity, intuition and freedom, and a deeper sense of purpose. It's our monsters, therefore, that can actually carry us back to the shore. Because, trust me, there is no rescue helicopter hovering overhead. And even if there were, we'd miss out on something quite wonderful by being airlifted to safety every time we felt we were out of our depth. What we need is to learn the lesson that surfer taught me of how to 'go with the water'. When we can do that, we can make use of our monsters and start heading in the direction we really want to go.

7
Control

Paving the Way to Authorship

My health is coming back in fits and (sometimes false) starts. I'm making it my mission to learn how to listen – not to my desires or my sense of obligation, but to my body. It's not easy to overrule the urge to train too hard or work out multiple times a day just because that's the standard I'm used to. But when I make the right decisions, I'm rewarded with spells of lightness and optimism. Finally, I can see a new version of myself up ahead, and although I'm not yet able to imagine her at full fitness, I am aware of a new kind of strength building within.

It's a wonderful feeling to realise that it's my responsibility to take control, and to know that I have the power to do that. After two years of futile attempts to fight my way through the emotional swell and physical debility, rather than being angry with myself, this insight brings me new hope. But it's not the same kind of hope that I used to attach to the supplements or the doctors or the diets. This is a hope that comes with a pregnant sense of ownership. It empowers me with a lust for living that I had all but completely forgotten until now.

On the days when my body tells me it's OK to train, I adapt my style and output to work with lower energy levels. I'm exercising my right to say 'no' to the coaches who ask for more than I can give, and I'm discovering for the first time what lies beyond the concept of competition. It comes as a revelation to realise that not everything needs to be about the win; that not every circuit needs to end in muscle failure or dry retching over the dustbin; and that, actually, there are far greater rewards up for grabs when I choose to take responsibility. Going 'with the water', it turns out, is not about relinquishing control. It's about claiming it in a way that feels coherent with the whole.

I know that this is an important part of the process for me; to understand that I don't have to compromise my health, my body or my happiness in order to be who I want to be. I'm learning that, even in a sport that's about breaking people, I don't have to break myself to have success.

• •

Responsibility

Responsibility to yourself means refusing to let others do your thinking, talking, and naming for you; it means learning to respect and use your own brains and instincts; hence, grappling with hard work.

Adrienne Rich,* *'Claiming an Education'*

The word 'responsibility' can strike fear into the heart of even the most hardened individual. When we hear it, we tend to think first of culpability, blame and the exaggerated ramifications of any error. It's our monsters that put these associations at the top of the pile. However, being responsible is not the same as being at fault. Yes, you can be held responsible for an error, but there's more to this word than that.

If an arsonist set light to your home and burned it to the ground, it would not be your fault, but it would be your responsibility. You would have to decide on a number of practical ways of responding first. Have you called the police? Do you need an ambulance? Are there still flames to put out or runaway pets to find? Then, you would need to make a decision about how you are going to respond internally and emotionally to the disaster. Do you get angry and look for someone or something to blame? Do you flee the country? Do you turn to alcohol or drugs to deal with the trauma? Do you search for silver linings? Do you reach out and then find yourself overwhelmingly thankful for the support of your friends as they help you back on your feet? Two people could go through exactly the same experience and come out the other side feeling entirely different about it.

Everyone, at some stage in their life, will be victimised by other people, by poor health, by nasty accidents or just by the evils of society. We're victimised because of the colour of our skin, our sexuality, our gender, our appearance, our level of income ... It's a horrible but entirely unavoidable

---

* American poet, essayist and radical feminist.

fact of life. Yet, whether we choose to *feel* victimised by the adversity we experience is down to us. There are survivors of serious abuse in this world who suffer less from a sense of victimhood than the old guy next door who thinks that our tree is blocking his sunlight. The objective intensity of our misfortune, it seems, can sometimes be quite irrelevant to the ongoing emotional effect. The real difference comes down to whether or not we choose to take responsibility for ourselves.

Response-ability

So, let's break the word into two halves. When considering the prospect of taking responsibility for ourselves, what we are talking about is developing an *ability* to *respond* (rather than react). Responsibility, in this sense, will be something that feels closer to liberation than liability.

To choose victimhood is to intentionally (albeit largely unconsciously) relinquish the right to take responsibility in the pursuit of personal happiness. Our method will vary, depending on which corner of the Drama Triangle we're currently residing in. While we're in the Persecutor position, we place responsibility in the hands of others by blaming them for our suffering; while we're in the Victim corner, we project our own sense of responsibility onto the Other because we don't believe that we're capable of taking it for ourselves; and while we're rescuing (even though we're likely to think of ourselves as doing the 'responsible thing' at those times), we deny ourselves the ability to respond autonomously by continually prioritising the needs of other people above our own. The end result is always the same; we give up the right to take control of our own wellbeing by depriving ourselves of the ability to actively choose our response.

But there is another option. We don't need to live our lives on a perpetual Drama Triangle. The answer to stepping away responsibly can be found by taking a look at one particular field of psychology.

Locus of Control

. . . you need to learn how to select your thoughts just the same way you select your clothes you're gonna wear every day. This is a power you can cultivate. If you want to control things in your life so bad,

work on the mind. That's the only thing you should be trying to control.

Elizabeth Gilbert, quoting 'Richard from Texas', *Eat, Pray, Love*

The study of locus of control focuses on the fundamental level of agency people credit themselves with, and how this affects their choice of behaviour and sense of wellbeing. The theory examines an important difference between two distinct types of thinking:

* **External Locus of Control (the victim mindset)** People in this mindset believe that external things (such as circumstance, luck or the actions of other people) have the ultimate power to influence the way that they feel and therefore act.
* **Internal Locus of Control (autonomy)** People with this perspective believe that they themselves are the only ones with any real power to control their own emotional state, behavioural responses and overall sense of wellbeing.

External Locus of Control

Externalising the locus of control is the very mechanism by which we end up feeling like a victim. Someone with this perspective may say (or think) things like, 'She made me angry', 'He made me do it', or, 'The weather was horrible so I was in a bad mood', etc. By presuming that things on the outside have power over us, we teach ourselves that our happiness, success and health all hinge on fate, luck and other people's actions, rather than our own. This can lead to a potentially deep and enduring feeling of helplessness.

This damaging externalisation can take place on the inside too. While in this mindset, we will put our own thoughts and feelings into the 'external' category and assume that those things have complete control over the way that our lives go. As a result, we can feel utterly powerless against our emotions, our urges to engage in habitual behaviours and any other type of negative thought process. It comes about as a result of resistance. We try to disown our most uncomfortable thoughts and feelings to distance ourselves from them, but in doing so we make them Other and they become monsters of the mind.

Internal Locus of Control

Internalising our sense of control, therefore, is the answer to escaping the trappings of the victim mindset and choosing a life of autonomy instead. It involves a deep appreciation of the fact that, even though we cannot control what happens to us, we always have a choice about how we respond and what meaning we take from our experiences. It also requires (and inspires) a willingness to begin taking responsibility for our own happiness.

I do not mention these things lightly. Escaping a sense of victimhood and dealing autonomously with the pain of life is not meant to be easy, and it would be irresponsible to claim that it is. Some inspirational stories with important messages talk about how the protagonist rose with apparent ease from their darkest moment to understand the positive value of their struggle. In retrospect, finding the silver lining might be a doddle, but while we're going through an emotionally painful time, the clouds and everything beneath them can turn to the blackest of black, and that darkness rarely makes a smooth or rapid exit.

The problem with the stories that gloss over the difficulty of the journey back is that they fail to elucidate the actual mechanism behind the hero's transformation. It's only by allowing ourselves to enter into and feel the most horrible of emotions that we gain control of how we respond to them, and no matter how great the thing on the other side might be, those moments will always feel close to hopelessness.

The next chapter is all about how to willingly enter into the darkness. However, before we get to that stage, we need to know how to build the confidence to do so by seizing control.

Control and needs fulfilment

An internal locus of control is not the magic answer to a painless existence, but it can make life a more varied, rewarding, connected, creative and potentially fruitful experience for those who take the challenge. It does this because it provides us with the ability to satisfy all of our needs with conscious volition, and therefore move into a state of growth, rather than protection.

Here are the needs categories again:

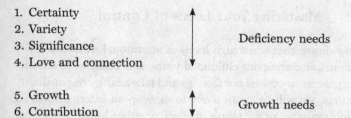

1. Certainty
2. Variety
3. Significance   Deficiency needs
4. Love and connection

5. Growth
6. Contribution   Growth needs

First and foremost, choosing an internal locus of control takes care of the need for certainty because it creates autonomy. This is important. With an external locus of control, certainty is virtually never up for grabs because things going well would depend on the stars aligning. Earlier in the book, I mentioned that those who feel the greatest sense of discomfort tend to be those who focus primarily on trying to fulfil their need for certainty. They feel the sense of lack because they have an external locus of control. An internal locus of control, on the other hand, can provide a sense of stability in the form of self-trust, even in quite precarious situations. Then, from that solid foundation, we can take responsibility for the ongoing satisfaction of all our other requirements.

People with an internal locus of control suffer less from lingering emotional problems like anxiety, resentment and shame. They're more productive and proactive because they believe their own actions to be of greater consequence. They enjoy a stronger sense of self-esteem due to the fact that they honour their own opinions and feelings. Ultimately, they're calmer, more optimistic, more motivated and in greater control of their behavioural choices because they choose to take responsibility for all those things.

People with this perspective can avoid the Drama Triangle because they'll be more likely to speak up, take action or simply exit when their current situation is doing them harm. They'll also take full responsibility for their part whenever things don't go according to plan because they choose not to play the victim and blame the outside world for their own shortcomings. This may sound undesirable, but in practice it's anything but. Every time we put ourselves in a position of (realistic) accountability, we teach ourselves that we do, in fact, have the power to influence things.

So, how is it that we might find ourselves in either of these two (vastly different) psychological camps?

Mastering Your Locus of Control

Studies have shown that when high levels of attention, love and security are made available during our childhood years, and when we're encouraged by our parents to express our feelings and take healthy responsibility for our actions, we will be more likely to develop an internal locus of control. Children who suffer abuse, neglect or other kinds of trauma, conversely, are more likely to develop an external locus of control.

That said, we absolutely do not have to suffer serious abuse during our formative years to find ourselves unwittingly playing the victim as adults. Even without the societal pressures of a world that encourages us to buy, acquire or achieve our way out of shame, it would still be natural to seek ways to offload responsibility whenever we're having a hard time, because when our most painful or frightening memories are triggered, we automatically regress to the emotional age of the original event. Seeing as most limiting beliefs are formed early on, and because all young children are naturally dependent on their environment (we're born with external loci of control of necessity), it's perfectly normal to find ourselves looking for someone to kiss our bruises better or for a baddy to blame when the water gets rough. Our victim moments happen when the mind goes searching for defence mechanisms and can only find the most (dis)comfortable of options to choose from. We're simply regressing to a familiar state of childlike powerlessness.

Training a better belief system

Something that you can do right away to begin reclaiming your sense of power is put your mind to the task of adopting the beliefs associated with an internal locus of control. Here are some key ones:

* 'I am the only one with any real control over my emotional state.'
* 'I can always choose my response.'
* 'I am infinitely more powerful when I choose to take responsibility.'
* 'Nobody and nothing (other than myself) can ever make me have a bad day.' (This one is stated in the negative, but I like it anyway.)

Remind yourself of these things regularly and your brain will physically adapt to accommodate them as truths. I'm not saying you need to stand in front of the mirror and repeat them as affirmations on a daily basis. However, these function in the same way as telling yourself that 'life is awesome' instead of 'life sucks'. Think these beliefs to yourself when you're in a difficult situation, or call them to mind when you see other people struggling with conflict, and you'll find it increasingly easy to opt out of internal drama going forward.

The control continuum

It is also important to remember that this is not a zero-sum game. When considering locus of control as a model for personal development, it's more productive to think of external and internal as two ends of a continuum than an either/or choice. We all have the ability to move quite fluidly between the states of victimhood and autonomy, depending on what our personal triggers are and how often we let them fire up.

EXTERNAL (VICTIMHOOD) ·················· X ·················· INTERNAL (AUTONOMY)

So much of this book is about limiting beliefs because these are the ideas that make our minds into monster territories. Working on them helps us to claim back a sense of power and move away from the trappings of the victim mindset. However, we need to back up that kind of psychological shift with the ability to take affirmative and responsible action. To simply reframe our childhood fears and hope that everything else will fall into place would be a decidedly Victim-like way of going about things. To really move on from the futile fight, we also need to lock down some important, self-empowering habits.

Taking Action

A key difference between those who operate from the victim mindset and those who maintain an internal locus of control is how much credence and time they give to the things that are beyond their reach. The fact of the matter is that our external environment will never be entirely within the scope of our influence; we simply cannot control other people's opinions, actions or wellbeing. Those things are up to them. With an internal locus of control, we can live by this rule and, as a result, it's far easier to make sure that we're prioritising our own wellbeing. It comes down to taking this attitude:

'If I don't like it and I can change it, I will. If I can't change it, then why bother wasting the energy it takes to worry about it?'

It's not that we won't care when the political situation is atrocious, or that we won't even notice when the weather is about to ruin our evening stroll. It's just that we will choose not to let the anger, fear or disappointment monopolise our thinking and ruin our day (or our life).

The Action Question

There is one simple question that someone with an internal locus of control will be far more likely to ask themselves than anyone stuck in Victim. It's a magic question that both highlights self-sabotage and inspires action. The question is this:

'Is there anything I can do about this right now?'

When the answer is 'yes'

On the occasions when the answer is 'yes', this question helps us create a new habit of taking responsible action (sooner). Perhaps a conversation needs to be had so that the 'awkward thing' (see page 157) can be said. Maybe we need to do something bigger, like research a new job, move house or even file for divorce. Any of these things are likely to make us feel uneasy, and change is always going to be a little bit frightening. Yet, to make things better, the courageous moments when we feel the fear and take action regardless are a necessary part of the deal.

When asking this question we must be sure to filter out any sneaky resistance options that might occur to us, like cancelling a flight because we are anxious about the turbulence. Any action that would 'help' us by avoiding the problem is unlikely to solve it – it would be the input of the inner Rescuer. It's easy to tell the difference. Thinking about some kind of avoidance will probably calm that sinking feeling we get when we consider doing something brave or vulnerable. The more powerful actions, on the other hand – the ones that ultimately help us to take control, and the ones that cause us to grow – will probably intensify it.

Very often, the key to taking (responsible) action when the answer is 'yes' comes down to acting quickly. If we stay in a moment of hesitation for long enough, our growing doubt will likely inspire a long stream of rationalisations about why we should definitely, absolutely, categorically *not* do the courageous thing. Every situation is different, so there's no rule here. Whether you adhere to the rationalisations of your conscious mind and do nothing, or ignore them and take action anyway, is entirely up to you. Just remember that skipping a flight will not cure your fear of flying. Unless you address the root cause, the issue will likely persist indefinitely. Motivational coach Mel Robins has a theory that it takes five seconds for the mind to talk us out of doing something new or difficult. Act within that period, and you can circumvent the inevitable siren song of the (dis)comfort monster.

When the answer is 'no'

The Action Question is perhaps even more important and powerful when the answer is, 'No, there is nothing I can do about this right now.' If we're feeling anxious, resentful or guilty about something that we cannot rectify or improve, then sustaining our current choice of emotional response is nothing but a self-sabotage. Continuing to engage in these kinds of feelings will also fall into the 'pointless self-destruction' category, when there is something we can do, but not until tomorrow. Asking this question and getting 'no' for an answer means that we can give ourselves full permission to honour, but then let go of the unnecessary emotion and choose to focus on something more productive instead.

In the case of anxiety, you might be surprised by how often you find the answer to be 'no'. For the most prolific worriers, 99 per cent of anxious thoughts concern things they can do nothing about at the time: something that's already happened, something that might happen in the future, comparison to people who are doing better than they are, whether or not the birthday present they bought for their granny last year was really what she wanted and so on. Of course, all these things are possible (actually they're probable; grannies can be really fussy), but just because life is full of things we could worry about, doesn't mean that we actually have to worry about them.

Susan's uprising

A few months ago, one of my clients – a deeply intelligent and caring woman who was subjected to unthinkable abuse during her childhood – reported putting this question to effective use for the first time, and it's possible that I've never felt happier during a session.

Susan lived in a near constant state of fear. Her severe phobia of vomiting and swallowing, coupled with histamine intolerance and a number of other physical and psychological issues, meant that she was able to tolerate only a handful of foods and a tiny amount of fluids, and that she rarely left the house.

When her husband required emergency medical treatment, Susan was faced with the challenge of managing her emotional response in order to take care of him, as well as herself. At first, she had felt too guilty and scared to even think about remaining calm. There was a part of her mind that equated worrying with caring and felt that if she didn't succumb to her usual anxiety, it would mean that she did not love her husband. Then, there was an even stronger part that believed worrying was a powerful thing to do – as if *not* worrying would cause the worst to happen because 'you are aware of the issue but don't do anything about it'.

The reality, of course, was that Susan's anxiety had no bearing on the outcome of her husband's treatment and would have been far more of a hindrance than a help during both the lead-up to his operation and the recovery period afterwards. She would not have been able to sleep or eat or drink, her mind would have been consumed by terrifying visions of disaster and she would have potentially undone all the progress she had been making. So, Susan made a pact with herself to cycle back to the Action Question whenever she felt the fear rising, and she used it like a permission slip to be the strong one. To her surprise, she found calm beneath the panic, and her sense of empowerment was tangible when she spoke of it. Susan had said a firm 'no' to her Inner Victim and proved to herself that even in the midst of all that chaos, she could still claim her right to a sense of control.

Exceptions

Of course, there are a few exceptions to the rule with this question. Grief (and sadness, some of the time) are necessary, yet uncomfortable, emotions that we usually cannot do anything about. It's absolutely OK and healthy to grieve for a loved one. We can't just think that pain away, and nor should we try. All the other 'negative' emotions – fear, anger, jealousy, frustration – must also be honoured (having an internal locus of control is not about sweeping things under the carpet), but many of us can hold onto those reactions for far longer than necessary. When we do that, we are self-sabotaging and we have every right in the world to let go and move on.

The more we practise this kind of thinking (and I'll emphasise the word *practise* here because that's exactly what it takes), the less of a threat all the things outside our control are able to pose. It's as if they shrink to occupy a smaller proportion of our awareness, making space for us to focus on all the things we actually *can* take ownership of – like our growth, our perspective, our sense of purpose and our chosen direction.

The Golden Linings Question

There's one more question that you can add in to the mix when the answer to the Action Question is 'no'. If you're in an uncomfortable situation, but there is nothing that you can do about it, then this question can help you to direct your attention away from (dis)comfort and onto whatever could help you turn the current problem into a solution. Here it is. And it's equally magic:

'What can I create out of this?'

Last Christmas, my boyfriend and I borrowed a (seriously old) car from a friend in order to drive a hundred miles to see my mum. We managed to get about ten miles from home before it broke down. This probably wouldn't have been so much of an issue if we hadn't been halfway down a slip road onto the A1, along which about fifteen massive lorries seem to pass every minute. With only the most basic insurance and failing phone batteries, we ended up waiting by the side of the dual carriageway for over twelve hours. We were wet and freezing and unable to sit in the car because of the lorry threat. But ... we genuinely had a fun day. This was only possible because we consciously chose to maintain our internal loci of control and to keep asking ourselves what we could make out of the mess we were in.

The temptation to succumb to a state of victimhood was strong that day, but instead we created games, emotional intimacy and a fortified sense of resilience. When we finally arrived at my mum's place at about 1 a.m. (having spent £120 on a taxi from London to Norwich), my sister looked at me and shook her head with disbelief: 'A few years ago, Hazel, you would have been *insufferable* right now!'

Task: What Can You Create?

Try applying the Golden Linings Question to your life right now. Is there a situation in which you are less than happy but know that there is nothing you can currently do about it? If so, consider that context with an entirely open mind for a moment. Or, better yet, imagine that the most sickeningly positive person you can think of has taken over your brain. See the situation through their eyes and then ask yourself, 'What can I create out of this?'

Make a list of everything that comes up (even the most outlandish and crazy ideas that occur to you). Then, allowing Sergeant Positive to retain control of your thinking, consider these questions:

If there were any skills, capabilities or resources that you could focus on developing in this situation, what would they be?

If there was someone with whom you could potentially develop a better relationship as a result of this, who would that be?

How could this situation help you to make better decisions in the future?

What have you learned from this situation that you wouldn't have known otherwise?

What has this situation brought into your life that you wouldn't have had otherwise?

Which of your values have been brought to light as a result of this (what do you now know that you find very important)? And, what can you do differently in the future to protect those values?

If there were a way for you to find fun in this situation, how would you do that?

I mentioned that I had a never-ending supply of gauntlets, didn't I? Well, here's another one. Even if you only have an answer to one of the above questions, and even if it seems like the most insignificant little glow around a massive cloud of blackness, make use of that information and act on it. It can take a surprisingly small amount of energy to get the control ball rolling, and once you have done that, you can use its momentum to make far bigger changes to your life.

David's concerto of control

David is a London-based concert pianist. We began working together to combat his issue with comfort eating, but when it took little more than an explanation of the locus of control for him to realise that neither cakes nor biscuits had any real power over him, we turned our attention to his career as a musician.

Regardless of his obvious ability, David had struggled with a lack of self-worth for as long as he could remember. One winter morning, his wife contacted me to book an emergency session for him. Later that day, David was going to be performing Rachmaninoff's Piano Concerto No. 2 – a piece that is renowned in the world of classical music to be one of the hardest to play. He had spent four months meticulously learning the score, and up until a week before the concert he had been playing it beautifully.

As the performance loomed near, however, David's confidence started to crumble. He was to play in an iconic London venue for an audience filled with visiting family members, friends and, crucially, some of his most respected peers. When we began speaking that day, he shed tears in anticipation of their negative judgement. His monster had taken over and dragged him into a state of utter helplessness. As a result, he had quite successfully convinced himself that he was not worthy of the piece, the venue or anyone else's attention.

David had fallen into an 'I'm-not-good-enough' trap. As a result, he was seeing every aspect of his upcoming performance as a potential Persecutor waiting to prove his inadequacy: 'Rachmaninoff's hands were so big that he composed music my fingers can't move fast enough to play ... I have to impress my peers but they're too critical ... The occasion is too big for me ... I'm out of my depth ... Everyone will think I'm a failure.'

While in the clutch of these thoughts, David was completely unable to recall the ease with which he had been playing this piece just a week earlier. Instead, he felt like the lost and powerless little boy he was when he first started learning the piano. And in that emotional state, all he could imagine receiving for his performance was something that felt like the reproving criticism of his childhood teachers.

The 'lost little boy' persona here was the key. In fact, it was his monster. For David to internalise his sense of control, he had to accept (rather than resist) the aspect of the self that he saw as weak, unprepared and 'not enough'.

To this end, David visualised the fearful child without his monster clothing. We discussed the kinds of thoughts that came from that part of his personality, so he could see them for what they were. Then, he took the 'lost little boy' on a tour of his present-day life. He was introduced to a loving, successful wife and wonderful friends, and he was shown some of David's greatest professional achievements. Incredible things can happen when we view our lives through the eyes of who we once were. It's so easy to lose sight of how far we've come until we choose to take a step back and see things from a different perspective. Doing this meant that David could see that all he had done must have been more than just fluke. Additionally, the more time he spent with this part of his personality, the easier it became to accept it. David wasn't just confronting his monster; he was learning to love it.

This shift made possible an empowered (and more adult) perspective on his performance. And as this was happening, his body language changed; he looked calmer, more relaxed, and he was sitting upright in his chair, rather than slumping forward. But the work wasn't finished yet. In order to let go of the sense of helplessness that stood in the way of a great performance, David had to turn his attention towards all the things that were actually within his control. Then he had to take responsibility for making the most of them.

For the remainder of the day, he would catch himself whenever he noticed the old, fearful thoughts and visualise the lost little boy they came from. This enabled him to recall his feeling of self-acceptance and then tell himself a better story. He chose to go for a run to reap the benefits of an endorphin boost; he practised breathing techniques to centre himself; he used positive visualisations; and he focused on relaxing his body during his final rehearsal, so he could get out of his own way and let his well-trained unconscious mind take him into flow.

All of these behaviours were in stark contrast to the tears of hopelessness he had shed that morning, but the performance anxiety had not vanished completely, and nor would we have expected it to. The difference was that David could now start accepting his nerves as a natural part of the process and know that he was more than those feelings; he was no longer that lost little boy.

His performance that evening was met by a standing ovation. As he rose to absorb the applause, he welcomed the feeling of knowing that he had played well. However, that buzz did not come from the audience; it came from somewhere within him. Because (rather than in spite) of the struggle he went through to get where he wanted to be that night, this entire experience enabled him to strengthen a far more productive and empowering perspective.

In those human moments of doubt, when his mind now tries to talk him out of a challenge, the story David tells his monster is this: 'If I apply myself, I can do anything.'

Internalising

Somewhat paradoxically, when we let go of the old desire to try to control everything on the outside, we often realise that we have far more influence over the things that happen there than we thought. Success, it seems, comes more easily when we take responsibility for our own emotions, and business partnerships, friendships and romantic relationships start to flow more cooperatively when emotional connection is made possible. It's as if the decrease in internal conflict correlates directly to a reduction in external discord too.

There's no reason why this shouldn't be the case. When we stop chasing ourselves around our inner Drama Triangles, we stop emitting all the negative emotions that might otherwise have coaxed people into defensive interactions with us (at least, we do so less often and we can catch ourselves when we slip). Additionally, when the external drama is not of our own doing, we can opt to stay at a safe distance because the gravity of our emotion has less power over us.

Internalised-control checklist

In summary, the key components for maintaining an internal locus of control and steering clear of victimising drama situations include these things:

1. Choosing courageous honesty (with ourselves first and foremost, and then with others as well).
2. Taking responsibility for the meeting of our own needs.
3. Using the Action Question – 'Is there anything I can do about this right now?' – to take action where possible and, crucially, give ourselves permission to let go of the self-sabotaging negative emotions that serve no actionable purpose.

4. Using the Golden Linings Question – 'What can I create out of this?' – to consciously choose to make something positive out of the challenging moments in life.

However, in order to do these things most successfully, there's one final missing ingredient. To claim an internal locus of control, we need to make sure we're taking ownership of our feelings, particularly those that may have caused us to feel 'out of control' before. This means braving an honest and open look at our emotional feedback and learning to embrace whatever we find when we do. We need to develop emotional intelligence.

8

Authorship

Making Magic Out of Monsters

The darker days are growing fewer and farther between, but I know not to wish them away completely. There's an unexpected beauty to the emotional world that I used to run from, and I'm discovering a stillness within it – a cocoon of certainty beneath the roughness of the surface. Gradually, I'm training myself to dive into the most fearsome of waters to find the quiet, and to my surprise there is nothing even remotely monstrous about this fluid realm that I'm making my own. With every descent, the more meaningful it seems to become.

I can still remember that old urge to flail wildly, gasp for air and pray for solid ground, but I'm learning to put those thoughts to one side and just trust that the quiet will always be there. Each time I dive, I dive a little deeper; and the deeper I dare to go, the easier and more beautiful I find the journey back out, with the water, to the shore.

I had no idea there was strength beneath the muscle and bravado until now. But there it is, teaching me how to shield myself from myself.

With this gradual building of self-awareness comes an even more important gift. I can see now that it's only by knowing the Self that we can ever hope to know the Other. As I dare to explore the world below the waves, the people around me transform before my eyes. Those I used to revere or fear now seem as beautifully human and fragile as the rest. Those who once seemed untouchable are now available via an entirely new means of connection. But it's not that understanding the vulnerability of others elevates me to a position above them. This is not about putting people in their place; it's about finally knowing that we are all in the same place. This water. The great leveller.

Getting in Touch

Fear is the main source of superstition, and one of the main sources of cruelty. To conquer fear is the beginning of wisdom.

Bertrand Russell*

When we start opting out of drama, our relationships can transform quite rapidly. Not only do we *self*-sabotage less often, but we can choose not to screw our loved ones over as well.

We already know that honesty is essential in order for us to make a responsible exit from most drama. However, without an authentic connection to our feelings, complete honesty simply isn't possible. Willingly listening to our emotional feedback is how we know who we are, what we want, what we need, or what we could benefit from changing.

Emotional Intelligence

Emotional intelligence involves getting real about what we feel. But it needn't be as daunting a task as that can sound. Just as a fear-of-failure monster can turn into a 'lost little boy', and just as the once petrifying ocean can become beautiful when we feel the sand beneath our feet, developing this ability means that we can take an entirely new perspective on our unconscious responses.

Don't shoot the messenger

The first stage in this process requires that we recognise the function of our feelings. Emotions are the unconscious mind's communication system. Everything we feel has been designed to motivate an action that the mind believes to be important. Of course, some of these messages are absolutely necessary, like the fear that tells us to step away when we get a little too close to the cliff's edge. Others are based on erroneous information, like the urge to scream and jump up onto a chair (and then scream some more and cry a little bit) whenever we see a mouse. Whether

* Mid-twentieth century British philosopher.

or not we think consciously that the beliefs generating our emotional reactions are 'true' or useful, the feelings themselves remain an important part of our personal experience.

Needs signposting

To boil it right down, emotions tell us how we're doing in terms of needs fulfilment. When we fail to take responsibility for the meeting of our needs – either because we don't know what they are or because we hear the message, but then ignore it – the unconscious will rise up and do it for us.

Sometimes, of course, it will get things right. When that happens, we won't have to question our self-control because everything will seem to automatically work out for the best. However, the unconscious mind can only choose its methods of meeting our needs from the stockpile of ideas that it's already familiar with. In other words, it'll select behaviours that fit the model of reality that we're calling the (dis)comfort zone. If we grew up with abuse, it may fulfil the need for connection by seeking out a violent partner. If we were brought up by an alcoholic parent, it might believe that vodka is the best way to feel calm and secure. If we learned to get attention through sexual activity while in our teens, we might find ourselves engaging in dangerous or regretful one-night stands whenever we feel lonely. The shame caused by these unwanted behaviours, of course, will only drive us deeper into our sense of victimhood and farther away from the autonomy that we need in order to make a change.

Emotional resistance

Emotional resistance will play a part in any self-sabotaging issue. It's by suppressing the feelings we associate with our monsters that we find ourselves locked into the victim mindset and causing ourselves further pain.

Yet, emotional denial is a widespread problem. We have been conditioned to take what should simply be a natural part of human existence and turn it into a story about our identity. We can confuse expressions of joy with immaturity or foolishness, fear with cowardice, enthusiasm with naïvety, sadness or hurt with weakness. We learn that the experience of sexual arousal means that we're bad or dirty, and we learn that to show anger is to be unkind or evil. As a result, we endeavour not to feel the most 'shameful' of our feelings and, consequently, shut them out.

The problem with this approach is that it's simply not possible. Firstly, we cannot deny any single emotion exclusively; we can't just decide that we don't much care for sadness but that we'll keep all the others like joy, excitement and love. To numb one feeling is to numb them all. Secondly, any emotion we attempt to disown will eventually show up somewhere or other to rain (or perhaps pour) all over our parade. Why? Because what we resist persists.

Bad Habits

With an external locus of control, we act habitually the vast majority of the time and without question. The more powerful our sense of victimhood, the harder we'll believe it must be to break a habit.

The habits we call 'bad' – like addictions, dependencies and repetitive negative behaviours (anything from fingernail biting to bulimia) – tend to fall into two categories. They are either a means to feel something when we've lost touch with our ability to feel anything much else (think gambling or sex addiction); or they're strategies that we use to keep numbing the emotions we don't want to feel. Some 'bad habits' will fit into both of these categories at once.

These kinds of problems, like all the others, are just failing solutions. They're coping mechanisms that we initially adopt because they make us feel better, but that cease to have the desired effect over time. The first nail we ever bite might feel like a satisfying little tidy-up, but once a nail-biting habit beds in (excuse the pun), it can make us feel decidedly *un*tidy. The first meal the bulimic ever purges is likely to feel like an act of control, but as the condition continues it leads to a complete loss of control. Equally, an alcoholic doesn't start drinking because it brings them a sense of isolation and loneliness. They start because alcohol offers relief from that kind of pain. The point at which a habit 'goes bad' is usually the moment when the resisted feelings catch up with us; it's when the emotions overspill.

The problem with any habitual coping mechanism is that, by its very nature, no habit is ever a response to our current environment. Whether it's a behaviour we've been repeating since childhood or something we picked up more recently, it will not be based on what's really happening right now, and may well be, therefore, an ineffective means of dealing with the situation.

Choice

The goal, however, is not to eradicate all habitual behaviour. If we did that, we would barely ever make it out of the house before nightfall. What developing emotional responsibility brings to the table is the all-important element of choice. It is cultivating the power to pick up and put down our habits at will in order to healthily satisfy our needs.

And it follows that increasing our awareness of our habitual patterns is an important step when it comes to taking control. Here are some questions to get you thinking about your potentially limiting coping mechanisms:

* In what ways are you most likely to try to deal with stress (either effectively or ineffectively)?
* Take a moment to think of some things that you failed to get round to recently. What did you find yourself doing in order to avoid those tasks/events?
* What might you find yourself doing to numb the feeling of fear or sadness?
* What might you find yourself doing to cope with embarrassment or humiliation (either effectively or ineffectively)?
* Finally, it's not just about the negative emotions. Many of us also suppress our positive feelings on a regular basis. If there was something that your mind might be doing to numb or otherwise sabotage the feeling of love, joy, excitement or enthusiasm, what might that be?

If you couldn't think of an answer to that last question, have a think about how well you take compliments. Do you pause to let the positivity sink in and then thank the other person for their comment? Or, do you look at your feet and mumble something about how wrong they are because actually you're a bit rubbish? If the latter, then please give yourself a moment to accept the next bit of well-meant praise that comes your way. It can feel surprisingly different, and not just for you; whoever gives you that compliment will also get a burst of good feeling when they see that you've let it land.

I'm sure (I'd hope!) that some of the things you have listed above will be healthy and effective methods of handling things. You might have written 'Go for a walk in the park' or 'Talk to my partner' for coping with stress, for example. Those options would likely help you to work through your emotion, rather than look the other way, and, if that's the case, then they're all good. It's the avoidance options that you want to keep an eye out for because rather than actually helping, they rescue you by enabling your suppression of the emotional feedback.

Over the remainder of this chapter, we're going to look at a simple process (I call it 'Diving Down'), which will help you develop your emotional awareness and learn how to step calmly and safely into the feelings you're most likely to automatically slam the door on. Cultivating this skill means that you can open up the possibility of opting out of the habits you might be tempted to put the 'bad' label on. This is about claiming your right to choose.

Going with the Water

Fear keeps us focused on the past or worried about the future. If we can acknowledge our fear, we can realise that right now we are okay. Right now, today, we are still alive, and our bodies are working marvellously. Our eyes can still see the beautiful sky. Our ears can still hear the voices of our loved ones.

Thich Nhat Hanh,* *Fear*

When we let go of emotional resistance and start to heed the messages sent by the unconscious, our experience of life can begin to feel fluid, rather than stuck. Water is a wonderful metaphor for emotion. As I learned in Nicaragua (see page 140), there are times when it can be frighteningly powerful (particularly if we're trying to swim against it).

* Vietnamese Buddhist monk, peace activist, poet and author.

However, it can also be beautiful. It can be deep and dark. It can be soft, vibrant or gentle. You can swim in it, float on it, surf it and dive down into it to discover a different world. Not to mention that it keeps you alive when you drink it. However, if you trap it in one place for too long, it will go stagnant and begin to spoil.

When we fail to listen to emotional information – when we choose to do nothing but feel victimised by it or the things that 'caused' it – we prevent our emotions from flowing as they should. As a result, anger festers into bitter, lingering resentment, fear extends to a chronic state of anxiety, guilt mutates into shame and we have to keep finding bigger (and usually more damaging) ways of trying to push it all away. I believe that my illness was little more than the physical manifestation of the emotions I refused to experience for so long that my body needed to make them 'real' in order to get me to stop and pay attention.

Feeling the feeling

Learning to feel our emotions is not about wallowing in shame or curling up into an anxious ball and letting fear take over. Rather, it's about enabling the communication of information that they are intended for. If we open ourselves up to the deeper meaning of our feelings by pausing to experience them, rather than engaging in knee-jerk habitual attempts to subdue them, then we can read the information in the same way that we might read a letter. The words themselves (the emotions) are not the point, it's the message that we're interested in.

In the case of uncomfortable or stifling emotions, the message will often be connected to some kind of shame-inspiring monster story that we're unwilling to hear. When we bring that piece of the jigsaw puzzle into the light, the emotions themselves tend to reduce in intensity because their job has been done.

Introducing certainty

Imagine you're on your way home from the supermarket and that you have a dinner party or hot date at your place that night. You want the evening to be special, but in the back of your mind there's a little voice telling you that you've forgotten something important. All the way home, you keep getting distracted by this nagging feeling that you're missing something: 'What *is* it?' Then, as you're putting the shopping away at home, it dawns on you that you've failed to buy the most crucial ingredient. Even though this realisation is not something that you could call 'positive', when you get the answer after all that searching, you may experience a subtle yet quite exquisite feeling of release. Your muscles let go and the little voice in your mind says, 'Yes. *That's* it!' That release is the feeling of something uncertain becoming certain. Even when the news is not good, that release will happen because certainty is the most basic of all the needs. And when we're deprived of it, the uncomfortable sense of *un*certainty can hijack our mental capacity indefinitely.

The process you're about to learn has been designed to help you find that release, as often as possible, in relation to any kind of lingering inner niggle that might try to commandeer your awareness. Only when you find the certainty your mind has been searching for will you have the option to let go. Perhaps most importantly, when you know what the problem is, you will be able to do something about it.

A note on breathing and relaxation

Frequent or chronic tension in the body – things like hunched shoulders, tight neck muscles, a clenched jaw, constricted breathing, some types of back pain or a permanently furrowed brow – are often indicative of emotional resistance. The body braces itself in anticipation of pain. To get a good visual of this, imagine someone who's taking part in the Ice Bucket Challenge waiting for their grinning friend to dump the water on their head. When we brace, we automatically either hold our breath or restrict our breathing to the upper part of the chest. This pre-emptive tension is a protective strategy that the unconscious uses for both physical and emotional pain. But it's not that effective for either.

Any midwife will tell you that resisting the pain of labour will prolong the process of giving birth and make it more painful. The same rules apply to emotional resistance. Tensing up and holding our breath while in the grip of a negative emotion will only ever increase the discomfort and block the flow (or even the birth) of important information.

I personally refused the idea of yogic or otherwise woo-woo-sounding breathing for ages. In fact, I spent the first few years of my practice completely dedicated to finding a way of calming the mind and developing psychological superpowers without the need for anything that smacked even vaguely of hippies. No tie-dye or incense here, thank you. However, just as I learned that controlled breathing was essential when I was training for physical power as an athlete, I conceded, before long in my role as a therapist, to the fact that breathing can make the world of difference when it comes to emotional strength too. When learning to feel our feelings, continuous and fluid breathing helps us to ensure that we are not resisting our monsters.

There are probably hundreds of different breathing techniques to choose from. If you already have a favourite, you can, of course, use that. If not, here's my preference. You can try it out as you read.

Task: Breathing Technique

To begin, rest your tongue against the roof of your mouth and focus on breathing slowly and calmly through the nose. Let the air flow right down into the base of your torso as you breathe in, so that your lower ribs and stomach expand like a balloon. Then let the air out slowly and gently, and repeat. As you do that, find the most natural position for your head to sit comfortably above your shoulders, so your neck isn't strained. Then, inhale through the nose for a count of four, and exhale through the mouth for a count of six (or eight if you're already skilled in controlling your breath). Fairly obviously, you don't need to keep your tongue against the roof of your mouth for the out-breath.

In order to extend your exhalation, you will need to restrict the air as you let it out through your lips. This just means almost closing your mouth or gently pursing your lips. There's no need to force anything. It's not about making the out-breath as long as humanly possible, just longer than the inhalation. The reason this is important is that breathing out automatically stimulates the part of your nervous system that enables you to relax, whereas breathing in stimulates the 'fight-or-flight' response. Each time you exhale, just imagine your muscles letting go and relaxing, especially those in your face, neck and shoulders.

This is an excellent skill to have to hand whenever you feel your emotions trying to get on top of you. If you're unfamiliar with this kind of breathing, follow the steps from the beginning again, so you can get a better feel for it. Here they are:

Step 1

Find the most comfortable position while breathing continuously and deeply through the nose and with your tongue resting against the roof of your mouth.

Step 2

Inhale for a count of four through the nose.

Step 3

Exhale for a count of six (or eight) through the mouth with your lips gently pursed, while intentionally relaxing your muscles.

Step 4

Repeat steps 2 and 3 for at least four cycles, allowing your spine to straighten and your muscles to release a little more each time.

Step 5

Close your eyes to continue for as long as you like, while focusing on the sound of your breathing. You may find a wonderful stillness of both body and mind as you do this, but your thoughts will still be there, and that's fine. Feel free to take a moment to just observe them. This will be good practice for the technique you're about to learn.

Peter's decision-making-monster

Peter had trouble making the decision to do things, particularly when saying 'yes' would involve going to some kind of big occasion or gathering. He visited me because he felt guilty about his lack of interest in attending social events, and was worried that he was verging on a full-blown social anxiety problem.

Quite serendipitously, on the day of his first session he was struggling with a decision about joining some friends at Glastonbury festival. He had been invited, last minute, by a group of people that he really liked, but rather than feeling excited by the opportunity, he found himself battling with something close to anger because he felt pressured to go. We used this as an opportunity to explore the deeper reality of his inner conflict.

Here's a transcript of the conversation we had at the beginning of his session:

Me: What are you thinking? Tell me what goes through your mind when you think about the Glastonbury offer.

Peter: Well, I don't want to get rained on, for a start. The line-up is good but I just don't think it's really my thing. It all feels like a hassle that I can't be bothered with and it really annoys me that people just expect me to go. I feel forced.

Me: How, specifically, do you feel that? Take your attention inside to focus on where you experience those emotions ... If you could point to that feeling of being 'forced', where would you point?

Peter: My stomach.

Me: And, if that feeling had a shape, what would it be?

Peter: I don't know ... like, a blob or a ball.

Me: Is that feeling heavy or light?

Peter: It's very heavy and black. No, it's a really dark beetroot colour. And it just sits there. It won't move.

Me: OK. I want you to imagine that you can drop your attention down into that part of your body, so you can think from right inside that feeling. Can you do that?

Peter: Yes.

Me: As you focus on that feeling, if there was a statement beginning with the word 'I ...' that comes to mind, what would it be?

Peter: I'm not comfortable.

Me: Imagine that feeling has a voice of its own. If you asked it to complete the sentence, 'I'm uncomfortable because ...', what would it say?

Peter (after a little time): Oh. I think this feeling might be more about the stress of the journey than the actual festival. Whenever I go to these things I almost always have a good time once I'm there, but I hate the stress of travelling on my own. I don't like the feeling that I might forget something or that I'll not be able to meet up with people easily when I arrive. So, I guess that feeling says something like, 'I don't want to travel'.

Me: I'd like you to just check that this feels right by saying to yourself, 'This decision is uncomfortable because a part of my mind doesn't want to travel.' Just repeat that in your head and see if it resonates.

Peter: Yes, it makes sense. The travelling feels more stressful than the event itself. When I imagine being there with my tent pitched, that feels OK. Actually, I get stressed out and angry before going on holiday as well. I think this feeling might have something to do with trust; like I don't trust myself not to screw it up in some way.

Me: OK. Well done. As you hold that in mind, just take a moment to relax your muscles, and breathe as if you can breathe right through that heavy beetroot feeling in your body, observing what happens ... Take your time and then tell me what you notice.

Peter: It releases a little when I breathe. It's still there, but it's shifted up a bit. Now I'm thinking of a time a few years ago when I had a panic attack on a plane. It's the only time I've ever had a panic attack. It came completely out of the blue.

Peter was a retired athlete. He'd been to a number of different Olympic games and many world and European championships. Travelling was a thing that he had done often, but rarely without the pressure of an upcoming tournament. Since he was a young teen, long trips had usually meant that he was on his way to a place where he would be pushed, judged and would have to live up to some high expectations. It made sense to Peter that his mind may have put performance anxiety and travelling into the same pot. Fear, as we already know, is very good at generalising. The stimulus for anxiety can jump from one thing to another like some kind of psychological virus.

An important part of Peter's problem had been concealed beneath the captain's rationalisations for years. His monster was more concerned with trust, travelling and performance than it was with socialising.

With the link between competition and his difficult decisions made clearer, Peter was able to get a better grip on the issue. As we continued talking, he found that the monster story with the most weight on that day was, 'I can't trust myself not to screw it up' or simply, 'I'm not trustworthy', which was something he could remember thinking in a number of different situations.

Here's how the next part of the conversation went:

Me: If your mind could let go of the belief 'I'm not trustworthy', how would the Glastonbury offer seem different?

Peter: Hmm ... Well, yeah. That would take the pressure off. The trip would feel very different. In fact, *I* would feel very different. That's a version of me that I would like to be.

Me: Take a moment to imagine that version of yourself; the one who can see himself as trustworthy. Notice all the ways in which he can think, feel and behave differently. Notice the kinds of actions that he takes as a result of his self-trust; and notice his body language, and the way that he speaks ...

Peter and I spent some time discussing and cataloguing the changes – large and small – that he would notice in his life if the 'I'm not trustworthy' story were to be edited out of the greater narrative. After the session, Peter took control by heading home to pack mindfully. He made solid plans for meeting people at the venue and reminded himself to change his body language on regular occasions. These things helped him to introduce a little more trust (AKA certainty) into the situation. Then he used the breathing technique on pages 190–1 to stay calm – or calmer, at least – while making the journey.

All of those responsible actions were things that he had already thought of; it's just that he hadn't done any of them because he'd been distracted by the externalisation of his inner drama and the confusion caused by his exaggerated emotional reaction. Until he taught his unconscious mind to let go of the anger he felt towards others for 'making him go', he wasn't able to address the real issue beneath all that deflection.

The remainder of Peter's sessions were spent unravelling his monster's 'I'm-not-trustworthy' story, which affected more than just holidays and trips to festivals. Doing this meant that he could rewrite his reality map. However, before we even began the bulk of that work, the little certainty release that Peter created with those few moments of self-reflection did provide him with the impetus to take (different) action. In doing so, he reclaimed some of the control that his monster threatened to take away, and I'm sure that the entire therapeutic process was made smoother as a result.

Diving Down: The process

I call the technique that Peter used to shine a light on his trust monster 'Diving Down'. It's a short, self-reflective process that helps us to feel our feelings, increase self-awareness and to encourage the release that comes from understanding why we behave in the way that we do, or feel the way that we feel. As a result, it enables us to challenge our reality map and start looking beyond the (dis)comfort zone.

This process can be completed in a matter of minutes (possibly even seconds), internally and in the moment. Once you're used to it, it becomes a tool that you can use to opt out of drama or bad habits, to calm down, to get to sleep, to keep moving through challenging feelings and, most importantly, to get real about your emotional experience, so you can take autonomous and effective action.

In brief, these are the four steps of the Diving Down process:

1. Ask, 'What am I thinking?'
2. Ask, 'What am I feeling?'
3. Ask, 'What is the monster story?'
4. Now breathe ... and challenge your reality map.

Let's go through the steps using an example. You don't have to complete this task yet, just get a feel for it. I'll repeat the instructions in brief for you to follow afterwards.

'I'm a bad friend'

Mary struggled to maintain close relationships. Over the last two decades she had many a friendship and partnership, but they all tended to either fizzle out or come to an unceremonious end after some kind of disagreement. When one of her current relationships seemed to be on the rocks, she chose to Dive Down into her own feelings, rather than go with the standard cold-shoulder response that she'd developed as a coping mechanism over the years.

Step 1: Ask, 'What am I thinking?'

This step is about thought awareness (it's basically a 'brain dump'). You can use it as an opportunity to explore and express everything that's currently going through your mind, including self-talk, mental images, opinions, judgements, knee-jerk emotional reactions, memories, urges and desires.

Here's what Mary found:

'I'm upset with my friend because she's angry with me for cancelling our arrangement. She's being unreasonable and unfair. This is just another person who'll eventually disappear. People are unreliable and mean. I feel like not talking to her for a while, so she understands how she makes me feel.'

What's important is that you give yourself full (non-judgemental) permission to express these ideas. If you're thinking something you'd never say out loud, like, 'What I'd really like to do is strangle my friend's cat', then don't edit that bit out. The ideas we'd most like to delete are usually the ones that help us get in touch with the important emotional content beneath them.

Step 2: Ask, 'What am I feeling?'

Exploring your thinking will have connected you to the emotions associated with this issue. This question helps you to experience them.

Much like you did with the driver urge in Chapter 4, you're going to pay attention to the physical sensation of your emotional reaction. By that, I don't mean the more obvious bodily reactions to stress, like a clenched jaw or sweaty palms. I mean the way you actually feel the emotion in your body. Common examples of this type of sensation would be 'butterflies in the stomach' or a 'frog in the throat'.

This is a level of awareness that we often skip. Many people will say 'I feel anxious' but they don't actually stop to notice what 'feeling anxious' really means to them. Perhaps there's a tightness or restriction in your neck or your chest? Maybe there's a heaviness or a churning feeling somewhere in your body? These feelings are usually subtler than the experience of something like a rapidly beating heart, so you may need to search a little deeper to identify them.

Some people find this stage all the more engaging if they get poetic about their experience. You might discover that you have a 'heavy feeling in your stomach, like bitter, black treacle', or perhaps a 'tingling, high-pitched screaming sensation in your chest'.

> **Here's Mary's response:**
> 'I have a hurtful restriction in my neck that feels like a spiky green conker has been lodged in my throat. I also have a heavy sinking feeling in my stomach that pulls me down into a slump.'

Step 3: Ask, 'What is the monster story?'

This question helps you to identify the anxious, angry, shameful, fearful or otherwise (dis)comfortable perspective that your mind is taking. What you're asking here is, 'Why am I *really* feeling this way?'

Asking this question of yourself is about pausing to acknowledge the internal cause of your discomfort, rather than buying in to the external-ised explanation (the Drama Triangle perspective).

Sometimes the story will be an obvious, full-blown limiting self-belief like, 'I'm not good enough', 'I'm a fraud' or 'I'm a bad person'. At other times it'll be less dramatic than that: 'I'm worried I might look a bit silly when I ...' No matter what you find, the act of asking – as counter-intuitive as it may sound – is empowering. You are daring yourself to know the worst of it: the shameful or frightening part that you might otherwise have tried to hide from yourself.

> **Here's what Mary found:**
> 'When I get in touch with that conker-like block in my throat, I realise that I'm actually feeling guilty. I'm afraid that she's right and that this all means that I'm a bad friend. I'm uncomfortable because I feel like *I'm* the one being unreliable and mean!'

The monster story that Mary had been resisting (and deflecting) was about her own inadequacy as a friend, which was a shame trigger that she had absorbed having grown up in a family of people who struggled socially. 'I'm a bad friend' was something that she had believed all her life, and because of her resistance to that story, she had learned to back away from anything that threatened to trigger it.

By acknowledging the monster perspective, you create the possibility of separating yourself from it and then seeing past it. Sometimes you might find something new, but often it's just the same old story trying to make itself real again. The beauty of this is that each time you catch your monster in the (repetitive) act, you get to know it a little better. You only need to discover the same belief at the root of an uncomfortable moment so many times before it starts to seem a little less believable: 'You again! Seriously?'

To affirm that this is just a perspective and not reality, you can organise your findings into a sentence like this:

> **'I am feeling (X emotion) because a part of my mind wants to believe ... (insert relevant monster story).'**

For Mary, the sentence went like this:

> **'I am feeling guilty because a part of my mind wants to believe that I'm a bad friend.'**

Finding the response-able answer

Taking care not to externalise the cause of your discomfort is essential here. We need to make sure that we're not blaming anyone or anything else for our own feelings if we are to take control.

For example, the real reason for your anger is not that someone else has said something mean to you. That would be the victim perspective. The real reason is that you've taken offence at their words. So, the question is: Why did you take whatever they said so personally?

Similarly, you are not anxious because the performance is fundamentally scary. You are feeling anxious because you fear that it might not go so well. So, what is it that makes you believe that it will be a failure? Or, perhaps, what do you fear it would say about you if it did go as badly as you're anticipating?

Examples
External (victim) perspective: 'The presentation I have to give on Monday is making me nervous.'
Internal (autonomy) perspective: 'I'm feeling anxious about the presentation because my monster is trying to tell me that I'm not good enough to wow the crowd.'

External (victim) perspective: 'This party is boring. I need a strong drink.'
Internal (autonomy) perspective: 'I'm feeling a little out of place right now and as if I don't quite fit in. I want a drink because a part of my mind believes that alcohol will rescue me.'

I have used numerous different permutations of this question with my clients over the years. Some other useful questions to consider here are:

* 'How am I making this about me?' ('How am I taking this personally?')
* 'What do I fear to be true about myself right now?'
* 'How do I fear that this situation might make me look to others?'
* 'What am I *really* afraid of right now?'

Step 4: Now breathe ... and challenge your reality map

This step is about ensuring that you are not physically resisting either the emotion or the monster story and then choosing to look beyond the (dis)comfortable perspective to see what else is possible.

You will start by focusing on the emotional sensations that you identified in Step 2. Then, you'll take a moment to breathe comfortably and continuously, while relaxing your muscles and adjusting your body language, so that you're sitting or standing in an upright and open position. Positive body language will strengthen the empowering message that you are allowed to feel OK in the presence of those ideas, and it will encourage your emotions to move from blocked to fluid.

Sometimes (but not always) you may notice a shift in the way that you feel the emotion as you breathe into it. It could seem to get more intense at first, just because you are giving it your attention. Then, it could begin to release a little as you connect it to the deeper and more authentic perception of the issue (the monster story). If you notice any shift, then that's a good sign. I think of it as the point when the emotion begins to flow. Sometimes it will be subtle and sometimes it can be quite dramatic. You might notice a change in the location of the feeling, or a change in its temperature or weight. You might find that the way you see the emotion changes; a difference in colour, size or tone. Or, you might just get that 'Ah! *That's* it!' release that comes from something uncertain becoming certain.

However, what we are not necessarily hoping for here is for the feeling to disappear completely – because sometimes the emotion you're experiencing will be vital and relevant. You might need to take action – i.e. write the email, search for the new job or say the awkward thing – before your mind will be happy to stop transmitting the message.

I'd suggest you breathe for a minimum of three breaths while taking stock of your inner experience before you ask the New Territories Question to challenge your reality map:

> **'If I were to edit out that monster story, how would I see this differently?'**

It's important to finish with this because it confirms that you have the power to change your perspective, and it redirects your thinking away from the problem and onto the solution. We've come across this question in various different forms already. It's very similar to the Golden Linings Question ('What can I create out of this?'), and the same as asking yourself how something would look if you chose to focus on the towards values rather than the away-from values, or how life would be if you chose growth over protection. The reason we're asking this question so often is because this is what it's all about. If the reality that we perceive is filtered, added to and warped to such an extent that we get a bespoke version, then why should we settle for a (dis)comfortable one?

To answer this question, you might want to imagine that an old lens has been removed from in front of your eyes, so that you can see the situation afresh. Reflect on the opportunities for positive connection to others, for growth or for contribution that you may have missed otherwise. Just considering what the situation would look like if your monster wasn't telling you its limiting stories trains your mind to start searching beyond the edges of the (dis)comfort zone for something better. Every time you consciously choose to make that search, you strengthen the synaptic paths associated with finding the Golden Linings.

For Mary, this meant looking beyond the drama that she was creating. Pausing to breathe through the experience helped her to calm down and let go of the instinct to shut her friend out, which would only have given her monster more ammunition for its 'I'm a bad friend' story. Recognising the deeper thinking inspired her to take ownership of the situation and choose a course of action that would fulfil her need for connection, rather than sabotage it once again.

As she asked herself what the situation would look like if she were to edit out the limiting perspective, the block in her throat opened up and she moved into an empathetic, rather than a defensive state of mind. What she imagined was herself being the one to take responsibility for resolving the dispute. The slightly awkward conversation that followed not only defused the drama bomb but also took her relationship to a previously unexperienced level of trust. Ultimately, Diving Down helped her to neutralise her monster's call to (dis)comfort and turn a difficult moment into the very thing that raised the height of her glass ceiling. Afterwards, she found herself looking back and knowing that she'd behaved in the way that she would consider a 'good friend' to behave.

Task: Diving Down into Self-awareness

Now it's your turn. Let's work through the four steps of the Diving Down process, while focusing on something in your life that causes you to feel blocked or limited. I've included optional journaling instructions if you would like to put pen to paper. Remember that the magic ingredient here is curiosity. Go into this with the intention of learning about yourself and you'll get the most out of it.

Before you begin, bring to mind something that's happening in your life right now (or that's soon to happen) that makes you feel blocked, victimised, powerless, anxious or angry. This could be an argument you've had, something that's coming up that makes you feel nervous or some kind of self-sabotaging behaviour that's currently affecting your health, success or happiness. This will be your focus.

Step 1: Ask, 'What am I thinking?'

Observe and describe your inner dialogue and other thoughts about the problem as if you're translating your thinking to someone else. Notice any images, sounds, memories, self-talk or Drama Triangle urges connected with your chosen issue. Be sure not to edit anything out. Just let your mind do the thinking it wants to do and stay curious about what you find.

Optional journaling: take a moment to transcribe your thinking.

Step 2: Ask, 'What am I feeling?'

Close your eyes and take your awareness inside your body to observe the way you actually feel the connected emotions. Then, describe that feeling to yourself, paying close attention to where it is in your body.

To get a more detailed sense of your physical experience, ask yourself the question, 'If this feeling had a shape or form, what would that be?' Then, ask yourself whether it's heavy or light, hot or cold, animated or static, whether it has any sound and if there's a visual that comes to mind. When you've done that, open your eyes and come back to the page.

Optional journaling: write a description or draw a picture of what you found.

Step 3: Ask, 'What is the monster story?'

Take a moment to acknowledge the most uncomfortable part of the situation or experience. What is the real, internal reason for your reaction?

Keep an eye out for any kind of limiting belief (e.g. 'I am/am not ...' or 'I can/I cannot ...').

Here are the other questions that you can ask if you need more prompting:

* 'How am I making this about me?' ('How am I taking this personally?')
* 'What do I fear to be true about myself right now?'
* 'How do I fear that this situation makes me look to others?'
* 'What am I *really* afraid of right now?'

To separate the story from reality and internalise your locus of control, insert your monster story into this sentence:

'I am feeling (X emotion) because a part of my mind wants to believe ... (insert relevant monster story).'

Optional journaling: write that sentence down.

Step 4: Now breathe ... and challenge your reality map

Start just by breathing for a minimum of three breaths as you take stock of your experience. Visualise the air flowing right through the part of your body where you experience the connected feelings, let your muscles relax and allow your body language to straighten up. As you do this, just observe your experience for a while, paying attention to any kind of shift in the way that your body feels.

Note: if you're doing this in public, it's absolutely fine to just breathe continuously through your nose.

Finally, take a look beyond your (dis)comfortable norm, so you can challenge your reality map. Here's the New Territories Question to help you do that:

'If I were to edit out that monster story, how would I see this differently?'

Imagine that the limiting perspective simply didn't exist. How might you see things differently if that was the case? Perhaps more importantly, how would you *like* to be seeing things differently?

Have a think about how your thoughts, feelings and actions might change, what might seem more valuable or important, what kinds of new and more positive self-beliefs could begin to seem true and what the opportunities for connection, growth and contribution might be.

Optional journaling: take a moment to write yourself a new story for this situation, describing all the changes you'd like to notice if you were to let go of your monster's limiting perspective.

———••———

Summary

That's all there is to it. If you have just completed that process, then you did these things:

* You identified a problem area;
* You went inside your head to see what was happening there;
* You gave some thought to the real reason for your discomfort;
* You breathed and took an internal-locus-of-control perspective on the situation;
* Then, you challenged yourself to look beyond your (dis)comfort zone.

That's a lot of good work, and all that's required for you to repeat it is that you remember the four key questions. To help you tattoo them into your mind, here they are once more:

* **'What am I thinking?'**
* **'What am I feeling?'**
* **'What is the monster story?'**
* And, while remembering to breathe: **'If I were to edit out that monster story, how would I see this differently?'**

I think of this process as a grounding tool – the ultimate reality check. You can do it any time you hit an emotional block (either in writing or not), and each time you do, you will increase your self-awareness, retrain your mind to seek the solution and strengthen your ability to act autonomously and authentically.

Diving Down Examples

For the sake of variety, let's return to the two examples that we looked at on page 198. In brief, this is how those issues might look if put through the full Diving Down process:

Example 1
What am I thinking?
I'm thinking about the presentation I have to give on Monday. The idea of performing in front of the whole team is making me really nervous. I'm worried that I'll fumble and trip over my words.

What am I feeling?
I have a hot, fluttery feeling in my chest.

What is the monster story?
I'm feeling nervous because a part of my mind wants to believe that I'm not good enough to wow the crowd.

If I were to edit out that monster story, how would I see this differently?
If I could let go of my fear of not being good enough, then I would be able to look forward to giving this presentation. I'm actually excited about the content, and I'm keen to share it.

Example 2
What am I thinking?
This party is boring. I need a strong drink.

What am I feeling?
I have a tight, groaning kind of feeling in the back of my stomach.

What is the monster story?
I'm feeling agitated because a part of my mind wants to believe that I don't really fit in here, and that alcohol will rescue me.

If I were to edit out that monster story, how would I see this differently?
If I could let go of the 'I don't fit in' story, I'd be able to relax and stop focusing so much on myself. If I could give my full attention to these people, I might learn something about them that engages me more.

Choosing Authorship

At the beginning of this book I suggested that the archetypal opposite of the Victim should be the Author, rather than the Hero. It's via the use of self-reflective processes like Diving Down that we can start to claim that title for ourselves.

The deepest level is where the important material lies; it's just that we're usually so busy treading water and refusing to look down that we hide it from ourselves. Asking the four questions above (and breathing through the hard stuff) helps us not only to know the resisted parts of the self that lurk beneath the surface, but also to understand them and learn how to use them.

What this means is that Authorship is not about a dogmatic rewriting of our negative beliefs. At least, not directly. It would be the Hero's approach to try to destroy all 'weakness' or slay the big, bad 'not-enough' monster. But you can't fight your way to self-esteem. I know because I tried, and the only thing I fought my way into was an even deeper state of self-loathing and sickness. The Authorship approach to finding strength is uncommon in this drama-obsessed world, but it's far more genuine and effective than fighting our fear, and it's available to everyone.

By acknowledging the fearful thoughts that we all have, the Author can encourage shame, doubt and any other daunting human experiences to evolve into things of merit and meaning. It's not supposed to be easy. Any writer, musician, choreographer, painter or any other kind of artist will tell you that the creative process is inherently difficult. You have to willingly dive into the darkest shadows before you find the beauty. However, the more you do it, the easier it gets to trust that what you're searching for is actually (always) there.

Known resistance

Fear and sadness are the emotions I'm most likely to resist. My mind seems to associate both of these with weakness. It says, 'Only cowards get scared, and only the feeble let themselves get hurt ... So let's just ignore those things, shall we?' It's because of this personal tradition, I'm sure, that I have such a penchant for melancholic music and psychological horror movies. I learned to love those things during my teens so that I could enjoy a second-hand and safe (if somewhat voyeuristic) experience of the emotions I habitually deprived myself of.

These days I'm not so keen to miss out on those fundamental aspects of life, so I keep a part of my mind on the lookout for things that could (or should) trigger those responses. I know when I'm resisting sadness because I feel a gnarled and knotted lump in my throat that stops me from breathing and hurts like hell. I'm well acquainted with this feeling. It says, 'Don't cry!' and it reminds me of the cinema lights coming back on after a screening of *E.T.* in the mid-1980s. Regardless of the fact that my sister had been in floods for about half an hour, I was determined not to shed tears in public, until my mum looked at me with a sympathetic (and probably mildly amused) look to say, 'It's OK, Hazel. You *can* cry!' At which point, of course, I completely lost it, causing rows of people to turn around and stare at me. It was a humiliating moment, and I would not be at all surprised if it contributed considerably to the permanent assignment of sadness to my monster, as well as the beginning of a stubborn Be Strong driver.

My dad died suddenly of a heart attack seven years ago. It was unquestionably the most horrible experience I could ever have imagined. Yet, I did not cry. At least, not properly and not for a while. An unwillingness to experience both fear and sadness will make grief a pretty impossible process for anyone, so my mind and I decided that we'd skip it. At least, we skipped the healthy parts of it by zoning out and going into overdrive with work and training at the soonest possible opportunity, none of which helped me to process my loss. What it meant was that right up until a couple of years ago, I still had difficult and unexpected emotional-overflow moments. When my mother moved out of our childhood home, for example, I had recurring nightmares about the house, even though I had been telling her to downsize for years, and had even said, 'Yeah, I mean, it's just bricks and mortar. Anywhere feels like home once you move your stuff into it. No biggie!' How wrong I was.

Just the other day, I stumbled upon an old group email between my mother, my sister, my father and myself. It was dated just a couple of months before his death. As I started reading, the knot in my throat swelled up and my neck started to feel as if it was burning. Reflexively, I reached for the mouse to click out of the thread and get on with some 'important' work. But then I caught myself, and I chose to Dive Down into the experience, rather than allow my monster to make me look the other way.

What I found, at the deepest level, was a contradiction of feelings. At first, I heard more from the part of me that felt reluctant to waste time on weakness, but as I started breathing through the knot in my throat, it shifted into something quieter, purer and more innocent. I found myself listening to a little voice that spoke directly to my dad about how much I love and miss him. It felt essential rather than shameful, and I had no intention of pushing it away. A few moments later the 'Don't-cry' feeling started to dissolve. However, the sadness beneath it grew richer; it expanded and deepened into something beautiful that reminded me of why I was sad about my father's death, rather than how much I wanted to refuse its happening.

The entire process took me all of five minutes, but it has occurred to me a number of times since and it inspired a quite wonderful and open conversation with my mother. What I have come to realise is that it was my resistance to sadness that made me feel the most ashamed of myself, not my experience of it. By pushing away my emotions and refusing to grieve the loss of my dad, I felt as if I was psychologically pushing away and rejecting one of the most important people in my life. It was that, not the emotion, that really wasn't OK.

Change vs acceptance

The more you practise Diving Down, the less likely you'll be to even want to change the essence of your limiting beliefs. This is because when you can see and accept them, they cease to have such a damaging effect. My 'not good enough' still crops up every now and then; it's just that she no longer looks like a monster and I no longer mistake her story for truth. These days, she teaches me where to focus my attention and invest in my growth. Doubt becomes a strength when you use it to highlight the areas of your life that you want to expand on, which is exactly what you get to see by asking yourself the New Territories Question and daring to let go of the fear of failure.

Ironically, my little 'not-enough' part also helps me to feel connected and worthwhile. I believe that when we're brave enough to face our fears and listen curiously to the language of self-doubt and even self-loathing, we gain access to the universal fears shared by almost every other human being on the planet (whether they know it or not). By stepping right into a shameful experience and developing the ability to empathise with ourselves, we gradually learn that the things we thought made us different, wrong, bad or unacceptable are actually just a standard part of being human. These are the experiences that bring us all together, not the personal flaws that separate us from the rest. I truly believe that being willing and able to 'go there' makes us more capable of finding love, not less.

Authorship is therefore more about rescripting our *relationship* to the deepest and most painful of unconscious reactions than it is about changing the reactions themselves. However, quite crucially, what can be completely rewritten when we choose Authorship is the material at the surface level: the habitual inclinations, Drama Triangle behaviours, our driver urges, and any other kind of desire to self-sabotage. These are the rough drafts that the Author applies the Tipp-Ex to. When we're able to feel what we once resisted, they become optional. Ultimately, out of self-awareness grows autonomy, and when we have that we can take control of our own story, in the moment, when it matters.

I'd like to conclude Part 2 with a quote from the Jewish psychiatrist and Nazi concentration camp survivor, Viktor E. Frankl. During his incarceration, Frankl quite literally authored his seminal work, *Man's Search For Meaning*, on scraps of paper and anything else he could find. Writing his book, which was on the importance of internalising one's locus of control, became the purpose that saw him through the unthinkable adversity of the Holocaust. These are his words:

> *Everything can be taken from a man but one thing: the last of the human freedoms – to choose one's attitude in any given set of circumstances, to choose one's own way.*[1]

Round-up of Part 2 – Power

Part 2 has been all about control: the ways in which we relinquish it and how we can claim it back. Here are the key points.

Victimhood (page 139)

We all have our moments when we slip into the trap of assuming that we're helpless, hopeless or that we have no choice. In the moment, relinquishing all responsibility can often feel like the preferable option. However, in the long run, routinely playing the victim can have a serious impact on our wellbeing because each time we choose not to take control we teach our minds that we *cannot* take control.

Drama (page 149)

Victimhood does not just come in one flavour. The Drama Triangle is a psychological model that describes the interplay between three different victim 'types': Persecutor, Rescuer and Victim. The Persecutor attempts to take control by blaming others; the Rescuer attempts to take control by saving others; and the Victim attempts to take control by manipulating others into saving them. What links all three types together (and sustains their sense of victimhood) is the refusal to take responsibility, which you could call 'real control'.

Locus of control (page 166)

Any time we're on the Drama Triangle (i.e. while we're in a state of victimhood), we externalise our locus of control by giving our power away. This causes us to feel as if our wellbeing depends on fate, luck, circumstance or the actions of others. Those with an internal locus of control, on the other hand, know that they alone can (and should) determine the way that they respond to the world around them. As a result, those with an internal locus of control feel calmer, more content and more in control of their own lives.

Two magic questions (pages 172 and 175)

There are two key questions that help to ensure we're operating from an internalised locus of control. Asking them inspires responsible action and trains the mind to opt out of victimhood:

1. The Action Question: **'Is there anything I can do about this right now?'**
2. The Golden Linings Question: **'What can I create out of this?'**

Emotional intelligence (page 183)

Emotional intelligence is the final ingredient required before we can escape drama (more often) and internalise our locus of control. All it demands is that we accept and experience our feelings and get real about what they mean.

Bad habits (page 185)

Emotional intelligence is made difficult, however, by our habitual inclination to fight against our emotional feedback, rather than accept it. There are many ways in which we can resist our feelings (drink, drugs, Drama Triangle behaviours, avoidance, etc.). The habits we call 'bad' are usually outdated coping mechanisms that are designed to enable our resistance. However, because 'what you resist persists', they cease to achieve their intended purpose over time. In a nutshell, emotional resistance results in self-sabotage.

Diving Down into self-awareness (page 194)

Diving Down is a process that utilises four powerful questions to help us build self-awareness, feel our emotions and, ultimately, take control of the life that we're leading:

* **'What am I thinking?'**
* **'What am I feeling?'**
* **'What is the monster story?'**
* And, while remembering to breathe: **'If I were to edit out that monster story, how would I see this differently?'**

This is how we can start to shake off the shackles of victimhood and claim authorship of our own lives.

PART 3
PLAY

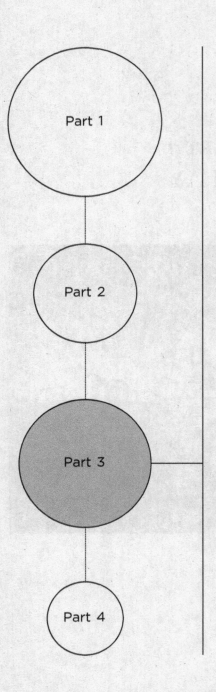

Play

This section is about making unconscious changes. Here, we'll bring everything from the first two parts of the book together by learning some in-depth processes designed to help you take control of your emotional reactions, rewrite your reality map and, ultimately, transcend the (dis)comfort zone.

Because people like to work in different ways, I've chosen three contrasting techniques. The first two chapters of Part 3 focus on lateral thinking and symbolism; the last two work in a more literal way by addressing the specific memories that lie at the root of your self-sabotage. It's my hope that you'll enjoy them all, but you may well have a preference.

Part 3 Contents

Evolution III
Monster Ownership   217

Chapter 9: Metaphor
Learning the Language of Symbolism and Imagery   219

Chapter 10: Narrative
Telling Better Stories   235

Chapter 11: The First Drafts
Going Back to the Beginning   256

Chapter 12: Meetings of Minds
Staging Your Own Reunion   269

You can listen to the guided meditation for Part 3 here:
http://hazelgale.com/home/mindmonsters-part3-recording

Evolution III

Monster Ownership

Until lions start writing down their own stories, tales of the hunt shall always glorify the hunter.

African proverb

We've used many different metaphors in this book; the conscious captain, the unconscious crew, water for emotion, mirages of the mind, etc. In Part 3, we'll take a look at why allegory and imagery play such an important role in the therapeutic process, but before that, let's take a moment to reassess the primary metaphorical symbol that we've been focusing on: the monster.

Task: Owning the Story

Step 1

First, bring to mind a key limiting belief that has a negative effect on your life.

The Victim perspective is that our monsters and their emotions are outside of our control and, therefore, that they can dictate our behaviour by *telling us* their frightful stories.

It's easy to look back on a memory about a hurtful parent or angry teacher and decide that those other people are our monsters, but they're long gone. Even if those people are still in our adult lives, the moment when they delivered the original message is a thing of the past. The monster that we carry within us – the aspect of self that we're too afraid to accept – is the part that took their message on and held it as truth.

The Author perspective, therefore, is that our monsters *are* us. When we can embrace that, we can see that they must be things we can influence. The Author knows that any aspect of the personality that comes connected to a negative message is actually believing it of itself. This means that the monster says, '*I'm* stupid/ugly/unwanted', not, '*You're* stupid/ugly/unwanted'.

This is how I'd like you to visualise this aspect of your personality now.

Step 2

Take a moment to imagine your monster telling its limiting story about itself, rather than you. How does it look when it owns its story?

Depending on how you've been documenting your monster's evolution, take a moment to note down or draw whatever comes to mind.

Step 3

When you've done that, I'd like you to have another think about one of the first questions I asked you:

If there was something you wish you could do with your monster, what would that be?

Make a note of the answer that comes to mind now.

————•●————

Playtime

In Part 3, we're going to look at the ways in which you can train the captain to communicate with the crew (monster included). If you started this book with a desire to kick your monster out, then I'd hope that by this stage you have a different idea about how best to overcome your self-sabotaging behaviours. (If you wanted to give it a snuggle at the beginning of the book, then that may not have changed.) Part 3 is where you'll have the chance to give your monster what it really needs to let go.

9

Metaphor

Learning the Language of Symbolism and Imagery

My coach is watching me punch the bag. 'You need to rediscover that vicious streak you used to have,' he says. 'You don't pressurise people in the same way any more. It's less ... convincing.'

He's right. Before I burned out, work rate and pressure were my biggest strengths. However, since getting back into my training I've been fighting much more tentatively. It's safer, I suppose. I crash and burn far less often now that I've found a way to temper my output. But it also means I'm getting a lot of split decisions, rather than clear wins. And yes, sadly, I have to acknowledge that I've lost some of the old spark.

I up my tempo on the bag, challenging my body to do just a little bit more. I don't want to be a boring fighter. That's not part of the plan. Maybe I can safely find another gear if I put my mind to it.

Later that evening, I sit down on the side of my bed to check in with how I'm feeling. I have a fight coming up this Friday, and I try to imagine myself being aggressive, but the imagery is mixed. One moment I look strong, the next, I'm sagging. In my chest, I can sense something that smacks of doubt. It's a heavy feeling, like a waterlogged sandbag, and it says just one word: 'Can't.'

This is all very familiar. Over the last six months, while I've been building my training up again, I've been careful to respect that 'Can't' and give my body a lot of rest. However, I'm no longer sure if it is really needed, or if it's just my monster finding another way to keep me from achieving my best.

I climb into bed and switch the light off. As I drift into and out of sleep, I have a half-dream – a semi-conscious fantasy infected by the weirdness of my sleeping mind's thinking. I'm imagining a lioness. She's strong and strikingly beautiful. Fearsome and impossible to ignore. I'm following her as she prowls through an alien landscape. It's an environment that I can't quite understand: part-wild, yet urban in feeling; uncomfortable, yet entirely known to me. The sky is intensely dark, but with shafts of bright sunlight that scorch through and illuminate little patches of the sandy ground beneath her paws. She is unperturbed by her strange surroundings and she moves – sometimes quickly, sometimes slowly – through the eerie, spotlit landscape, as if it belongs to her. Silent footfall after silent footfall, she makes the space her own, driven forward by nothing but the instinct that tells her what to do. And then she's gone, and her wayward world along with her – all swallowed strangely by the welcome black darkness of sleep.

Vehicles of Meaning

… most people think they can get along pretty well without metaphor. We have found, on the contrary, that metaphor is pervasive in everyday life, not just in our language, but in thought and action. Our ordinary conceptual system, in terms of which we both think and act, is fundamentally metaphorical in nature.

George Lakoff and Mark Johnson,
Metaphors We Live By

Metaphor is not just a flowery literary device used by poets to communicate the depth of their love or the darkness of their sorrow; it is a deeply ingrained and indispensable part of being human. We think in metaphor, talk in metaphor and, of course, we dream in metaphor.

In 1980, George Lakoff and Mark Johnson wrote the book *Metaphors We Live By*, in which they explored the pervasive influence that metaphor has over the lives we lead. In the decades since, their studies have sparked a complete reconsideration of some of the most fundamental ideas about how the mind works and how we take meaning from the things that we experience. The study of metaphor has gone on to contribute considerably, not just to the expected fields of art, literature and communication, but also to the worlds of cognitive science, law, politics, religion and even mathematics and the philosophy of science.[1] It has done so because we have woken up to the deeply suggestive nature of even the most basic and everyday use of metaphorical comparison.

We use metaphor in our language far more often than we're likely to realise. It has been estimated that the average person employs roughly six metaphors per minute of speech.[2] We just don't register the majority of the metaphorical words and phrases that we use because their meaning has been normalised. Have you ever told someone that they're 'sweet'? Well, unless you just licked their face, that was a metaphor. Ever said that you're 'flying' through your work, that the conversation 'flowed' or that the exam was 'tough'? These are all metaphors.

Scientists have argued for decades about how the brain processes linguistic metaphor. Some still believe that we understand metaphorical phrases like, 'He gave her a cold look' simply because we have learned that the word 'cold' in this context actually means 'unfriendly', and so we process it as such. However, recent studies have turned up some results that indicate a much more interesting possibility.

Neurologist Krish Sathian of Emory University in Atlanta (along with his students) conducted a study on the processing of metaphorical and literal meaning using fMRI brain scanning. The scientists scanned the participants' brains while they listened to both literal and metaphorical phrases describing the same thing.

Example
Literal: 'He had a bad day.'
Metaphorical: 'He had a rough day.'

Literal: 'He is naïve.'
Metaphorical: 'He is wet behind the ears.'

Literal: 'It was a precarious situation.'
Metaphorical: 'It was a hairy situation.'

The part of the brain that processes language was active while the subjects listened to both the literal and metaphorical phrases. However, the metaphorical phrases also stimulated the region of the brain involved in feeling different textures through the sense of touch. They also took longer to process than the literal descriptions. These results suggest that the brain's understanding of metaphorical meaning could be grounded in sensory perception as well as linguistic comprehension, which would have important implications about the breadth of meaning we take from such simple-seeming descriptions.

Of course, the above experiment was carefully designed to include only a single metaphorical word in each phrase. If you imagine someone hearing a story that invokes metaphorical meaning from all the different sensory modalities – sight, sound, touch, smell and taste – then you might see many, many more areas of the brain firing up to get a grip on the story's overall meaning. What's perhaps the most fascinating about this, though, is that we've all had different experiences of these kinds of sensory encounters. That is, we all hold different memories in our minds that give individualised meaning to words like 'rough', 'wet' and 'hairy'. Now, I can only apologise for having to put those three words next to one another in a sentence, but any image that may have sprung to mind will probably – quite conveniently – prove my next point.

Because we can only understand the world through the empirical senses, we can only grasp the concept of, say, 'roughness' by having experienced it for ourselves. Therefore, even though we are all likely to think we know what 'having a rough day' means, the phrase could invoke an entirely different kind of emotional response in different people. Was the day rough like sandpaper (did it wear us down)? Was it rough like a boisterous older sibling or an angry prison guard? Maybe rough has some positive associations? Rough like the hands of a hardworking grandfather perhaps. Because we each experience our own, personalised version of reality, we will all have our own unique version of 'rough'.

Freudian slips

It is the unconscious mind that is largely responsible for our choice of metaphorical descriptors. Of course, some metaphors can be carefully and rationally thought out (like many used in literature), but the ones that just show up in our spoken language rarely fit into this category because we can't think quickly enough to consciously select every word that we speak. Furthermore, even when we think we've given complete consideration to the meaning of the metaphor that we've chosen, there's likely to be a wealth of implicit associations that our unconscious mind is aware of – and using – regardless of the fact that they escape the attention of the captain.

In this respect, to use a metaphor to describe itself, the full meaning of a metaphorical symbol is a little like a tree with far-reaching roots. Consciously, we perceive the symbol (the visible part of the tree), but beneath it grows a much greater structure of meaning. Regardless of whether or not we make an explicit reference to them, the unconscious mind will be well aware of those invisible parts of the tree, as well as their function, their connection to the earth and how far they extend. All of that information will be condensed into – and then implied and expressed – by any tree-like symbol (e.g. leaves or bark, etc.).

What this means is that the metaphors that occur to us or crop up automatically in our language can be used to expand our conscious understanding of the unconscious perspective. All we need to do is a little digging.

Equivalence

Imagination is the beginning of creation. You imagine what you desire, you will what you imagine and at last you create what you will.

George Bernard Shaw,* *Back to Methuselah*

The mind is an association-making machine. It continuously hunts for patterns and similarities between the things we encounter and the things we have already experienced. It does so in order to understand and to save time. We don't need to work out what a chair is every time we walk into an unfamiliar room full of them, because the mind already has a mental blueprint for 'chair'. Anything that satisfies the key conditions – stable, four legs and a back, etc. – will automatically trigger all of our chair-related knowledge and behaviours. So we sit down.

The mind's love of equivalence is what makes metaphor such a powerfully suggestive tool. You can think of the mind like a conscientious mathematician: it will always aim to balance its equations. You probably learned in your very first algebra class at school that if $x = y$, then $10x = 10y$. Well, the same goes for metaphorical equivalences. The mind will strive to keep all equated things the same:

* Irish author and playwright.

$$10x = 10y$$
$$massive\ x = massive\ y$$
$$tiny\ x = tiny\ y$$

And also:

$$my\ love = a\ wild\ rose$$
$$my\ love\ withers = the\ wild\ rose\ withers$$
$$my\ love\ blooms = the\ wild\ rose\ blooms$$

It usually makes sense to people that once a metaphor for something like love has been decided upon, any change in the love will represent itself in the metaphorical image. If we have called our love a rose, then when our love dies we can quite easily imagine the rose withering away too. What's perhaps less obvious is that this is another two-way street. If we wanted to encourage our minds to focus on the blossoming of our love, then we could use the metaphor to make that suggestion by imagining the rose coming into bloom. As long as the request is within reason, the mind – conscientious as it is – will strive to get both sides flourishing equally.

Of course, it's not always that simple. There will usually be some obstacles to overcome along the way. If the love is not yet blossoming, then that will be for a reason, and the unconscious mind is far more likely than the conscious to know what that reason is. What metaphor allows us to do is work through the challenges in an abstract and resistance-free way, largely because we don't have to think directly about the problem that we're addressing. And so, instead of trying to create unconscious change by issuing orders, using metaphor is more like a collaborative problem-solving conversation with a friend; a meeting of minds where both parties can make suggestions based on their individual understanding of the situation, as well as learning more about the opposing point of view. This makes it infinitely less likely that either side will feel the need to fight back.

Getting past the 'Can't'

The lion imagery that I used to rediscover my lost aggression (see page 219) helped me to get past the 'Can't' that could well have stopped me otherwise. Somehow, my abstract self-to-self conversation that evening allowed me to honour and work through my unconscious resistance.

The morning after my half-dream, I could still remember the feeling I got from watching that lioness prowl through the wastelands of my symbolic dreamscape. She stayed in my awareness as I trained the following day, and I found that I could create a sense of strength and control by flashing the imagery up in my mind and then moving in a certain way. My body responded to my visualisations with a smooth sense of authority and forceful bursts of forward momentum, as if I had access to her ferociousness. That lion became an inner coach. She focused my mind on what I wanted to do, and she informed me quickly and automatically about how I needed to do it.

As I warmed up for the bout that Friday night, in a darkened backroom of an Essex nightclub, I imagined her leading the way. I watched her getting into the ring; strong, decisive and certain of her purpose. I visualised her moving with powerful poise, physically grounded, as if her feet were somehow magnetic, yet able to leap into action whenever that was needed. She was my guide – my mental blueprint for how I wanted to perform.

When I climbed through the ropes for real, I stepped right into that metaphor. I imagined the sensation of the canvas beneath her paws and I felt that same feeling of intense energy surging through my body. When the bell sounded, without needing to think, I moved forward, ducking and rolling underneath my opponent's jabs, driving her back with a strength of intention that I'd not felt in years.

Before the end of the second round, my opponent's corner-men threw in the towel to call a stop to the contest. I had won by TKO (technical knock-out). But it wasn't the result of the bout that made me feel the most proud. The real win was that I felt, for the first time that night, as if I had some command over my mental state, even in the midst of battle. Rather than being paralysed by a lack of self-trust or my fear of fatiguing, I fought that day in the way that I actually wanted to. That was the victory I relished the most, and it marked a pivotal point in my fighting journey.

Metaphorical Emotions

Sensory descriptions are used as metaphors for many things: 'The future is *bright*', 'The situation was *sticky*', 'The manifesto *stank* of lies'. When it comes to emotion, we instinctively use descriptors from all five senses – visual, auditory, kinaesthetic (feelings), olfactory (smell) and gustatory (taste) – to describe how we feel.

As already covered, negative emotions themselves are not the problem – they are just the connecting channel between the unconscious and the conscious. However, they are linked to the problem and they will change when the problem shifts. That sounds obvious, but it's an important point because it means the mind must have made an equivalence between the emotional reaction and the problem as a whole (if 'big anxiety' = 'big problem', then 'small anxiety' = 'small problem'). This equivalence means that once we have gained access to our unconscious reactions by diving into them (and once we have started to build a contract of trust with the part of the self that creates those reactions), then our feelings become a powerful resource for making a change, not just to our current experience, but to the bigger picture as well.

Metaphorical fluidity

The second Diving Down question – 'What am I feeling?' (see page 196) – encourages us to create a metaphorical representation of the emotional state associated with our self-sabotage. The examples in the previous chapter included a spiky green conker-shaped feeling that was lodged in the throat, and a dark, heavy, beetroot-coloured blob in the stomach.

By playing curiously with this kind of metaphorical imagery (we're going to add a section for this into the 'Now breathe ...' stage in the process), we can encourage a shift in the way that we feel, as well as the important move from a state of protection into growth. If the original symbol represented a stuck, stagnant or frozen emotion, then any change made to that symbol (if accepted by the unconscious mind) should mean that the feeling can begin to shift into a more fluid state. This means that every time we play with the feelings that the unconscious mind creates for us, we compound two important ideas:

1. That emotions change; we don't have to get stuck in any emotional state.
2. That our emotions belong to us; we can influence them (as long as we choose not to resist them).

Ultimately, human beings learn and grow through play. By having fun with the very things that are otherwise likely to shut us down, we can choose growth at the most crucial of moments.

Teaching the captain how to 'play nice'

Of course, a feeling will not necessarily always improve when we make a metaphorical suggestion, and this is not a substitute for self-awareness, because if all we do is try to 'metaphor away' our emotions, we could be entering into dangerously resistant territory. However, it does mean that rather than relying entirely on our awareness to shift our unconscious reactions, we can join the conversation and put in our metaphorical tuppence-worth.

If the unconscious reaction is intense anxiety when we encounter a spider, but the conscious perspective is that the spider is most definitely not dangerous, then the metaphor creates a space for that conversation to be had. Visualising the fear as getting smaller (or something similar) is just metaphor-speak for, 'No, that little spider isn't dangerous, my dear mind! We'll be OK, honestly!'

The Art of Playing with Your Feelings

You know those people who can just lie down, and the moment their head hits the pillow, they fall asleep? I'm not one of those.

The moment I climb into bed, my previously sleepy brain comes alive. Sound and language are almost always involved. Sometimes it's as though a band has taken up residence between my ears. It likes to play songs for me – occasionally just one line of them – over and over. On other nights, an overly enthusiastic part of my mind (one that clearly drinks too much coffee) will talk at length, discussing every nuance of every detail on some random topic that I'm not really interested in.

While writing this book, that overly enthusiastic, coffee-drinking part of my mind has been intent on chatting about theory into the wee hours of the morning. It talks in my writing voice and it explains whatever I've been focusing on that day. Sometimes it does this better than I can, and I'm forced to grab my journal and transcribe its ideas. I enjoy this process and I budget a little extra time in bed to make space for it. However, there comes a point (usually just after 1 a.m.) when I decide that enough is enough.

I'm an auditory person, so my mind will probably always be a relatively noisy place. I think primarily in a very clear voice, and it goes on and on constantly, no matter what I'm doing. Right now, you're probably either thinking, 'Everyone does that' or, 'She talks to herself in her head? She's clearly bonkers.' But we don't all think in the same way. Some people use a voice, while others think more in images, sounds or feelings. Most of us will be able to do all these things, but we'll often place preference on one or two of those modalities. My preference is to think in a way that I can hear.

Regardless of my noisy thinking, however, I'm not naïve enough to consider my difficulty in falling asleep to be 'just the way I am', because it's changeable. When I'm at my calmest, that voice talks gently about nonsense for about ten minutes until it just fades away dozily. When I'm under pressure, however, it could probably keep me up for hours if I wasn't prepared to do something about it. I've used many different sleeping aids over the years. Back in my adrenaline-addled fighting days, before I brought the problem to therapy, I took supplements religiously. I wanted a magical remedy for my persecutory insomnia, even though those pills made me feel as if I was swimming through treacle the following day. Now, thankfully, I have a healthier repertoire of options. Diving Down and then making metaphorical suggestions for sleep is my preference.

A few nights ago, when I lay awake talking to myself about this chapter, I decided to call it quits after stealing two ideas from my chatty, insomniac part. The question, 'What am I thinking?' gave me ramblings about metaphors and trees and their wide-reaching roots, as well as a couple of slightly anxious thoughts about needing to get to sleep, so that I'd be fresh for my clients and my writing the next day. 'What am I feeling?' revealed a tightness in my upper chest, which was angular, light, rapid, busy and seemed to be made of some kind of metallic material. Then, as I focused on that feeling, I heard the familiar sound of screeching brakes. It was faint, but definite, as it rang right in the inside of my ears.

The question 'What is the monster story?' confirmed my suspicions: this was driver activity. Hurry Up (see page 106) is a frequent character in my late-night Diving Down sessions, and this time it was trying to make me believe that I wasn't going to get this chapter written to meet my deadline.

As I started breathing, I asked myself what needed to happen to the emotional symbol in order for it to shift. I had two options to play with: the shape and the sound. First, I adjusted the sound. I slowed it down, as if it was playing on an old tape recorder that was running low on batteries. As I imagined the pitch getting deeper and drowsier, the muscles in my forehead started to release, but the feeling hadn't changed that much yet.

Next, I visualised the angular, metallic shape from my chest as if it was floating just in front of my eyes, and I gently encouraged it to get smaller. At first, it was resistant. Hurry Up wasn't ready to sleep yet, apparently. I had to start spinning the metal structure as if it was on an axis for it to begin to budge. As I did this, I was vaguely aware of some kind of release. It was as if a different, more adult part of my mind patted my Hurry Up driver on the head and said, 'You always feel this way but you always get it done, don't you?' Then, almost like watching a sci-fi spaceship disappearing into hyperdrive, the metallic shape shrank down very rapidly and vanished into the black. Silence.

The last thing I remember from that night was thinking something like, 'Huh. Cool. I should use this as an example.' But I didn't write it down. I was too busy falling asleep.

Time to Play

Once you've learned how to add metaphorical suggestions to the Diving Down process, it becomes a fantastic tool for when you need a way of managing your feelings in situ. Obvious options would be times when you're suffering from pre-performance jitters, nervousness before a stressful event or, as described above, failure to sleep. However, you can feel free to try this anywhere you like.

The idea is to use the Diving Down process to 'go inside' and get real about what you're responding to, and then play with a metaphor for your current emotional state, so that you can suggest a shift in the way you feel.

A key thing to remember is that whenever you're stressed, no matter what your situation, you're reacting to your own perspective, rather than reality. That doesn't mean your perspective is necessarily wrong – your situation could really be quite dire. But that's not to say you have to keep suffering from the feeling that you're creating in response to it. By taking ownership of your emotions, you can claim some power over your reactions, and that will put you in a far better position to take control, where possible, of the reality.

Making your suggestions

Before we jump in, let's take a little look at the different options you have for making metaphorical suggestions.

Types of suggestion 1: Simple changes

Very often, quite simple changes to the shape, size, location or movement of the symbol can make the biggest difference. These are known as 'submodality changes' in NLP and form a large part of many state-changing techniques. Try altering the feeling's colour, spinning it on an axis (as I did, above), changing the pitch of any sound it might have or imagining it feeling lighter. Anything that occurs to you is worth applying.

Note: I find that making the symbol smaller can very often create the most tangible shift. If other suggestions fail to make a noticeable difference, I'd recommend coming back to this one, perhaps a few times in one session.

Types of suggestion 2: Creative metaphor

The metaphorical change may not always be the most obvious thing, so remain open to any suggestion the unconscious presents to you. Maybe imagining it washing away like water feels right. Or maybe your mind would like to imagine sunlight shining onto it. We are creative beings. Anything goes. One of my clients used this process to address a rising feeling of panic he experienced whenever his ex messaged him. What he imagined happening as he relaxed was that he could breathe the feeling out. As he did, he saw the panic fluttering away in the form of butterflies. What's more, not only did this visualisation help him to stay cool whenever That Name appeared on his phone, but he later found that it helped him to pitch his ideas better at the office too.

Conversing

As you imagine making a change to the symbol, observe the feeling in your body while continuing to breathe comfortably and relax your muscles. If the feeling shifts in any way, then you're probably on the right track. Perhaps repeat that change again to see if it can shift some more. If it doesn't, then use a different metaphorical suggestion and see if that's more effective. You might need to try a number of different ideas before one sticks and you notice a physical change in the way you feel.

Remember that you're having a conversation here, rather than issuing an order. There could be a bit of back and forth before you resolve the problem, and you need to respect the input from your unconscious self. Just as it would be in a conversation with another person, if your suggestion isn't accepted, you will have to find a better way of articulating yourself. (I think we'll all agree that saying the same thing again BUT LOUDER rarely works.)

Sometimes, when things start to change, the initial shift can be quite subtle, so you will need to keep a part of your mind focused on your internal physical experience. But, whatever you do, please remember that reducing the emotion down to a completely neutral state is not necessarily the goal. It *will* happen sometimes, but on the occasions when it doesn't, even a 5 per cent shift can be claimed as a success as far as the bigger picture is concerned.

Making sure that you're open to learning

Remember that Diving Down is a process for increasing self-awareness, which remains true even when you use it routinely to fall asleep. Sometimes, a shift in the emotion brings with it a novel insight or a change in perspective. So, keep an eye out for new ideas about things you could do or say to improve your situation in a practical sense as well.

Note: please remember that this is not something that can be expected to work for deep, important emotions like grief.

Task: Diving Down into Emotional Fluidity

If you're ready to have a go, let's run through the process. There is no need to reach for the pen. You can do all of this in your head.

These will be the steps for this version of the Diving Down process:

1. Ask, 'What am I thinking?'
2. Ask, 'What am I feeling?'
3. Ask, 'What is the monster story?'
4. Now breathe ... and play with the metaphor.

Start by choosing a focus. What is there that's going on in your life right now that you'd like to feel differently about? Alternatively, is there something coming up that makes you feel unnecessarily agitated? We need this to have some tangible emotional impact, so I'd recommend selecting something you currently feel quite anxious, angry, sad or guilty about.

Step 1: Ask, 'What am I thinking?'

To gain awareness of your surface-level thought processes in relation to your chosen focus, observe and narrate your internal dialogue as you consider the problem situation.

Step 2: Ask, 'What am I feeling?'

Now, drop down into your body to observe the physical presentation of the connected emotions. Pay close attention to how you actually feel those feelings, so you can create a metaphorical symbol to represent them.

If nothing comes to mind immediately, here are some questions to help you develop an idea. As always, just go with whatever comes to you. There is no right or wrong, because once you've decided on an answer, your mind will have made the equivalence:

* If you could point to the position in your body where you feel the emotion, where would you point?
* If that feeling had a shape or form, what would that be?
* Is it two-dimensional or three-dimensional?

* What does it seem to be made of?
* Does it move in some kind of way or is it static?
* Is it large or small?
* Is it heavy or light?
* Is it hot, warm, cool or cold?
* If you could touch it, what kind of texture would it have?
* Would it be soft or hard?
* Does this feeling have any kind of sound associated with it? If so, what does it sound like?
* If it had a colour, what would that be?
* Are the edges of this symbol spiky, smooth or something else?

Spend a moment focusing on that emotional symbol, allowing it to develop in your mind so that you have a clearer idea of what it looks, sounds or feels like.

Step 3: Ask, 'What is the monster story?'

To make sure that you know what you're dealing with, and that you're taking an internal-locus-of-control perspective, listen to your deeper experience to discern what it is that you're really responding to. Then, complete this sentence:

'I am feeling (X emotion) because a part of my mind wants to believe... (insert relevant monster story).'

Step 4: Now breathe ... and play with the metaphor

Breathe fluidly and comfortably through the ideas that surface for at least three exhalations. As you do that, consciously relax your muscles and observe the emotion (as you see, hear or feel it) in your body. Then, ask yourself the following question about that symbol:

'If there was something that I could do with this symbol, which would encourage a positive shift in the way that I feel, what would that be?'

Close your eyes to focus on the metaphor while you consider the possible answers. For any idea that floats up, try it out. Stay relaxed and curious as you play with the options, repeating those that work and continuing the conversation by changing those that aren't accepted. When you notice a shift, open your eyes.

Finishing up

Sometimes this final stage will feel more appropriate and needed than others, depending on what you experienced while playing with the metaphor. Still, I would suggest that it's always good practice to ask the New Territories Question whenever you've identified a limiting belief at play. Here it is:

'If I were to edit out that monster story, how would I see this differently?'

———— •• ————

Summary: Metaphorical Emotions

The Diving Down practice that we've looked at in this chapter is just that: a practice. You may have created a shift this time round, or you may not have seen much change. However, nothing I'm including in this text is intended as a quick fix because I don't really believe those things exist.

When I first learned how to make these kinds of suggestions for myself, I'll admit that I lacked a little faith. Because I wanted something to make a magical difference, anything less than that felt like failure. However, just the fact that you're choosing to pause and take action is actually a pretty big deal. Sometimes these kinds of processes work wonderfully and make us feel as though we're the masters of our own minds. Then, at other times ... nothing. When the latter happens, it's all too easy to decide that 'it doesn't work' and assign ourselves back to the (dis)comfortable Victim corner on the Drama Triangle. Please don't do that. You've already come so far!

Having said that, we've only just touched on what's possible when it comes to making metaphor work for us. In the next chapter we're going to look into narrative and how to work with more complex allegorical imagery to tell our minds a better story.

10

Narrative

Telling Better Stories

The Danish boxing club is in a quiet suburban area surrounded by frosty basketball courts. It's 4.30 in the afternoon when we arrive from the airport. The chill in the air is razor-blade sharp on my skin. I retreat further back into my hoodie and start shuffling from foot to foot in an attempt to warm up.

As my coach sips from a hot cup of coffee, the steam mists up his glasses. I look on longingly. I haven't eaten since last night and even then all I had was two boiled eggs and some chopped tomatoes. I'm really hungry, but the hunger is nothing compared to my thirst. I'm used to dehydrating for weigh-ins, but this time has been extreme. I haven't had a sip of water in just under twenty-four hours.

As is often the way in ABA boxing, the call-up for this bout was short-notice. When my coach asked me if I wanted to take the fight I was about five kilograms heavier than I needed to be, and I had less than two weeks to get the weight off. This would have been relatively easy to do before I got sick – I would have cut my carbs, gone on a long run every morning and then dehydrated a little for the weigh-in. However, my body is no longer willing or able to go completely crazy for two weeks, so I accepted this fight knowing that I would need to stay dry for an entire day in order to get close to 67 kilograms. Thankfully, I'm able to jump on the scales this evening, rather than tomorrow just before the competition, but as we wait impatiently outside the club, I'm aware that I still have between two and three kilos left to lose.

Finally, our host arrives and – after a little friendly banter – my coach turns to me with a serious look. 'Right. Let's go and get this done.'

We find the sports hall, which is mercifully empty, and I disappear into the store cupboard at the back to get changed. First, I dress up in thermal tights and a long-sleeved top, then I put on a tracksuit, T-shirt, jumper, sweat jacket, massive woolly socks and a woolly hat, and I start working out.

Skipping, running, more skipping, shadow-boxing, more running ... Curse this cold Danish winter. I'm thirty minutes into the session and I don't think I've even started sweating. More skipping, more running, more shadow-boxing ...

Almost two hours later – and after a few heartbreaking failed attempts on the practice scales, followed by the agony of putting all those (now sweat-soaked) clothes back on to continue training – I'm finally down to 67 kilograms. Feeling relieved, we head straight over to the hotel where the official weigh-in takes place. I meet my opponent, they sign me off as on-weight, and I head up to my room to desperately glug down the rehydration fluids that I've been dreaming about since I woke up this morning.

Even after eating and drinking I still feel pretty terrible, and without the goal of weight-making to occupy my mind, my thoughts turn to the fight. I'm feeling nervous; more nervous than I'd like because my opponent is vastly more experienced than I am and I've already put my body through the wringer. But these thoughts aren't helpful. Right now, I need to focus on the positive, so I climb into bed, pull the duvet up to my chin and decide to channel my nervous energy into the construction of a metaphorical story.

I start by asking myself a simple question: 'What would I like to have happen?'

More than anything, what I long for is to sleep well and then wake up in the morning feeling clear and fresh. Yes, those two words resonate with my yearning. Too many times now I've slept poorly before a bout due to my racing, anxious mind and woken up feeling foggy, slow and sluggish. I didn't travel all this way for another one of those days. I need to have a conversation about 'clear and fresh' with my unconscious self.

As I ask myself the question, 'Clear and fresh like ... what?' an image of the vast, blue ocean comes to mind. There's a flying fish making a sprightly exit from the water and, as I allow myself to get lost in my imaginary scene, I notice that there are icebergs near by and stars twinkling brightly in the night sky.

The fish, it seems, has the leading role in this little narrative. I imagine the feeling of ascending through that fresh water and using it to gain the speed needed to fly. I enjoy the contrast in resistance: from water to air. It feels liberating somehow, like a release or perhaps just a new perspective. I replay the story a few times in my mind, distracting myself from the less than soporific fighting thoughts, and enjoying the simplicity of the repetition. Before long, my eyelids are getting heavy, and I snuggle down deeper into my duvet for a long and restful sleep.

------••------

Spinning Yarns

Narrative is everywhere we go. We read, watch and listen to stories in books, films, on the TV and radio, in songs and in plays. We are sold products via the stories used in advertising. Commercials don't just tell us that a particular fruit juice is good, they sell us that idea by narrating a little section of someone's life – a life that has been made better by the presence of said juice. Why? Because story helps us to learn.

The science of storytelling metaphor

Stanford University's professor of biology, neurology and neurological sciences, Robert Sapolsky, suggests that the human brain acquired the ability to think in metaphor as a 'necessary shortcut'. In his article, 'This Is Your Brain on Metaphors', Sapolsky kindly encourages the reader to imagine taking a 'bite out of a struggling cockroach' (for which we all thank him greatly). In doing something like this, neurons in the particular part of the brain that processes gustatory disgust will fire up, just as if we imagined tasting or smelling rotten food or any other unwholesome thing. This is a reaction that our brains evolved in order to prevent us from doing things like eating cockroaches. Good.

According to Sapolsky, the same area of the brain (the insula) will also activate if we read a story in the newspaper about something we consider to be morally disgusting – say, a massacre or the abduction of a child. We might then refer to the perpetrators of such crimes as 'rodents', 'maggots', 'rotten scum' or even 'lousy cockroaches'. We make these comparisons quite automatically because in considering a morally disgusting act, we will automatically stimulate the same neurological functions that remind us how much we really, really don't want to take a bite out of a struggling cockroach. Sapolsky puts it this way: 'When we evolved the capacity to be disgusted by moral failures, we didn't evolve a new brain region to handle it. Instead, the insula expanded its portfolio.'[3]

But the effect of this kind of mental crossover extends further than just triggering a nasty feeling. Emotions lay the groundwork for our judgements and our behaviour. Frighteningly, a study conducted at the University of Kansas demonstrated that people who read two articles – one that used the metaphor of the nation as an organic organism (including statements like 'Following the Civil War, the United States underwent a growth spurt') and one that discussed the dangers of airborne bacteria – were more likely to express negative views about immigration afterwards.[4] The metaphorical overlap got under their skin by evoking emotion; it encouraged them to fear immigration in the same way that they might fear an infection.

On the inside, our monsters are also capable of using metaphor to keep us in a state of protection. They can co-opt the multitude of metaphorical possibilities available to them at any given moment to make menacing the most mundane of information. However, the beauty of narrative is that even our monsters are willing to pay attention at story time. This chapter's task will enable you to write the kind of story that can teach your mind how to resolve unconscious conflict and to strengthen desired, positive attributes.

Using Metaphor to Solve Problems

Just as my lion half-dream helped me to get past the 'Can't' that could otherwise have stopped me back in Essex, the flying-fish narrative in Denmark got through to my unconscious and unravelled some of my fear. As I lay there in my hotel bed thinking about taking flight, it made me smile to realise that I was using a 'fish out of water' metaphor for fighting. It also made sense. Walking willingly into any kind of danger is an unnatural thing to do, and in the past, my fear had certainly caused me to flounder. The way I interpreted my metaphorical story that night was that I was making this decision OK for myself: 'Yes, I'm doing something that my instincts would prefer I did not do. But that doesn't mean I can't make it somehow beautiful.'

I won the bout the next day. In fact, I think that fight may have been my best-ever performance. My opponent had probably competed in something like forty or fifty more fights than I had, but I chose to take control from the beginning of every round nonetheless, striking fast and then moving before I could get hit back. I knew it was going to be a good bout before we even began. I can clearly remember how it felt to hit the pads in my warm-up. I was sharp, powerful and accurate, and that feeling continued when I stepped into the ring. A good night's sleep will do that for you, but I think there might have been more to it than just that.

Unlocking hidden strengths

In spending a little time thinking creatively about the positive things that we want to have more of, we can deepen our understanding of what it will take to achieve them. This comes about as a result of that problem-solving conversation between conscious and unconscious. While we speak metaphorically about some kind of desired attribute — say, the confidence to talk to someone we find attractive or the motivation to get out on our morning runs — the unconscious is exploring the vast structure of roots that extend below the surface, providing the water, nutrients and stability to whatever it is that we want to nurture. Furthermore, because we needn't think directly about the end goal, we can more easily avoid the trap of chasing mirages.

I often use metaphor with the people I train to box. There's perhaps no better situation than the middle of an exhausting training session to demonstrate how much more easily people respond to imagery than they do to logical, technical pointers. My longest-standing boxing client – an investment banker who I've been coaching for over a decade – has an entire repertoire of symbolic commands to which he'll react almost instantaneously. He didn't need to sit down and put serious thought into any of them; they're all just images that he came up with during our conversations mid-workout. It might sound ridiculous for a coach to shout 'Flamenco!' (snappier punches) or 'Steel cube!' (tighter guard) at a fully grown man while he trades blows with another. But it works.

Diversity

In my practice, I have witnessed the development of some incredible and varied metaphorical landscapes over the years, and I can safely say that no two have ever been the same (or even that similar). People have imagined handcrafted pocket-watches to regulate their timing and holographic brains with multicoloured electrical impulses to sharpen their thinking. I've very much enjoyed conversations about laser-eyed robots that can focus exclusively on the task at hand and magical bubbles of light that deflect drama, yet allow meaning and love to permeate.

Not everyone will find themselves wandering through quite such rich imaginary fantasies immediately. However, you might be surprised by what people can access when given the freedom and the platform to get creative. Even the most literal-seeming and straightforward of clients – CEOs of big companies and success-driven, businesslike pro athletes – can find themselves getting lost in the almost childlike imaginary world of their creative minds. What's more, in my experience, they tend to make changes at a faster rate when they do.

Hello Trouble, My Old Friend

Trouble is the fat red thread that ties together the fantasies of pretend play, fiction, and dreams, and trouble provides a possible clue to the function they all share: giving us practice in dealing with the big dilemmas of human life.

Jonathan Gottschall, *The Storytelling Animal*

In *The Storytelling Animal,* Gottschall looks into the history and evolutional function of narrative. He suggests that story makes up the very backbone of what it is to be human, calling it our 'evolutionary niche'. At first glance, the human love affair with story as entertainment might suggest that the function of fiction is escapism. But, as Gottschall points out:

If fiction is escape, it's a bizarre sort of escape. Our various fictional worlds are – on the whole – horoscopes ... We are drawn to fiction because it gives us pleasure. But most of what is actually in fiction is deeply unpleasant: threat, death, despair, anxiety, Sturm und Drang.[5]

It certainly seems to be true. Watch children submerged in their fictional playtime worlds and you'll see them engaging with the dark forces of evil: dragons, aliens, bad people and, of course, monsters. Rehearsal of fearsome conflict seems to be the way in which children prepare to navigate the inevitable turbulence of real life, and it doesn't stop when we grow up. You only need to view a couple of films or an episode of a soap opera to realise that trouble pretty much always plays a leading role in adult storytelling too.

Gottschall's argument is that 'The human mind was shaped *for* story, so that it could be shaped *by* story.'[6] We learn to act like a human, uphold human values, solve human problems, and enjoy human life largely through the medium of storytelling (in its various forms). Our mirror neurons enable us to model the behaviours, emotions and other experiences of a story's protagonist. Then the brain rewires itself as if we, ourselves, have been on the same journey and solved the same problems.

This is also true of the metaphorical stories we write for ourselves; we mentally recreate the journey taken by the key symbols, whether they are animal, mineral or vegetable. When I imagined my fish soaring effortlessly through the fresh air, therefore, my mind was physically changing to incorporate an allegorical blueprint for me to take my own flight.

What this means is that for a metaphor to help us overcome an issue, there will often be some kind of obstacle to navigate within the story. When working with clients, the 'trouble' (AKA unconscious resistance) sometimes shows up as a big and difficult issue that we spend multiple sessions working through, and sometimes it's subtle and just seems to resolve itself quite naturally as the narrative unfolds. Either way, whenever or however it turns up, our old friend Trouble is always welcome to the party.

'Smooth and Cool' Presenting

A few years ago, I conducted a corporate workshop on the use of metaphor. Initially the topic was (unsurprisingly) met with some resistance. The team had just finished a long string of in-depth technical workshops and probably wanted to head to the pub rather than listen to some 'touchy-feely' therapist-type talking about creative problem-solving. Still, there I was, and I wasn't going to let any raised eyebrows dampen my enthusiasm. A few years earlier, I would have approached this subject with a similar level of scepticism, so I knew exactly where they were coming from.

The aim of the workshop was to teach the attendees how to coach one another into their desired flow state for work: the perfect pitching persona, perhaps, or a state of focus for challenging tasks. One woman (let's call her Janet) was looking for a 'smooth and cool' mindset for public speaking. She clearly thought the workshop was difficult and a bit ridiculous. She sat with her arms tightly folded across her chest and looked down at her knees while her partner asked the questions I'd put together, starting with one designed to evoke a metaphor: 'Smooth and cool like what?'

'I just don't see the point!' she said. 'What do you mean, "Smooth and cool like what?" I just want to feel calm when I talk to large crowds, rather than nervous and tetchy ... like I do right now.'

One of the most magical things about working with metaphor is being able to watch the story solve the problem in real time. It's normal (in fact, it's very helpful) if the client finds themselves in their 'problem state' at some stage in the process. It means that any development they make is being mapped and learned right then and there in both a practical and allegorical way, and it's then easier for the conscious mind to recognise the change as it happens and log it as possible.

Janet's partner bravely pressed on with the questions, taking care to focus on the positive descriptors that Janet used ('smooth' and 'cool'). Eventually, Janet said, 'Well, I dunno. Maybe smooth and cool like a lake. Maybe that.' She was far from converted, but at least she was playing ball.

As the pair continued with the process, that lake turned out to be in the Alps. It was surrounded by snow-capped mountains and the lush green of dense fir trees. The sky was a bright blue, and its enormity was reflected in the glassy water's surface. But ... there was a problem. At some point, a figure appeared in Janet's metaphor to swim in the serene blue water. She was dressed in her swimsuit and ready to take the plunge, but when she dipped a testing toe in, she recoiled in horror. This lake was *too* cool. Swimming in it would have been anything but calm. In a flash, Janet's frustration returned and she started to close down again. 'This doesn't *work* for me!'

Responding to the resistance, Janet's partner asked the two most important questions for problem-solving within a metaphorical scene. First, she said, 'What would you like to have happen?', to which Janet replied: 'I just want her to be able to enjoy the lake.' Then she asked about the conditions for that outcome, 'What needs to happen for her to enjoy the lake?'

I watched for a moment, as Janet started coming up with ideas to get around her metaphorical problem. Maybe the swimmer needs a wetsuit? Maybe it needs to be summer? She was back in the game.

Satisfied that these two were on their way to a resolution, I moved on to help another pair in the group who were talking quizzically about a rocket launch (honestly, it was a brilliant day). When I returned ten minutes later, Janet and her partner were deep in conversation. The Alpine lake had frozen over and the swimmer had become a figure skater. She was turning pirouettes and jumping into triple salchows – the type that make that wonderful, arresting sound on the ice just before take-off.

Everything about Janet's demeanour had changed. She was upright and open, her hands and arms gestured to emphasise her descriptions and she spoke clearly and eloquently. What's more, her partner appeared to be completely locked into the story, emphatically nodding in approval as Janet described her ice-skater's brilliance. You could say that Janet had adopted the grace, composure and fluidity of a highly skilled athlete, practising what her body knows how to do beautifully. Or, you could say that she was delivering a brilliant presentation.

This is what the power of metaphor can do. We don't just come up with a nice idea, we *become* the idea as it develops. What's more, Janet had done more than just access her desired performance state – she had built on it. Perhaps she knew when she said 'smooth and cool' that she also wanted 'exciting and captivating', or perhaps it hadn't occurred to her. Either way, it was clear that this style suited her, and that she was very good at it.

The following day I received an email from the group coordinator saying that a few people had fed back that they had already accessed their performance states using their metaphors that morning. I don't know if Janet was one of them, but I dearly hope so.

Let's jump in to the task to see what your mind can come up with.

Task: Telling Your Own Story

Before we begin, you will need to choose your focus. What would you most like to improve or achieve as a result of doing this task?

I'd suggest you focus on something relatively simple here. You could work with an objectively serious self-sabotage like panic attacks or binge eating, but it might be better to save those issues for the memory process coming up in the second half of Part 3. Perhaps you can think of a psychological skill that could help you with those bigger problems though: a state of confidence, focus for reading or studying, increased enthusiasm at work, productivity, a sense of connection to other people while you speak to them. Alternatively, you may be able to think of a physical action that you'd like to improve: a technique in sport, better posture in a certain situation or a clearer speaking voice for presentations. Or, as many people do, you could use this process to access a simple, yet so often longed-for state of calm.

If you're stuck, here's a question to help you come up with an idea:

If there was something that you would like to be able to do differently in order to feel more productive, confident or happy with yourself, what would that be?

While you chew that over, there are a couple of key points for you to consider. Firstly, the most common concern that people have about this process is that they think they're not going to be creative enough for it. You don't need to be the type of person who can write poems or paint pictures to get something useful out of this technique. It's true that some people are more inclined to think laterally than others. However, I used to curse my stubbornly literal mind and I have learned to work with metaphor by practising with exercises just like this one. I'm sure that your unconscious will have some wonderful ideas for you if you just relax and go with it.

You should also bear in mind that working with metaphor can sometimes take you into your problem state before you find your way back out. Occasionally, as Janet did, my clients will start to feel a little anxious or frustrated as they develop their narrative. This isn't just because they're finding the storytelling difficult. It's because working with a metaphor for the solution to their problem has triggered some resistance. Remember that the unconscious mind doesn't want to solve the problem because it sees it as a solution. It may look for a way to fire up your limiting beliefs and keep those negative stories feeling true. So, if you find yourself feeling incapable, angry or any other kind of 'not ... enough' while developing your story, I implore you to stick with the task, because that emotion could be a very important part of the process.

With that out of the way, if you've thought of a skill, psychological state or other attribute that you would like to enhance, let's begin.

Step 1: Exploring your focus

You're going to start by creating a more detailed description of your goal. This does not need to be metaphorical. However, it's crucial that you make sure it's all stated in the positive rather than the negative because you cannot create a metaphor about something you don't want to do or feel without encouraging your mind to do or feel that thing.

For example, let's say your goal was to use more positive body language while speaking to people you see as authority figures. If so, rather than saying, 'I *wouldn't* slump when talking to my boss', you will need to think up a positive counter to that problem. What would the situation look, sound or feel like if the slumping problem simply didn't exist? Your answer will look more like this:

'I would be able to stand up straight, with my shoulders back and my chin lifted when talking to my boss. I would be breathing more easily, I would speak more clearly and calmly, and the way I will act when standing this way will inspire more confidence in my work.'

Take a moment to think up (and perhaps write down) your description. Just let the words flow without self-criticism. The more detail you consider, the better.

When you've done that, consider which of the words you've used might be the most resourceful. From the example above I might select 'stand up straight', 'chin lifted', 'breathe more easily', 'speak clearly and calmly' and maybe 'inspire'.

We want a good selection of descriptive words to choose between in the next step, so to expand on your initial idea (especially if it's fairly literal), try asking this question of any particularly key words:

'What kind of ... ?'

Example

'What kind of *straight*?' 'A kind of strong, tall and confident straight. Or, a proud and commanding kind of straight ...'

We now have even more resourceful words to add into the mix: '*strong*', '*tall*', '*confident*', '*proud*' and '*commanding*'.

Step 2: Developing your metaphor

Next, you're going to pick one word or phrase to use as a jumping-off point for your story. There may already be some metaphors in your description. Perhaps you've talked about the desire to 'flow' through your work or 'zoom in' on your task. Maybe you've mentioned speaking more 'freely' or having more 'strength' of mind when you assert your opinion. Any of those words would present a great opportunity. However, if you can't find a ready-made metaphor, you can simply choose a descriptive word. For example, from the options above, I could stick with 'stand up *straight*' because it seems to encapsulate the main aim.

Note that your focus can just be the original goal. If your aim was to achieve a state of calm, for example, then you could easily use the word 'calm' for this step.

Decide on the most resourceful word or phrase to use as a jumping-off point for your story. Then, to encourage a metaphor to come to mind, take your selected word or phrase (let's call it 'X') and ask this question:

X like what?*

---

* The structure of this question and some others that I'll ask in this chapter has been borrowed from a series of coaching questions designed by psychotherapist David Groves. Groves created the Clean Language™ approach to help counsellors and therapists work with their clients' metaphorical language without contaminating the resulting imagery with their own associations. If you'd like to know more about this approach, I've included a book on this topic (*Clean Language*) in the Bibliography (see page 361).

Example
Stand up *straight*.
Straight like what?
Straight like a giant redwood tree.

Just sit with the question for a moment and see what comes to mind. There's no need to second-guess your answer here; just trust the crew and go with whatever crops up. If nothing comes, then pick a different starting point.

Optional journaling: note down your answer.

Step 3: Developing your metaphorical scene

Next, you're going to expand on the metaphor by developing the scene in which your key symbol exists (e.g. the redwood tree). This step is about breathing life into your idea, so that it becomes more detailed and real in your mind. Before you start writing or visualising, consider the following:

Questions for developing your metaphorical scene:
* Where do you imagine your primary symbol (the protagonist of the story)?
* What kind of environment is it in?
* What else can you see in the scene?
* How does it relate to those other things?
* What kind of attributes does your key symbol possess?
* What are the standout visual components in the scene?
* What kind of sounds come with this imagery? (Either those made by your symbol, or the sounds made by things around it.)
* What other kind of sensory information does it evoke? (Is there anything to smell, taste or feel in this scene?)

Example
'The redwood tree is tall and solid. It's growing in the middle of a Canadian forest, but it's taller than the other trees near it. Its bark is a beautiful, deep red colour and it is very thick and strong. Hundreds of species of birds, insects and other animals make the tree their

home, and they live there harmoniously together. At the top of the tree, the thinner branches allow the leaves to sway gently in the wind, which makes a soft, relaxing sound. Because it stands so tall, the view from the top of the tree reaches for miles and miles ...'

Take a moment to develop your scene. You don't need to think about what it might mean yet. Just absorb yourself in the imagery and allow it to come to life.

Optional journaling: write fluidly and expressively about the scene that comes to mind.

Step 4: A beginning, middle and end

Of course, for this to be a true story, it needs to have some duration. So, to give your narrative a beginning, middle and end, answer these questions (insert a brief description of your key symbol behaving in the desired way into the brackets):

What happens before (X)?

What happens after (X)?

Example
What happens before the redwood stands tall? 'Before the redwood stands tall, it needs to grow from a tiny sapling, just like all the other trees. When it's small, the forest gives it shelter and protection.'

What happens after the redwood tree stands tall? 'Once the tree is big enough to stand taller than those around it, it can see beyond the other trees. It also becomes a part of that protective canopy that gives shelter to the new saplings growing at its feet.'

Take a moment to explore your narrative, going with anything that comes to mind (even if it feels as if it could be taking your story somewhere unexpected).

Optional journaling: write fluidly and expressively about the beginning and end of your story.

Step 5: Checking

For this step, I'd like you to imagine that you have a cinema screen in your mind. Then, in a moment, I'd like you to play the story from beginning to end with these two aims:

1. To notice how the full narrative makes you feel.
2. To pay attention to any unconsciously generated imagery or ideas that crop up in addition to what you've already imagined.

Take a moment to do that before reading on. When you've played the entire story, open your eyes and consider the following questions:

Is there anything else that needs to happen before your story feels complete?
If so, add it in.

Does everything feel OK with your story?
If so, that's great. You can skip forward to the section entitled 'Mapping back to reality' on page 251. If not, answer this next question:

What was it that prevented the story from either feeling right or playing out fully?

If you found a glitch, then you've come across our old friend Trouble. Take a moment to describe the obstacle to yourself.

Example
Trouble: 'When I try to imagine the redwood growing from a tiny sapling to full height, it feels too crowded and intimidated, as if the trees already living around it could prevent it from standing as tall as it would like.'

Optional journaling: make a note of the obstacle that arose in your story.

Step 6: Making use of Trouble

If you found Trouble, then the creative editing you do to solve the problem in the story could be the most important part of this process. This is how you can converse with your unconscious mind in order to map out the solution for the real-life problem. You will need to ask yourself the same questions that Janet's partner asked to help her evolve her swimmer into a figure skater.

Here they are:

(Checking the intention) When you consider the obstacle, what would you like to have happen?

(Checking the resources) What needs to happen for that to take place?

Example:
When you consider that the sapling feels too crowded to grow tall, what would you like to have happen? 'I'd like the redwood to be able to find its own place among the others.'

What needs to happen for the redwood to find its own place among the others? 'The sapling needs to gradually take root, so that it can build its strength as it grows. When it trusts in itself to find its own space, it can work its own way through the canopy. Because it does this slowly and naturally, the other trees in the forest accommodate it; they welcome it'.

When you've found a potential solution, ask this question:

And can that happen?

If the answer is 'yes', then you've made use of our old friend Trouble. Well done.

If it's 'no', then you need to do a little more editing. Have a think about what needs to happen for your solution to work (e.g. 'What needs to happen for the sapling to gradually take root and build its strength?'). If you can't find a way to make your original solution work, then consider a different one. There are always options, and the more creative you get, the more new connections your unconscious will be making – and that's a good thing.

Keep rewriting and adding to your story until it plays out in a way that feels positive, empowering and in line with what you want. Be sure to finish with the question, 'And can that happen?' When you get a 'yes' to that, you have completed the task.

Optional journaling: if you'd like to make the most of your story, take some time to write it out in full. You could even consider storyboarding it if you like.

———•• •———

Mapping back to reality

You don't actually need to know what your metaphor means in order for it to be effective (we can never fully understand the extent of the implicit meaning). However, I believe that the more informed we keep the captain, the better. Looking into the meaning of the different symbols in your story can shed light on the practical actions that could move you more swiftly and easily towards your goal.

When I imagined the icy ocean scene in Denmark, the fish initially struggled to build enough speed and power to take flight. That was my Trouble, and it almost certainly represented a lack of trust in my own energy levels after such a gruelling weight-cut. I worked around the problem in the story by allowing the fish to begin its ascent from a deeper position. When it did this, the beginning of the build-up was more enjoyable because there was more to see under the water, but the fish had to start slowly and increase its speed very gradually in order to jump as high as I wanted it to when it got to the surface.

I used that section of the story as a blueprint for my warm-up the following day. I started getting ready early, so that I felt in control; but I made sure to stay relaxed for as long as possible before ramping up the energy just before the bout. This approach meant that I enjoyed not only that wonderful feeling of smacking the pads with sharp accuracy, but also that I had fun during the day before the contest. I chatted with my coach and some of the other fighters and I met some really interesting people in the audience – all because I'd given myself a pass to swim very slowly until I actually needed to fly.

Take a moment to have a think about what the different elements of your story could stand for. How could you put those ideas into action in your life?

Keeping it Alive

Developing your story may or may not have unlocked some previously inaccessible unconscious resources or perspectives (it could be fun to keep an eye out over the coming days for any evidence of positive change).

Either way, it can be used to keep your mind trained on the solution, rather than the problem.

Making it work for you

To keep your metaphor in the forefront of your mind over the coming days and weeks, consider making a note of it somewhere you'll see it regularly. What the imagery does is condense a potentially large amount of implicit information down into one, easily recalled picture, sound, scene or movie clip. Each time you bring that imagery to mind, your brain will strengthen the synaptic paths associated with the positive change you're going to make. With time, even without having made the changes in real life, your mind will begin to feel as if it has lived that story many times.

If your metaphor will be particularly useful in a specific environment, then find a way of reminding yourself to bring the imagery to mind just before entering into that situation. For example, if the redwood tree was your metaphor, and you had a meeting with your boss tomorrow, you could set an alert on your phone to remind you to imagine the redwood standing tall and naturally co-existing with the other trees. It would only require that you focus on the imagery for a few seconds before walking into the meeting room to make that positive suggestion to your unconscious mind.

You can also consider these optional tasks:

* Draw aspects of the landscape to develop the ideas even further and better 'imprint' them into your neural circuitry.
* Make a note of any particularly resourceful insights that you might have gleaned.
* Keep a reminder of key words or phrases on the screensaver of your computer or phone.
* Talk your metaphorical story through with a friend (this makes it easier to remember).

There's one more thing for us to do before we move on. I saved the best bit for last.

Different Angles

Back in the hotel room before my fight in Denmark, resolving the Trouble and letting that flying fish do its thing provided a welcome distraction for my mind. But I wasn't quite finished yet. I wanted to know more about the metaphor, so I decided to play one of my favourite games with it: perspective shifting.

This is a tool that can be used in pretty much any situation, metaphorical or not. It just requires that you take a moment to look through the eyes of someone or something other than yourself. It can be helpful, for example, to imagine stepping into the shoes of another person when you're in some kind of disagreement, so that you can see things from their point of view. That sounds obvious, but if you take the time to really engage in that process – to imagine literally being the other person: standing as they would stand, using their facial expressions and then viewing yourself through their eyes – you could be surprised by the insights you can glean.

When working with a metaphorical story, however, this will be a more abstract process than that. What you have to do to gain a bigger-picture perspective on your story is to step into the different symbols to view the scene through their 'eyes'.

In Denmark, I started by imagining that I was the ocean. I looked at the icebergs, the stars and the fish from that perspective. The ocean felt as though it had a symbiotic relationship with the stars and the sky, and about the fish, it felt protective. It cared for it and offered it sanctuary.

Next, I imagined being the fish. From the fish's point of view, the sky looked wonderfully exciting, full of possibility. The little fish felt safe in the water, but it loved to rise up powerfully and reach for the stars that it could see in the night sky.

Finally, I stepped into the position of the stars and I experienced something quite extraordinary. The fish looked impossibly small in that massive blue ocean and it was getting progressively smaller, as if I was zooming out. In a flash I found myself looking not only at a tiny fish, but also a tiny ocean on a tiny planet that appeared like a little speck on the background of the infinitely enormous universe.

Now, I'm aware that this might sound strange, but the insignificance of me and my little fight comforted me enormously that night. I drifted off to sleep with two ideas in my mind about the competition the following day:

1. It's exciting to reach for the stars. I do this because I love it.
2. None of it really means anything beyond that.

Task: Accessing the Bigger Picture

Let's return to your narrative one more time. To view your scene through the 'eyes' of the different elements in the story, start by making a list of all the symbols (e.g. fish, ocean, icebergs, stars). Then, one by one, step into the position of each symbol and ask the following question about all the others:

'From this position, how do I see (the other symbol)?'

Example 1 (from the fish's perspective)
Question: 'From this position, how do I see the icebergs?'
Answer: 'They look big, calm, still and solid. I know that I can depend on them being there.'

Example 2 (from the perspective of another redwood tree)
Question: 'From this position, how do I see the central tree in the story?'
Answer: 'It's just a tree like me. I enjoy seeing it stand so tall.'

In practice, I often find that perspective shifting can provide the most meaningful insights during metaphorical work. Another boxer, who had originally seen her aggression as a gentle wave lapping at the shore, stepped into the position of a person on the beach and realised that her wave looked more like a tsunami to others. A golfer I worked with imagined his career like the flight of a paper aeroplane through wispy clouds. However, when he looked at the plane from the position of those clouds, it looked 'intimidating' as it powered through the sky.

What do you get when you view your scene from all the different perspectives available?

Note: if you find more Trouble when you play this game, then you know what to do. Skip back to Step 6 above and make use of it.

------●●------

The take-away insight

Zooming out to recognise the insignificance of my little fight (the tiny fish in a tiny ocean on a tiny planet) became a standard pre-fight visualisation for me, and I still use it now when facing a challenge. So, here's my final question for you:

> **If there was one key insight that you could take away from your story, what would it be?**

In the next chapter, we're going to look at how to get creative with perhaps the most fundamental and influential type of metaphor around: memory.

11

The First Drafts

Going Back to the Beginning

We're poised shakily at the starting line, waiting for the race to begin. My heart is pounding, but I'm not entirely sure why. In the back of my mind, I have the sense that something important rests on what happens next. It's sports day at Coton Village Primary School. I'm five years old.

As I look down the stretch of lumpy grass ahead, all I can see is my dad at the finishing line. He's egging me on enthusiastically: 'Come on, Hazey!'

Dad likes sport and poker and other games, and he usually wins when he plays. Winning is important, I think, because it makes him happy.

Ready. Set. Go!

Suddenly my legs are moving as fast as they possibly can, so quickly that it doesn't really feel as if my feet are touching the ground. I'm not even sure if this is what I'm supposed to be doing, but right now everyone else is running fast, so I do too, desperate to get to the crowd of mums and dads before anyone else. It feels as if my body is carrying me as rapidly as it is able, away from something too terrible to even think about. There's no looking back. No thinking. Just running.

As I cross the finishing line the parents' shouting turns to applause and I make a beeline towards my dad, who proudly scoops me up into his arms: 'Well done, Hazey-babes. You won!' But my heart is still beating too loudly for me to hear his words. All I can feel is relief.

Relief. It's over and I have done something that made my dad happy. It's over and I won.

The Ever-shifting Memory Map

Perhaps the most powerful way of claiming Authorship of our own story is to go back to the beginning. In this chapter, we're going to explore the metaphorical nature of memory and time, and how our earliest stories can be rewritten, so that our minds have better scripts to refer to.

As you'll see over the remainder of Part 3, the above memory played perhaps the most significant role in the process of my coming to terms with my own little monster. I relate it so vividly here to make a point. For a long time, this was my recollection of that day, along with all the anxiety and uncertainty that I was feeling. Until I was given the opportunity, I didn't question it or consider addressing it because in my head it was just a normal thing that happened. It certainly didn't seem that important. However, the way my mind chose to remember that day speaks volumes about the (dis)comfortable version of reality that I had been sustaining for myself. Rewriting the story has helped me to reframe not only my relationship to competition, but also to life, love, companionship and the very idea of what it means to be 'me'. We'll explore exactly how I did that during this and the next chapter.

No matter whether or not you can think of any stand-out moments from your childhood, and no matter how 'good' or 'bad' you consider your powers of recollection to be, there will be stored moments in your memory bank that can provide you with a similar opportunity. You just have to know how to identify them.

Before we jump into the mechanics of how to do that, though, I have some news for you about everything you've ever experienced. Brace yourself.

The plasticity of memory

Can you remember where you were when you heard about the 9/11 attacks or London's 7/7 bombings? Me too. Do you have clear pictures or auditory impressions of what was going on around you at the time: conversations you had, the looks on people's faces and so on? Me too. Would you swear on your life that you were in that exact place, with those people, having those conversations? Me too. At least, I would have done some years ago. Now, I wouldn't be so confident.

The vivid recollections that we store after experiencing something particularly poignant are called 'flashbulb memories' – a term coined in 1977 by psychologists Roger Brown and James Kulik, who studied people's recollection of the John F. Kennedy assassination. In 1986, researchers interviewed people the day after the explosion of the *Challenger* space shuttle. Details recorded included how the interviewees heard the news, how they felt about it and what they had been doing at the moment they learned of the disaster. However, when those same people were interviewed again two and a half years later, a quarter of them had misremembered every single detail and not a single person told consistent stories in the two interviews.[7]

I don't know about you, but that fact blew my mind. Of course, the very first thing that I did was call my mum to say, 'Hey, you remember when we heard about 9/11? Do you remember me coming out into the garden to tell you the news?' 'No,' she replied, 'I was ironing when I heard about 9/11.' Damn it!

Reconsolidation Theory

This may not only be true of flashbulb memories. Some groundbreaking studies made towards the end of the twentieth century have indicated that memory is malleable by nature, and in a constant state of change.

Initially, the understanding was that once a memory had passed through the temporary archives, our original record of that event would be preserved as a permanent physical imprint in the neocortex (the outer part of the brain). Imagine a family photo album collecting dust in the attic. The thinking was that memories were like the photos in that album. Each time we decided to bring it down and reminisce, the photos would look the same (if a little faded).

However, Reconsolidation Theory, which resulted from a study conducted by neuroscientists Karim Nader, G. E. Schafe and Joseph LeDoux in 2000, suggested that the very act of recalling a memory renders it unstable, and that the instability means that memories can be updated automatically to accommodate new information.[8] So, rather than flicking through an old photo album, the act of recollection appears to be more like retrieving image files from a computer hard drive, editing them in Photoshop, and then saving them over the originals.

Here's how they worked it out (if you don't like experiments on rats, look away now).

The science

The scientists began by sensitising rats to an auditory tone. They did this by repeatedly playing the tone and then administering an electric shock simultaneously. With time, the rats developed a phobia of the tone. Poor rats.

Next, they administered a drug that blocked protein synthesis in the amygdala, the part of the brain responsible for the formation of fear-related memories (live-wires). What the drug did was prevent the amygdala from consolidating a memory into long-term storage. When they introduced the drug at moments when the rats were unaware of the tone, their phobia was not affected (i.e. the live-wires stayed live). However, if they did the same after reminding the rats of the tone, they found that the rats forgot their phobia altogether, indicating that the act of recollection must have made the difference. In short, remembering the memory opened up the possibility of changing it.

The implications

The reality of cognitive function is that memories are altered every day when we learn, and every time we remember. In a sense, therapy is a way of rerouting memories, by interpreting them differently.

Joseph E. LeDoux,*
'Manipulating Memory'

This discovery could be wonderful news for people with anxiety issues and mental illnesses like post-traumatic stress disorder (PTSD) because it means that rather than just coping with the stress triggered by reminders of past trauma, those traumatic imprints themselves could be available for a rewrite. However, this needn't only benefit those affected by serious upheaval. As we have already covered, we don't have to be standing in the middle of the road looking at an oncoming bus to experience fear; human beings can learn to be afraid of pretty much anything (like school sports days, for example). If Reconsolidation Theory holds true, then we should be able to *un*learn our unnecessary fears by reconsolidating some useful and positive information into our formative memories.

* American neuroscientist.

Memory as Metaphor

If we're all just making it up, then why not make it up better?*
Trevor Silvester

In light of all this, as counterintuitive as it can feel, rather than considering memory to be a record of moments gone by, I believe that it's better to see it as a collection of stories told by the mind – using the familiar language of our own experience – to keep important messages alive. 'Important', that is, as far as the change-averse unconscious mind is concerned.

To keep us 'safely' sheltered beneath our respective glass ceilings, the unconscious needs a way to keep our limiting beliefs alive and true. A little like the narratives employed in advertising, maybe our minds use our memories to sell us the (dis)comfortable sense of identity that fits with our pre-existing belief systems. It certainly seems that we instinctively use the plasticity of memory to recall the version of the past that justifies our actions. We write the 'Not-my-fault' parts and the 'They-deserved-it' bits into our stories to protect ourselves from the pain of guilt. However, as we already know, to adopt the position of victim is far from pain-free in the long run because it adds even more fuel to the 'not … enough' fire. So, if our memories are potentially running in our minds like a chain of victimhood commercials, then taking the opportunity to do a little rewriting could help us to promote a far more empowering product.

The birth of a little monster

My first race may not sound like a typical childhood 'trauma'. However, there are many reasons why this moment might have been – or perhaps more accurately, might have become – a pivotal live-wire recollection for me.

Firstly, there's the race itself: a baptism of fire into a competitive world and a concentrated echo of the sibling rivalry my sister and I shared while we were young. This aspect of the memory means that it functioned as a tidy metaphor for the combative, 'win-or-be-beaten' life of fighting.

* Reproduced from our work together with the kind permission of Trevor Silvester.

Then, on a deeper level, there was my relationship with my dad. I loved my father enormously, but he was a scientist who travelled for work and was away half the time when I was little. Remember how young children tend to make everything that happens about them? While my mind was functioning in that way, Dad's absences would have raised some quite distressing questions in my unconscious: 'Why is he leaving me? Is he coming back? What did I do wrong?'

As an adult, I know without a shadow of doubt that those fears were unjustified, but as a child whose world only extended as far as my own interests and desires (for things that I didn't understand could only be provided if my dad went to work), I tried everything I could to stop him from disappearing. And then, every time I failed, that increasingly painful message replayed in the back of my mind: 'I'm simply not enough to make him stay.' My monster was born.

The making of a mirage

Retrospectively, it's easy to see the significance of my sports-day memory. When I went from the heightened and frightening experience of running to winning the race, *and* Dad was there *and* he showed the love and acceptance that I had so craved whenever he was away, my young mind was bound to come to some conclusions about the importance of my achievement. Winning on that day earned me the affection of someone I yearned to connect with more, and clearly my mind logged it as an effective – well, essential – strategy for feeling OK going forward.

That sports day wasn't the only example of my dad taking pride in my physical prowess. These things happened often because he valued sport and it was a great way for him to spend time with me. Another memory from around the same period in my life, and which I worked with in a different therapy session, involved him calling me down to his fortieth birthday party, so he could show his friends my biceps. Of course, I happily complied, but these things meant that being strong, fast or physically skilful quickly fused with my experience of my dad's somewhat scarce attention, and I wasn't yet capable of understanding the unconditional nature of his affection in those moments. Instead – thanks to my limited processing – I unconsciously concluded that I had to be stronger, faster or fitter than the rest in order to deserve (his) love.

Anything less than winning, as a result, was simply unthinkable, and that sports day sealed the deal in my mind: 'When I win, I am loved. So, when I don't win, then ... I'm not?' Oh dear.

Suddenly, both my Be Perfect driver and a life of fierce competitiveness zoom into perspective. Every thumb war, every board game, every arm wrestle (many of which were with my dad) absolutely had to be won, lest I felt that horrible sinking feeling that said, 'I'm not enough'. Embarrassingly, for decades my primary dating strategy involved taking a poor, unsuspecting victim to a late-night drinking hole and thrashing them at pool. I mean, what's more lovable than a person who shakes with adrenaline at the mere prospect of a casual bar game?

My 'winner' value was a coping mechanism, and because it seemed to work well while I was young, my mind continued to run mental commercials advertising the importance of victory to keep me investing in it. However, beyond the point when beating the opposition would get me a cuddle from my dad, victory-seeking failed to bring me what I actually wanted. Adult disconnection issues are too complex to solve with childish strategies, so winning quickly became a mirage. No matter how many people I beat at arm wrestles, my monster would continue chasing me into the scorched and lonely wastelands of 'not ... enough'.

Jenny's fear of baring her soul

Jenny was a professional dancer. She visited me because she felt unable to express or show emotion on stage. The only feeling she could connect to while dancing was an emptiness in the pit of her stomach, which she experienced as shame. This feeling caused her to back away from open and honest self-expression, rather than to share her experience with an audience.

Her live-wire was a memory of being disciplined through an act of humiliation. Her father had forced her to walk through the crowded town centre with bare and dirty feet as a punishment for not washing them after playing outside. When we first worked with this memory, the message that she felt it conveyed was: 'It's not OK to reveal myself' or, 'I'm dirty and unacceptable'. This became her monster's story, and as a result she had learned to lock down her emotional self entirely for fear of the ramifications of exposure. After decades of using this coping mechanism automatically, her emotions had come to feel like dangerous substances – certainly not things that it would be safe to reveal to others while on stage.

The reframe that made the difference for Jenny involved an understanding that her father's choice of punishment resulted from his own strict upbringing and was, ultimately, an attempt to teach her something that he felt was important. Her relationship with her father had never been a loving one, however, so a truly positive connection to him wasn't an option. Instead, she used the memory of other people from her life to help her younger self feel loved and fully accepted.

Then, in order to move into a state of growth, rather than protection, she gently introduced her child self to the joy of emotional expression. The method she chose for doing this was, of course, metaphorical. First, she lovingly cleaned the bare feet of her younger self to wash away the old residue of her shame. Then they danced together on the rocks by the shore in her home town, until it began to feel safe for her to communicate in that way.

Quite wonderfully, after this session it was only a matter of weeks before Jenny was complimented on her emotional performance at an audition.

Task: Creating Your Temporal Map

In order to prepare for the memory task in the next chapter, you need to answer some questions about how your mind thinks of time. These may sound a little odd. Just go on gut instinct for now and I'll explain their relevance afterwards.

First, imagine that the past and the future – as concepts – have spatial orientations in relation to your body. Now answer these questions:

If you could point to the direction of the past, which way would you point?

If you could point to the direction of the future, which way would that be?

Take a moment to close your eyes and settle on your answers before reading on.

This process gives you an idea of how your mind likes to organise time spatially. For example, the past could be in front of or behind you, to your left or right, up or down or somewhere else; and the future is likely to be in the opposite direction (although not always). By joining the dots, you can imagine your life's metaphorical timeline. To make sure that you can visualise this, answer this third question:

If you could see your timeline, what might it look like? (So, if it had a colour, what would that be? Or, if it took some kind of form, what might that be?)

Close your eyes for a moment to visualise the dots connecting in whatever way they do for you, then come back to the page. We're going to use this idea in the next chapter's memory task.

A spatial metaphor for time

We all automatically (and unconsciously) connect space and time together in this way. It's a metaphor that seems to be shared across most – if not all – cultures. Of course, it's not normally a conscious thing, which is why those questions can seem bizarre when considered in such a direct way, but the unconscious mind appears to think of space and time as almost interchangeable. You can hear it in everyday phrases like, 'Put the past *behind* you', 'Look f*orward* to the future', 'Put it all *down* to experience', 'The future is looking *up*', '*Here* in the now', etc.

Our body language can also betray the unconscious connection between time and space. Have you ever noticed someone talking about the holiday they took last year and gesturing over their shoulder? I would bet that wasn't actually the geographical location of Marbella. It's more likely to have been their personal placement of the past, and if you pointed the gesture out, they probably wouldn't even be aware of having made it.

If this all sounds like madness to you, then keep an eye out for these things over the next few days. I'm sure you'll notice someone giving you an indication of their timeline at some point. ('*Point* in time': that one slipped out naturally.)

Timeline organisations

The most common timeline configurations are:

Horizontal Most commonly, this will be *left* for the past and *right* for the future for English-speaking people. However, this is often reversed for left-handed people and those from cultures that read from right to left.

Forward/backward For English speakers, this will usually mean that the past is behind and the future lies ahead. However, this changes in some other languages. In the language of Aymara, which is spoken in Peru, the word for future (*qhipuru*) means 'behind time', referring to the idea that the future is unknown (so you can only see the past).

Vertical Occasionally a client's timeline will run vertically (up and down). This is often the case for people speaking languages like Mandarin, in which the future is expressed as down and the past as up, but it crops up with English speakers as well.

The effect that language has on perception is demonstrated by the fact that bilingual people who speak languages with varying typical timeline organisations will switch their sense of temporal orientation depending on which language they are speaking at the time. So, if someone spoke both Aymara and English, for example, they might gesture behind them when talking about the future to another Aymara speaker, but then gesture forward when talking about the future with an English person.

All that is to say that there is definitely no right or wrong when it comes to the direction of your timeline, and although the English language would seem to suggest that the future lies ahead of us, very many people (60 per cent, according to the estimates made by NLP practitioners) will imagine their timeline running from left to right (or vice versa).

Taking control of time

Timelines aren't just a way of understanding our unconscious perception of time; they can also be used to affect it.

There are certain traits that seem to correlate with the way we choose to arrange our timeline. Left/right and back/front are the two most common configurations. As a rule of thumb, those who have their time-line laid out laterally, like something they can read, tend to be more aware of the passage of time – as if they are the observers of it. They may be the type to know exactly what the clock says without needing to look, and they are more likely to be quite punctual (or at least feel very uncomfortable when late). Those who have their past behind and future ahead may be the type to get so lost in a task that they forget about the concept of time altogether. They could also be more likely to leave a job until the last minute and miss their deadline. This doesn't mean a person with this timeline organisation can't learn to be punctual or get things done early; it just might not come as naturally as it would to others. (I can personally testify to this.)

But, of course, the timeline we see isn't fixed. I don't believe that we're doomed to run a little late just because we imagine the future stretching out ahead of us, and I've known people to create visualisations based on a repositioning of their timeline to take control. One client, a freelance designer who struggled to meet his deadlines, found that imagining he could pin a day-long stretch of his timeline to his desk when he started work helped him allocate time more effectively to the individual tasks he had planned. Then, when he was ready to finish work for the evening, he would detach it and allow it to ping back into its usual place until the next day.

Maybe you could benefit from a similar trick? Start the day by thinking of the jobs that you intend to get done. Then visualise them along a lateral timeline (drawing it can be even better). This could give you a more effective means of quantifying and distributing time, both practic-ally and emotionally.

Timeline configuration and emotional states

A person's chosen timeline metaphor can be indicative of much more than just their ability to show up on time. People with high levels of anxiety sometimes find that the future section of their timeline is invis-ible or otherwise inaccessible, as if they are so worried about what's to come that they can't even conceive of it. (Or, conversely, it could be that their anxiety is a result of their not being able to see the future in their minds.) People who strongly fear death or who feel that they're running out of time can imagine their future timeline to be alarmingly short. I've seen clients who had traumatic childhoods and imagined their lines to be circular, so that they felt as though they were always heading in the direction of their unthinkable past. With English speakers, this same kind of issue can sometimes be represented by a flipped front-to-back timeline, so the past lies ahead (presumably, this would be less of an issue if you spoke Aymara). Configurations like these can be strong indicators of depression ('I have nothing to look forward to' or 'I'm going nowhere'), and a common symptom would be the feeling of being 'stuck' or unable to progress.

Every now and then people will surprise me with unusual timeline metaphors: a cloud of water vapour, a dangling rope or a knotted ball of yarn. These things don't need to spell disaster, but they will usually provoke a conversation. If your timeline is out of the ordinary, then the question to ask yourself is: does it feel OK? If so, then that's fine. If not, then you might want to have a think about evolving your metaphor, so that it better suits your needs. You already have the tools to do this, of course. Just ask yourself these questions:

1. If there was something you could do with your timeline that would mean it felt more positive or effective, what would that be?
2. What needs to happen for that to take place?
3. And can that happen?

Subjective Time, Morphing Memories and the Role of Resistance

We all know that time is subjective, even before we start to think of it in terms of a metaphorical visualisation. We try to put time into concrete units – seconds, hours, months, years – but those labels mean very little when five minutes waiting for the bus can feel ten times longer than five minutes doing something we love.

Whether a moment drags or dashes by is all about emphasis. We resist the things we don't want to experience in an attempt to avoid the discomfort they bring. But to resist something we have to focus on it and, by doing so, we allocate it more space in our awareness rather than less.

This means that its duration can seem to stretch out ad infinitum. In contrast, unresisted events (the positive moments that we'd actually like to hold onto) can fly by because the unconscious doesn't sense any attention-demanding threat within them. Just like unresisted emotions, they're allowed to flow through comfortably.

When applied to the bigger picture, this phenomenon can mean that the mind will automatically expand all of the most uncomfortable experiences along our timelines. Imagine dropping a few beads of black dye onto a long, thin piece of blotting paper. Over time, the dye will spread and, as it does, the lighter stretches will be dominated by the darkness. Likewise, when we take our past into consideration, the painful moments can overwhelm the happy bits. As that continues to happen, both our experience of the present and our expectation of the future can become tainted by the murkiness of our overall (perceived) experience of life.

This is why the malleable nature of memory is so crucial for change. Fail to utilise it and the bad times could just continue to get bigger and more monstrous indefinitely. Grasp the opportunity to reframe our live-wire memories, on the other hand, and we can release the pain that would otherwise encourage our minds to give the (dis)comfort even more time-distorting attention.

Shrinking the memory = shrinking the monster

Reworking and minimising any stored event that once contributed to a limiting belief means that you can give yourself a way to meet, face and interconnect with the aspect(s) of the self that you have been resisting. In doing so, you can shrink your monster, as well as its contextual habitat, down to a manageable size.

So, if you're ready to let go of whatever the darkness looks like for you, then it's time to take a trip down memory lane.

12

Meetings of Minds

Staging Your Own Reunion

I imagine floating up above my timeline and I position myself so that I get a sense of it mapping out my life below. My line is thin, crisp and black, as if it's been drawn using a biro and a ruler. The past is behind me and the future in front, where the line just fades out gently, as if the pen is running out of ink.

Trevor asks me to find a recent example of the problem that I'm dealing with. I don't need to search for long. Last week I felt nervous to the point of shaking, purely because I was about to spar with an experienced girl who had just joined our club. I have already come so far on this therapeutic journey; I'm back in the game and my body has started to work with me more often than against. However, I still have a lingering, unnecessary tendency to invest way too much into the competitive moments that crop up in my life. This particular training session triggered my anxiety because all of my teammates were ready to watch me spar the newbie, and I wanted – no, I needed – to impress them.

Within moments of thinking about that day, a familiar feeling starts to spread through my torso. It's not as intense as it was in the gym, but I can remember it clearly: first a tight vibration in my chest and then a piercing sensation like a knife to my heart that says, 'I'm not good enough.'

Trevor has another question: 'If your unconscious mind were to know the very first event connected to that feeling ...' I've stopped listening because my mind is whirring. It's as if I've suddenly awoken every moment I've ever felt that way. I consider recent examples first – competitions and squad training sessions ... But then, as if I've been pulled physically back along my timeline, it's the events from my childhood that start to dominate my thinking.

Like a group of children competing for my attention, there are a number of early memories trying to make themselves heard. One seems a bit bigger than the rest. At least, I think it does. Maybe I've just chosen to focus on *it, but now that I am, I can't think of anything else, so I start talking about it. I tell Trevor about that nervous little girl waiting to race, desperate to do well and longing to win the love of her father. As I speak, the connection between this moment and my performance anxiety becomes clear. Just like I did in the gym last week, that little girl feels as though she needs to 'get it right' in order to be worthy of those looking on.*

When I stop talking, Trevor pauses for a second, as if to give me time to absorb myself in the memory. Then he asks another question: 'If there was something you could teach that child, which, by learning it, would mean that she could let go of that old feeling, what would it be?'

It's funny how obvious it seems from up here above my timeline. That little girl's fear is just so misplaced. Her dad loves her. A lot. As do the rest of her family. She doesn't need to win his or anyone else's affection because she is already worthy of connection. Just like everyone else, she's enough as she is.

I feel quite maternal about the younger me that I'm looking at, and I yearn for her to see things the way I can. As I imagine handing this new truth down, I'm relieved to see the moment when it dawns on her. First, she opens up. Then, she starts to smile. And then, she's running – with clumsy and wobbly steps, like a five-year-old should do – right into the arms of her doting father.

A smile appears on my face as I watch the little me toddling through her happy little race. Then I feel a deep, deep, sad love as I imagine my father picking her up. He looks so proud, but – of course – the race means nothing to him. Nor me. This memory is about Dad much more than it is about a primary-school sports day. Our relationship is the main event.

As I zoom in on the connection between us, I find that it's warm and close and tangible, as if I could reach out and touch it, or perhaps grab hold of it and use it. I can see my dad's love streaming powerfully from him to me, as if it has its own colour: a soft but vibrant gold, like the light of the morning sun. It flows in through my heart and then around my entire body, like the circulation of my blood. As it flows, any remaining traces of panic drain from my young face, and then I'm able to send that same golden colour back to him and watch as he responds to our connection. The shift in direction is liberating. It's like some kind of release; as if the permission to focus on something other than my own struggle is curative in itself. Put simply, it feels good to give something back.

A few minutes later, I'm travelling back along my timeline, through all of those other memories that tried to get my attention earlier. As I make the trip, I can see that colour sweeping along my timeline, connecting with all the different versions of me who most need to feel it. Child me, teenaged me, adult me ... all of them being fortified with that same important message: 'You don't need to win anyone's affection. You're already worthy of connection.'

By the time I'm back above the present moment, the entire timeline below me is glowing with that vibrant golden light; and when I search inside my body – even while thinking about the sparring from last week or the competitions I have coming up – the old piercing, knife-like feeling has gone.

Enough is Enough

The past beats inside me like a second heart.

John Banville,* *The Sea*

Working on that memory helped me turn the context of competition from a largely fear-filled concept into something that it was possible to enjoy. In other words, my away-from motivation was flipped to the positive. (See page 115 for a reminder about the difference between 'towards' and 'away-from' values.) On that day, I gave myself permission to move *towards* involvement, sharing and connection, rather than run away from the prospect of failure.

I did this by countering the old 'I'm-not-enough' belief, right at its root, with the more adult idea that everyone is worthy of connection, no matter how much or how little winning they do. This is something that I had probably tried to tell myself hundreds of times before, but the captain had never quite managed to get through to the crew. However, by delivering the message to the little me who first felt the pain of disconnection, I was able to pique their interest.

* Irish novelist.

Rerouting

I see memory reframing as a way to reroute established thought processes. When I think of that sports day now, I no longer feel the fear or confused disconnection that was there before because my mind automatically directs me to the hug at the end. It means that I can understand the event for what it was: evidence of my dad's unconditional love and *not* the moment when I narrowly escaped exposing myself as unworthy of his affection. I guess you could say that the plot has changed, and with the new theme being absolute acceptance and the memory of a very important person's presence in my life, I can now use that moment as a reminder that challenge and endeavour are more important than results, and that when we share those things with others, we can enjoy the races that we run so much more fully.

What's more, it turns out that when we 'race' with a smile on our faces, we tend to do much better than when we do so without.

Robert's unexpected dinner guest

Robert, a scientist in his forties, visited me because he felt he was drinking too much, eating the wrong foods and making a number of other 'bad choices' on a near daily basis. The life he described to me in our first session was defined almost entirely by the 'rightness' and 'wrongness' (primarily the 'wrongness') of all his decisions. He was living a binary existence: unless he had the most virtuous and perfect of days, he would feel like a fundamentally bad human being.

Robert had tried everything he could think of to beat his 'bad' urges into submission, and his primary strategy for resisting the temptation to buy a bottle of wine or packet of crisps was truly heartbreaking. For years, Robert had been routinely punishing himself with images of his wife and children crying at his graveside whenever he was about to make the 'wrong decision'. As we already know, this kind of negative motivation rarely works (certainly not over prolonged periods of time), and Robert was no exception to the rule. Over and over again, he would imagine his own death as the consequence of his imminent 'bad decision', and then he would make that decision anyway. The result was that the deepest and darkest of shame monsters followed him everywhere he went, telling him constantly that he was responsible for the future misery of those he loved the most.

When I asked Robert what he thought might be the cause of his deep-rooted sense of 'wrongness', he reluctantly expressed some concern that it could have been connected to his mother – a woman who set impossibly high standards for herself. Her house had to be spick and span, every meal needed to be perfect and manners were of the utmost importance. As a result, Robert and his two younger sisters were impeccably behaved, but they also felt a weighty sense of duty when it came to getting things 'right', because the consequences of not doing so had such a tangible impact on their mother.

One night, while the family were sitting at the table eating dinner, someone knocked at the door. The unexpected visitor, who was promptly invited in to share their meal, came through to the dining room to sit down. But there was no spare chair. Keen to do the 'right thing', six-year-old Robert leaped out of his seat and offered it to their friend, saying that he was happy to stand for his meal. Then, proud of his decision, he turned to beam at his mother and receive some credit. However, instead of the praise he had hoped for, all he got was a petrifying, steely glare that struck him like an icy blow to the heart. He had done the wrong thing.

Robert's mother, it turned out, was too embarrassed by the awkwardness of the situation to recognise her son's good intentions. In fact, she was appalled by his decision to give up his own seat. The way she saw it was that he had humiliated their guest by making himself look like the martyr. And so, under the instruction of her own monster, she punished her son severely.

Robert remembered that day for forty years because it had wounded him so deeply; but it wasn't just the eventual punishment that was painful. In the moment he received that icy glare, he learned that, even when he was trying so hard to get it right, he could fail seriously enough for his mother to withdraw her love. Or, at least, so it seemed to his six-year-old mind. As a result, the experience punched holes in virtually all of his needs. He felt unloved, alone, unsafe, uncertain, insignificant because his efforts were invisible and, of course, incapable of making a valuable contribution. That sense of lack lived on, and every time his unconscious mind caught a glimpse of anything even remotely similar (i.e. whenever he considered making a 'bad decision'), his damning self-judgement bedded in even more strongly: 'I'm a bad person.'

To reframe the memory, Robert began by understanding his mother's reaction in an adult way. When he took the time to view it from an objective position, he could clearly see that day was more about her anxiety than it was about his fundamental badness. The most transformational part of the session involved building a connection between the two selves. Robert saw his younger self a lot like his own son, and he felt a deep and easy sense of loving acceptance when he looked at him. However, it was when his younger self accepted him back – even after all the 'wrong choices' he had subsequently made in life – that something really seemed to click into place.

Robert imagined the innocent little boy hanging a Saint Christopher pendant around his adult neck and, as he described the exchange, tears of relief rolled down his face. He could feel then, that even though – just like everyone else – he was not perfect, he remained a worthy and lovable human being. It meant that he could begin to let go of the binary notion of good versus bad and right versus wrong. Because absolutely everyone makes mistakes. Even picture-perfect mothers.

I said goodbye to Robert feeling certain that he had touched on something important that day. When he returned to the office for his next visit, he told me that (unlike the catastrophic visions of his own funeral) imagining his younger self gifting him that pendant was enabling him to make healthier decisions. When he brought the imagery to mind – even months later – he would experience his body filling up with a feeling of warmth that could, on occasion, completely overwhelm his urge for alcohol or junk food.

Robert needed something to smile about in order to run his race the way he really wanted. The aspect of self that he had been trying to fight was the part he saw as incapable of getting it right. However, when he chose to explore the origin of his limiting beliefs, that part turned out to be a loving child with only the best of intentions. It was this realisation that gave him something to smile about. There was no monster at all; only a misunderstanding.

Memory Reframing: The Process

In many ways, this process is what we've been gearing up to all the way through this book. In practice, I have witnessed people make some of the most staggering changes after 'earthing' their live-wire memories. By choosing to engage in this work for yourself, you'll be able to shift your perspective on the part of your personality that we're calling the monster. Then you can rewrite your relationship to – or perhaps even nullify – some of its most destructive stories. As Robert discovered, this is made infinitely easier when you can recognise that your monster was only ever a frightened, innocent and childlike thought process, rather than a terrifying and shameful fact about your personality. Let's take a look at how it's done before we jump in.

Using your timeline

Establishing a timeline enables us to create a defined and easily navigable metaphorical landscape to represent our lives, which we can then use to identify our live-wire memories. Because memory is state-specific, our timelines can be thought of as train tracks that lead us through a specific and relevant sequence of events: jump on the train when you're feeling afraid and it'll take you to a scary memory; jump on it when you're feeling happy and you'll take a trip to something positive. What this means is that by connecting to a recent moment of fear, anger or some other kind of self-sabotaging emotion, that train can transport us through all of the memory stops associated with the problem at hand, right back to the live-wire (or sometimes, live-wires).

Locating a live-wire

The idea is that if you reframe the earliest memory in a problematic chain, then your perception of all the later connected events will also shift, because you must have viewed them, at the time, through the lens of a negative belief that was already formed. For this reason, even if the memories that come to mind seem somewhat innocuous at first glance, it's a good idea to start with the earliest that you can think of. Because this is a tool that you can use for the rest of your life, you always have the option to return another time and tackle later memories if needed.

Reframes of events that occurred before the age of eight often yield the most profound effects. This is because those are the moments that link directly to our core beliefs and values, and therefore set the limits of the (dis)comfort zone. Additionally, they're likely to represent the childlike thinking associated with an external locus of control because they come from a naturally powerless stage of life. Any reframe of a victim thought pattern is likely to create an important ripple effect through the mind's map of associations.

Not everyone finds a singular and defined event the first time they do this. Some people recall a longer period of time, like the years spent in a certain house, for example. Occasionally, what comes to mind feels more like a combination of similar events than one stand-out moment (e.g. not one particular maths class, but the feeling of every maths class attended with a particularly nasty teacher). Or, you might think of something that you very much doubt could actually have happened. None of these things matter. Given that memory is not 'real' anyway, you can work with anything that comes into your head as if it is a document of the past (because if you're thinking about it, then your mind is probably using it in that way).

Getting a new message across

Regardless of the limitations that can grow from it, childhood is a fertile period of life in terms of creativity. Young minds are capable of incredible feats of wonder. Children can spend hours lost in fantastical worlds of magic or imagined battles, where She-Ra defeats hordes of their younger sister's My Little Ponies (just me?). One of the most delightful things about working with memory is that when we reframe the earlier events from our lives, we can tap back into that creativity. The symbolism that results can be greatly beneficial to the therapeutic process because it allows us to bridge the gap between conscious and unconscious quite effortlessly.

When we run through the process in just a moment, I will give you some prompts, but you have absolute creative freedom when it comes to your reframe because it's your story. You can choose to have a conversation with your younger self to teach them what they most need to know, you could hug them, show them something important or give them something symbolic. Perhaps you want to dance by the shore like Jenny did with her child self (see page 263).

Whatever you choose, as you engage with the reframe, your mind will tell you when you have achieved a satisfactory resolution (and when you're not quite there yet) via your emotions and your automatic imagery. If your younger self continues to look or feel unsure, then you may need to find another way to get the message across. When you've got to where you need to be, you'll know it – you'll either feel a new and more positive emotion or you'll see your younger self joining in, looking happier, feeling at peace, playing or, perhaps, looking older and more in control.

Anchoring

The process of connecting sensory stimuli – i.e. anything that we can see, hear, feel, taste or smell – to a particular emotional state is called 'anchoring' in NLP (or 'classical conditioning' in some other therapy styles). It's something that happens quite naturally. If I hear the song 'When Will I Be Famous' by Bros, I am instantly transported back to a Blackdale Middle School disco, hoping to slow dance with the boy I liked. That's because my mind has connected that particular set of sounds to my emotional state from the time ('painful, nervous and angsty longing', I think would be an appropriate label).

My Bros anchor, of course, came about automatically. However, anchoring is also something we can do intentionally in order to keep hold of positive and useful feelings. All it takes is a little emphasis on a certain sensory cue while you're experiencing something that you'd like to be able to repeat (think: a state of calm, the feeling of confidence or a sense of connection).

There will likely be a number of options for finding positive anchors in the process you're about to do. We're going to focus on one in particular; but, of course, everyone is different, so I'd suggest you keep an eye out for anything that feels positively charged. We'll discuss how you can use this tool after you've completed your reframe.

Connection

No matter what kind of problem someone is overcoming, when working with young live-wire memories, a focus on human connection can often be tremendously curative. By introducing an 'important other' into the memory, we can use the feeling of connection that we create to replenish needs that were at a deficit during the original live-wire moment. There is a specific step in the process that allows you to focus on building and anchoring some kind of self-to-other bond.

However, please bear in mind that your 'important other' does not need to be a parent. Not everyone is lucky enough to have had stable or caring parents to fall back on for a feeling of connection, but that doesn't mean they can't get what they need from this element of the process. Whoever (or whatever) you choose need only be someone (/thing) who can effectively communicate the message that needs to be heard. In practice, my clients have had imaginary conversations with present-day partners or friends and family, as well as spiritual figures, film stars, sports personalities, toys and animals.

The transformative point of connection in my sports-day reframe was with my dad, as he held me after the race. Seeing as that session took place only a year or so after my father's death, this was enormously emotional and I'm sure only half of what I said out loud was audible through all the snot and tears. But it also felt immensely pure and authentic. I could see the proud and caring look on my dad's face as we conversed, his twinkling eyes, brows faintly raised and his head cocked slightly to one side. And I could feel the doting affection that I know he had for me. The entire process was potent and visceral, and I'll remember it for as long as I live.

It was the emotional meaning of our connection that my mind chose to represent metaphorically with the soft, golden light. Even now, just imagining that anchored colour relaxes and soothes me. It reminds me to let go of my old Be Perfect driver and to focus instead on the present-moment enjoyment that I can take from whatever it is I'm doing. It is my hope that, by the end of this chapter, you'll have an anchor of your own that you can use in a similarly powerful way.

Choosing Your Focus

A word to the wise

This process is an adapted version of Trevor Silvester's *Timeline Reconsolidation*. It's probably the most involved and emotional process in this book. If you know that you have something particularly challenging in your past, I recommend that you consult a private therapist to work through those memories under their guidance. Even if you don't consider your past experiences to have been traumatic, if anything that comes up during this process feels too uncomfortable to explore on your own, then you should stop. I have very rarely found this to be the case, but I want to make it absolutely clear, nonetheless.

This process works by rerouting the thinking that prevents you from experiencing what you want. For this reason, you need to have a limiting belief in mind before you get going.

Have a think about the monster stories that have the strongest impact on your life and pick the one that feels the most limiting or uncomfortable.

Identify a recent moment

Next, I'd like you to identify a recent moment when it felt true. For example, in order to work with the limiting belief 'I'm a failure', you would pick a time from the last few years when you felt like a failure. Or, if you are working with a self-sabotaging habit, then you would bring an example of that behaviour to mind and the limiting belief would be how that habit makes you feel about yourself.

Ideally, we want an emotional connection to the problem, so it's best to choose something that still has some intensity of feeling when you think about it. You probably won't feel the emotion as strongly as you did on the day, and that's fine.

Step into the moment and feel the feeling

As you recall the recent moment, I'd like you to identify what needs to go through your mind in order for you to experience the negative emotions at their strongest. Step into the memory and notice how you feel as you remember the sights, sounds and sequence of events. Try replaying the worst part to yourself, and say the connected limiting belief in your mind as you do. Take a minute to close your eyes and do that now. Then, when you can start to remember how you felt on that day, come back to the page and answer the question below:

On a scale of 0–10 (10 being the most powerful), how strongly can you remember those negative emotions?

Make a note of both your score and what it was that brought the feelings up to that level before jumping into the task.

Task: Earthing Your Live-wires

Step 1: Finding a live-wire

Call to mind the timeline metaphor you created in the previous chapter (see page 264). Then, imagine you can float up above it, so that you can look down on it like a map. Close your eyes briefly to get a visual.

Now, reconnect with the problematic emotional state by stepping into the recent negative event again and doing whatever you did earlier to ramp the emotional intensity up. When you start to feel the associated emotions in your body, read the question below and give your mind all the time it needs to search through the connected events and settle on the earliest (if you're struggling to find the live-wire, it can help to repeat the limiting belief in your mind to keep yourself on track):

If your unconscious mind were to know the very first event connected to that feeling – the earliest event, which by going back to it would enable you to let go of the connected self-sabotage – when would that be?

Take your time to settle on a memory before moving on.

Step 2: Observing the memory

If you haven't already done so, move back along your timeline, so that you are floating above the selected memory.

Now, just look down and observe the situation – almost as if you're imagining it happening to someone else. Watch the sequence of events as they play out. Remember whether your younger self was on their own or with other people, if it was daytime or nighttime, whether they were indoors or outdoors ... If you're thinking of a relatively long period of time, just observe all the key moments that come to mind, then choose one to focus on here.

Spend some time observing your younger self and their reactions. Notice what their body language was like and what they may have said or done as the situation occurred. Pay attention to the thoughts that must have been going through their mind and consider how they could have arrived at the limiting belief you're working with. Take a moment to close your eyes and observe the scene in detail. Then, when you can remember as much as you think you can, come back to the page and answer the following question:

If there was a connection between this event and the problem(s) you've had up until now, what would it be?

Take a moment to think of all the things that connect this event and the way your problem presents in your adult life. What seems similar or the same?

Optional journaling: spend a few minutes writing fluidly and emotionally about this memory. Describe what happened, how it made you feel and all the connections between it and other areas of your life.

Step 3: New lessons

Answer this question:

If there was something that you could teach your younger self – which, by learning it, would mean that they can let go of this event and the old limiting belief completely – what would it be?

Take a moment to consider the options.

Once you've thought of a new and more positive message to counter the old discomfort, ask yourself: 'And what *else* do they need to know?'

I suggest you think of around three different 'lessons' for your younger self. What do they need to know about themselves, others or the world before they can feel better about this situation?

Take a little time to ensure you've thought of everything before moving on.

Now, just imagine that you can pass those new truths down to the younger you in the memory. You can do this in any way that would seem the most powerful. It might be something that you would see happening – some kind of visual metaphor, perhaps, like a beam of light or a paper aeroplane with the message written on it. It could be something for your younger self to hear – words spoken or a certain piece of music being played. Or it could be that you imagine an emotional way of passing on the positive ideas. Just pay attention to anything that comes to mind, and allow your unconscious to do whatever it needs for your younger self to fully absorb the positive message(s).

Close your eyes to take a moment with that visualisation. When you can see that your younger self is beginning to understand, come back to the page and continue.

Optional journaling: write about whatever you imagine, as if you're telling a short story. Start at the beginning and then describe the moment of learning as it plays out. Take some time to connect with the emotional experience of both your younger self and your present self as you write.

Step 4: Interpersonal connection

Now it's time to connect the younger you to an important other. This could be someone from whom they felt painfully disconnected at the time, or it could be someone who simply has the knowledge, emotional ability or expertise to communicate the message your younger self most needs to hear. Consider people you love, people who love you, people you admire, etc. To choose someone, answer this question:

> **If there was someone who could communicate a positive message to your younger self – which by hearing it from *them* would mean that you can let go of the old problem – who would that be?**

When you have someone in mind, consider what would be the most powerful way for them to communicate their transformative message.

This could be done with actions or language, or it could be entirely metaphorical. Close your eyes to let an idea begin to bubble up before coming back to the page.

When you've thought of something, watch the scene playing out as if on a cinema screen in your mind. If words are involved, listen to the tone of voice in which they're spoken. Observe the other kinds of interaction that help your younger self to let go – gestures, physical contact, play or other shared activities – and notice the body language and facial expressions of all involved. Spend a moment visualising this in detail, making sure that you allow your younger self to respond in any way they like.

Next, I'd like you to consider the way this important other feels about your younger self. Step into their shoes for a moment. Observe the situation from their position and consider how they feel about the limiting belief your younger self was trying to form. Then, look at the younger you through their eyes and dive into the emotions they feel. What would you call those feelings? It could be something like 'love' or 'a nurturing feeling', or it could be 'pride', 'respect', 'optimism' or something else entirely. Really spend a moment getting in touch with that positive emotion. Then, when you can feel it for yourself, answer this question and go with the first response that comes to mind:

If that feeling had a colour, what would it be?

I'd like you to imagine that colour beginning to flow from the important other to your younger self, connecting the two of them together. Spend some time engaging with the detail that your mind can create as you imagine this. Is that colour soft or bright? Does it flow quickly and powerfully or is it gradual and gentle? Consider whether it would stream into a particular part of your younger self's body in order for them to feel it the most intensely. Or perhaps it would be even more powerful if it could envelop them entirely? Close your eyes and visualise this connection now.

Then, take a moment to notice how it feels as the connection grows stronger. Does that colour feel light or heavy? Is it hot, warm, cool or cold? What kind of effect does it have as your younger self absorbs it fully? Is this feeling energising, comforting, empowering or something else? As you allow your younger self to absorb it, just take a little time to visualise the emotion circulating around their system and helping them to feel secure, significant and connected.

If appropriate, you can let your younger self send that same colour back to the other person, as I did with my dad, and notice how they respond to the shared emotion.

Finally, allow the important other to repeat their positive message as you visualise this metaphor for connection, and watch as your younger self absorbs the full understanding.

Optional journaling: write fluidly and expressively about this exchange, making sure that you describe anything that feels particularly emotionally charged.

Step 5: Self-connection

The final reframe here is to ensure that you are creating a self-to-self connection too. Imagine that you (your adult self) can enter into this memory and meet your younger self as they are now. When you've done that, take a look at the younger you and consider the three things that you love, respect or like the most about them. How do *you* feel about this version of yourself?

Now, I would like you to use that same important colour to connect your adult and younger self together. Take a moment to close your eyes and visualise the colour flowing between you. Again, make sure that you notice how the younger you responds, what happens to their body language and facial expression and how this connection can help them to feel. Consider this question:

Is there anything else that your younger self needs to hear, see, be shown or be taught before they can let go completely?

Here's where you can get really creative. Is there an activity that would help your younger self to feel better about themselves? Do they need to know something about their own future? Is there love or success on the horizon for them to see? Does there need to be some kind of metaphorical exchange, like Robert's Saint Christopher pendant? Just notice what comes to mind and take your time to imagine it taking place.

Note: if you wanted to give to your monster something positive when asked the question at the beginning of Part 3 (page 218), then – if appropriate – you may want to consider giving that thing to your younger self here.

Optional journaling: make a note of the three things that you love the most about the younger you, and write a description of any additional interactions that you have envisaged.

Step 6: The most powerful message

Now, take a step back from the memory and observe the way you see it now. Let the new version of this event play out and consider what might be the most important and positive message of the entire reframe.

When you have an idea, put that message into a single, big-picture phrase or sentence. For example, 'You're worthy of connection just as you are' or, 'You're already enough'.

I'd like you to imagine that your unconscious mind can store this memory in this new way, so that every time anything reminds you of it, you'll be able to remember that positive message.

Now, float back up above your timeline, so that you can see the entirety of the map below you. Then, imagine that – just like a pebble being dropped into a pond – the ripples of this change can flow out from this memory and all the way along your timeline towards the present moment. As you observe that happening, allow the colour you chose as a metaphor for positive connection to flow along the timeline as well: into and through all of the other events that used to be connected to the problem you once had. Take a moment to visualise that happening.

Then, start travelling forward along your timeline yourself. As you pass over any other important events along the way, just take a moment to pause and communicate the positive message to all the different versions of yourself that most need to learn it. Let the colour flow into each of them, and imagine how they feel to receive the warmth, lightness or other sensations that come with it.

Give your unconscious mind all the time it needs to let that colour, feeling and message flow all the way back to the present moment, so that by the time you're back above the position of now, your unconscious has everything it needs to be free.

Step 7: The future

Finally, imagine those ripples and that colour flowing right out into your future. Just as the ripples made by that pebble in the pond would get bigger, broader and more all-encompassing as they continue to expand, so too can the changes that you're making here.

So, follow your colour out into the future to an event, which if it had happened before *would* have been connected to the problem you once had. To avoid the mirage trap here, imagine something that will happen relatively soon – where you can see the improvements as they're being made. Then, make sure that your future self is also connected to the important colour and the message it can teach. When you've done that, answer this question:

How different does it seem?

For the final visualisation of the exercise, just take a moment to imagine all the ways that your future self might think, feel, behave and speak differently. Notice what you can achieve when you keep this new message in mind, and how it could help you to better meet your needs. Consider the way your relationship to others might change, and what kinds of choices you might make in terms of career, hobbies or direction. Be sure to imagine that your future self can keep hold of that colour, feeling and understanding as they go about creating the life they most want to lead. Then, when you're ready, step down into that future moment, so that you can experience it as if you already have all of those resources, skills and abilities. Notice how it feels to be this new version of yourself.

Optional journaling: describe your imagined future. As always, make sure that you're stating the changes in the positive, rather than the negative.

When you've finished, give yourself a moment to come back into the present, and please congratulate yourself on the work that you've just done. Before reading on, you might want to have a little break, so feel free to put the kettle on. However, I'd recommend that you read the final few pages of this chapter before you put the book down for the day. You've just created a really powerful tool, and I'd love to tell you how you can start to use and strengthen it straight away.

A Colourful Anchor

The reason you used that specific colour to represent both the self-to-other and self-to-self connection during your memory reframe was so you can use it as an anchor. By repeating the imagery in those two key moments, you will have allowed your mind to create an equivalence between your colour and a state of acceptance, love, pride (or whatever word you would use to describe the shared emotion). It's also likely to represent a moment of needs fulfilment, because the effect that kind of connection can have on our younger selves usually helps them to feel either safer (certainty), more capable of relaxing and enjoying themselves (variety), more important or acknowledged (significance), more loved (love and connection), more open to the enjoyment of learning (growth), more capable of making a difference to others (contribution) or all of the above.

This means that your anchor can help you to move out of a state of protection and into a space of emotional fluidity and growth. It's also likely to serve as a metaphor for self-acceptance because it's based on a positive feeling that you generated while looking at your (younger) self.

If you've reframed a memory connected to a limiting belief that you had been fervently resisting, then the anchor could capture the point at which you allowed yourself to accept and love the aspect of your personality that you once tried to disown because of the pain that it felt. What this means is that the anchor can serve as a reminder to let go of your resistance; it's a tool for 'de-monstering' your monster.

Firing your anchor

Using a colour to represent this kind of positive emotional content is particularly useful. Firstly, it's quick and easy to bring to mind (most people don't even need to close their eyes to think of a colour). It's also very versatile because you can potentially separate it from the original scene without losing the emotional cue. Then you can use your anchor in a number of different situations.

We are going to call the process of bringing your colour to mind 'firing your anchor'. Here are some ideas for how to do that:

Confidence/calm

Your anchor can function as a confidence booster or a tool for accessing a calmer state of mind. Take a moment to fire your anchor now by imagining that colour flowing into your body and just notice how your muscles respond. Do they relax? Many people also notice a feeling of warmth, lightness or tingling as they do this. It doesn't need to be pronounced, but if you sense something like this, then it's a very good sign that you have just created a powerful tool for suggesting a positive emotional shift.

Relationships

You can also use this colour to improve your relationships and your ability to communicate. Emotions like shame, fear, self-doubt or anything else that might trigger a state of protection can drastically hinder our ability to connect authentically and freely with other people. By using your anchor as you speak with others, you could be giving your mind a metaphorical 'permission slip' to be the calm, self-accepting version of yourself that they will respond to the most comfortably.

Take a moment to imagine the colour connecting you with someone that you love. Close your eyes, bring a loved one to mind, notice how they are sitting or standing and the expression on their face, and then let the colour flow from you to them in the same way that you did with your younger self. Pay attention to how this makes you feel about them and about your relationship to them. Then notice how they respond to the connection as well.

Next time you want to make sure that you're fully connected to someone that you're speaking with, you can imagine this happening in situ.

Other self-sabotages

Once you have set an anchor like this – just like Robert learned to do with his St Christopher pendant imagery – your colour can be used to counter your moments of self-sabotage.

You can think of this as a 'pattern interrupt'. It's our emotions that inspire our choice of behaviour. This means that any time that we can interrupt the usual emotional sequence just before doing something we don't want to do, we can break the circuit and open up a window of opportunity for change. Making it count, of course, requires that we take responsibility in that moment. The powerful thing is that each time we do that, we will strengthen our sense of internal control in the very situations we might otherwise have felt the most 'out of control'.

Think of a common example of your own self-sabotage – something like procrastination, nail-biting, performance anxiety or giving in to peer pressure and smoking a cigarette while out with your friends. Then, fire your anchor by imagining your colour flowing into your imagined self in that situation. Let that colour change your behaviours, thoughts and feelings, so that you can respond to the challenge in the way that you would like. Then, the next time you feel the urge to engage in that behaviour, pause to repeat this imagery, and then grasp your opportunity to take control.

Any of the above are things that you can use in a matter of seconds when challenge arises. In a moment we're going to look at how you can integrate your anchor into the Diving Down process to maximise its effect. Before that, though, let's put the tool that you've created to the test.

Testing your anchor

Anchors grow stronger as we continue using them, but you can test yours right now to see how effective it already is.

Bring to mind the recent memory you used to connect with the old, negative feeling right at the beginning of the process. Then, imagine your anchored colour flowing into that memory. You might choose to visualise it tinting the entire scene, focusing on a certain object or simply flowing into the remembered version of yourself from that day. Take a moment to do that now, letting the colour permeate all of the elements that would benefit the most from a shift. Then answer the following questions:

1. With your anchored colour flowing into that memory, if you try to find the old emotions, what do you notice?
2. If you were to rate those old feelings on a scale of 0–10 now (0 being completely neutral), where would they be?

If you've reduced the emotional intensity of that remembered moment, or if you just think about it differently now, then you've done some very good work. Well done!

If not, don't fret. You may just need a little more time to process your reframe. If it continues to feel ineffective in a few days' time, it could be that a different memory – an earlier one, perhaps – will hold the key. Or it could be that you need to do a little more work on this reframe. You can travel back along your timeline to that memory as many times as you like, adding new messages, metaphors, resources and connections, until you create the shift you need.

Task: Diving Down into Self-acceptance

Finally, your anchor could now make a persuasive new addition to the Diving Down process. Whether you use it to access a state of calm, to connect to other people more fully, or to alter your perspective on a challenging situation, this colour can serve as a quick yet powerful means of redirecting your attention and changing your emotional state.

This is how the steps will go for this version:

1. Ask, 'What am I thinking?'
2. Ask, 'What am I feeling?'
3. Ask, 'What is the monster story?'
4. Now breathe ... and fire your anchor.

If you'd like to have a practice now, start by choosing a focus. Bring to mind a situation in which you'd benefit from a stronger sense of self-acceptance. Now, here are the steps to follow:

Step 1: Ask, 'What am I thinking?'

To gain awareness of your surface-level thought processes in relation to your chosen focus, observe and narrate your internal dialogue as you consider the problem situation.

Step 2: Ask, 'What am I feeling?'

Now, drop down into your body to observe the physical presentation of the connected emotions. Pay close attention to how you actually feel those feelings, so you can create a metaphorical symbol to represent them.

Step 3: Ask, 'What is the monster story?'

To make sure that you know what you're dealing with, and that you're taking an internal-locus-of-control perspective, listen to your deeper experience to discern what it is that you're really responding to. Then, complete this sentence:

'I am feeling (X emotion) because a part of my mind wants to believe ... (insert relevant monster story).'

Step 4: Now breathe ... and fire your anchor

Breathe fluidly and comfortably through the ideas that surface, for at least three exhalations. As you do that, consciously relax your muscles and observe the emotion (as you see, hear or feel it) in your body. Then, fire your anchor by doing one of the following:

a) Imagine the colour flowing into your own body as you breathe.
b) Imagine the colour flowing between you and someone with whom you'd like to either connect or communicate with more effectively.
c) Imagine the colour flowing away from you and into a context in which you'd benefit from a stronger sense of self-assurance.

Finishing up

As always, I'd recommend that you finish by challenging your reality map. Here is the New Territories Question to help you do that:

'If I were to edit out that monster story, how would I see this differently?'

Use it or lose it

Anchors are things that grow more effective the more you practise with them. They don't 'run out'. In fact, just like building strength in a muscle, the way to think about this psychological exercise is that you either 'use it or lose it'. You don't get big biceps by doing bicep curls just once; you have to keep picking up the barbells. Luckily, firing an emotional anchor takes considerably less time than completing a workout, and although I recommend that you practise regularly for the next two or three weeks to make sure you've patterned in your new skill, after that you won't need anywhere near that kind of frequency. You can keep your anchor alive by just firing it a handful of times a month.

Before moving on to Part 4, have a think about the contexts in which your anchor could benefit you the most. Then, I'd suggest you practise Diving Down into each of them and firing your anchor when you hit the monster story. Just hold the negative belief in mind, breathe and imagine the colour flowing through you. This can be one of the simplest and most powerful ways to self-compassionately reclaim control of your self-sabotage. In doing this, you will give your monster — the fearful child inside of you — what it really needs to let go of its story.

Round-up of Part 3 – Play

Part 3 has been about building a bridge between the conscious and the unconscious. In order to teach the captain the language of the crew, we've looked at how to use the magical mechanism of allegory and the metaphorical nature of memory.

Here are the main points:

Metaphor (page 219)
Because of its naturally persuasive nature, metaphor plays a key role in most therapeutic styles. Once we know how, we can utilise the mind's love of equivalence (if x= y, then 10x = 10y) to make powerful suggestions for unconscious change.

Diving Down into emotional fluidity (page 232)
One of the options we have is to work some metaphorical suggestions into the Diving Down process. This technique enables us to exert some control over the way that we feel, especially when we know that our unconscious reaction is unwarranted.

Narrative (page 235)
Like metaphor, narrative shapes the way we think and helps us to learn. In Chapter 10, we looked at how to use metaphorical storytelling to make more complex suggestions to the unconscious mind about the way we'd like to think, feel or act.

Metaphorical memory and timeline visualisations (page 264)
In Chapter 11, we looked at the science of memory reconsolidation and considered the idea that memories are metaphorical. We developed a visual metaphor for time that can be used to map out our lives and trace our live-wire memories.

Earthing live-wire memories (page 280)
In Chapter 12, we learned a key process for the reframing of problematic past experiences. We also set an anchor (the colour of connection), so that we can repeat the positive emotional state that can be used as a counter to moments of self-sabotage.

Diving Down into self-acceptance (page 290)
Finally, we looked at a third variation of the Diving Down technique, which integrated the use of anchored imagery at the 'And breathe...' stage.

PART 4
PURPOSE

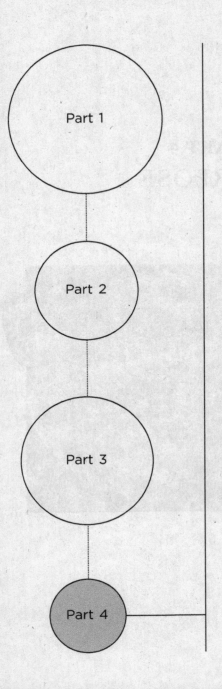

Purpose

Part 4 guides you in applying all of the tools you have developed over the course of this book to your life as a whole. The aim here is to move away from the anxiety that can naturally stem from too much 'navel-gazing', and into living a life of meaning and motivation instead.

Part 4 Contents

Chapter 13: Mentors
Self-acceptance and Interpersonal Connection   299

Evolution IV
A Metaphor for Wholeness   316

Chapter 14: (Re)Purpose
Beyond Winning and Losing   322

You can listen to the guided meditation for Part 4 here:
http://hazelgale.com/home/mindmonsters-part4-recording

13

Mentors

Self-acceptance and Interpersonal Connection

It is the fifteenth of December 2013. Today has been a curious experience. The peaceful ring walk and the snowily silenced sound of the crowd made the bout that I just won feel more like a dream than the fighting nightmare I've previously known. It's not that I wasn't nervous beforehand. Of course I was. Today was important. But I was able to use that energy differently this time. Instead of a tidal wave, I found a steady flow; instead of dread, I experienced excitement and focus, and it's all because something is different within. My internal world feels less desperate, less conflicted and less alone, and in the absence of all that old discomfort – as if a golden ray of morning sunlight has been allowed to shine into the most shadowy parts of my self – new space has been created for something much more fertile.

As my hand is raised in victory, a rush of warm emotion floods my body, and I break out into a rare in-ring smile. It strikes me as quite fitting that it's here, in a scruffy Essex sports hall where the Women's National Championships are being held, and not at any of the more glamorous, international events I've competed at, that I've finally learned how to feel something more than relief after a win.* Even though I know that I'll be able to pick holes in my performance when I watch it back, the anticipation of witnessing the little imperfections no longer fills me with dread because I can accept myself along with them.

I look out across the crowd of spectators and locate my friends and training partners, so I can share my success. And then, with tears

---

* Thankfully, the women's event is no longer held independently from the bigger and more prestigious men's one. This was actually the final year in which female boxers had to compete at a separate event in order to claim a national title in the UK.

gently welling, I realise that there's a deeper feeling of joy beneath the pride and achievement. It comes from the knowledge that victory simply isn't 'all about me' in that fearful way that I used to see it. I don't think we can keep these things for ourselves without tainting their meaning. The satisfaction, it turns out, comes from letting others in on the win.

In the car on the way home after the competition, growing sleepy as the adrenaline fades, I get the feeling of a new sense of purpose beginning to ignite.

••

Revolution

At the beginning of this book, I told you that this fight meant much more to me than just the acquisition of a boxing title. This wasn't the biggest on-paper achievement I ever had in fighting, and although I had regained a good portion of my fitness by this stage, I was still a way off 100 per cent, so I doubt it was even the best demonstration of my boxing. But none of that mattered because the objective achievement had little to do with the importance of this moment for me. It was the internal victory that made it count.

Up until the final year of my time fighting, the concept of winning had been nothing but a shimmering mirage ahead of me. No matter whether I got the decision or not, I had never really let myself drink from the oasis until this day. As my hand was raised, that 'rare in-ring smile' came from a sense of inner togetherness. Finally, I had allowed that little girl in her sports-day kit to join me in battle, and when we triumphed, she was the one who showed me how to feel it.

The irony is not lost on me. After all this time running from her, it was my 'little monster' who turned the mirage from a shifting, fake and intangible dream into something real that I could reach out and touch. What's more, I learned that when I looked away from myself I could also look away from the anxious need to prove myself. Facing out, rather than in, on that day meant that I was finally able to connect fully with the people my shame would once have kept from me.

Parent, Adult and Child

In Transactional Analysis, the self is divided into three 'ego states', which are essentially the three main parts of the personality: Parent, Adult and Child. We've met this concept before; it's another way of understanding drama. However, rather than just showing us what we need to step away from, this take on the theory shows us how to evolve the aspects of our personality that are most likely to gravitate towards conflict.

Adult The Adult is the captain. It is our conscious, rational, thinking self. This part is unemotional. It's all about logic and reasoning.

Child The Child is our feeling self. It will have been the protagonist in our early live-wire memories, and it's what we meet when we Dive Down. When we're out of balance internally, the Child is likely to play the role of Victim.

Parent The Parent is the experienced self; the part that has been through everything we have, and so bases its judgements and decisions on that information. It is the Parent that sets our goals and decides how to go about achieving them, but what do you think is most likely to happen when a parent makes their child do something that they really loathe or are afraid to do? The child will rebel, of course.

Happy families

Self-sabotage results from internal discord. To avoid this kind of psychological drama, all three of these main aspects of the self must work in harmony together, and there are two specific conditions for this to be the case:

1. The Parent part must come from a nurturing, rather than critical place if it is to avoid persecuting the Child and inspiring disobedience.
2. The Child needs to be allowed to experience and express its emotions freely if it is to move on healthily from challenge, and grow as a result.

When those conditions are met, all three parts will be able to communicate effectively in their own, particular language, and contribute to a sense of harmony within the self as a whole. Failure to satisfy these requirements, however, will result in some kind of energy-draining inner squabble.

The dark side of the Child

The monster is the dark side of the Child self. It is made of the emotions and the resulting behaviours that we attempt to disown. But we can't just get rid of the Child's dark side, and we can't ignore our emotions without inviting an overspill (a temper tantrum or panic attack, perhaps). When resisting our monsters, we attempt to punish them in the same way that an exasperated parent might ground or smack their naughty kid. But as many a parent will tell you: when you punish a child, they will usually find a way to get you back.

The little girl that felt a fearful need to win the love of her father is my Child self and my monster. If I were to repress her messages and deny her voice, then I would be acting like a critical parent to that part of my personality and it would rebel (as she did when I got ill, or every time I shook with adrenaline at the prospect of a game of pool). I had to let go of my instinct to beat her into submission before I could healthily step away from my internal shame-drama. Nurturing and listening to my emotional self meant that I 'de-monstered' her and then invited her back onto my team. Now I'm quite happy to have my little 'not ... enough' on my crew. What's more, I can tell you that I'm much wiser for it.

I should make something clear here. When I talk about allowing the Child to play their part, I'm not suggesting that we should act childishly. The emotional self will make some unwise suggestions from time to time. Sometimes we can't just go out and have fun because we really do need to fill in our tax return, and sometimes screaming the house down because our partner changed the TV channel really isn't a great idea. Keeping the internal family happy does not mean giving in to every Child-led whim, but rather honouring and respecting the motivation behind our emotional calls to action. Then, to allow all three parts – Parent, Adult and Child together – to come to an agreement about the best way to proceed.

The other thing that integration makes space for is the re-education of the Child. By opening up new and more effective channels of communication, we create a means to teach our emotional selves how to let go of genuinely unnecessary reactions, like jumping onto a chair whenever we see that cursed spider. Processes like those you learned in Part 3 allow the Adult and Parent to step in and untangle the bad logic of the Child's limiting beliefs. It's just that in order to do this, we first need to have invited the Child back in from outside.

The contents of this book – everything from the self-awareness we can build by learning about the functions of the mind, to the emotional intelligence we can develop when Diving Down and the creative reframing we can do through the use of metaphor and memory – has been included to help you 'de-monster' your own thinking by shining a light on the dark side of the Child. The aim, ultimately, is to invite that part back, so you can move towards a place of integrated and harmonious self-acceptance. Of course, this is an ideal, but the closer we get to it the more easily we will grow and develop, because the Child is the part we need to hear from in order to know what we really want, who we really are and what we need to change before we can realise those things.

Learning from the Monster

Owning our story can be hard but not nearly as difficult as spending our lives running from it. Embracing our vulnerabilities is risky but not nearly as dangerous as giving up on love and belonging and joy – the experiences that make us the most vulnerable. Only when we are brave enough to explore the darkness will we discover the infinite power of our light.

Brené Brown,* *The Gifts of Imperfection*

It's easy to forget that parents learn from their children, as well as the other way round. Many new mothers and fathers talk about rediscovering their love of playful growth when they have their first child. That stage of life is so often about reprioritising – cutting back the office hours so that more time can be spent with the things that 'really matter'. Children can also teach their parents a great deal about friendship, trust, the joy of novelty and having the conviction to stand up and speak from the heart.

The difference, of course, between inner and outer children is that, even though the external ones can act like little monsters from time to time, we're usually able to remember that we love and value them regardless.

---

* Research professor at the University of Houston and author.

Listening

The Child is a crucial team player who is there to provide us with important information about how to best live our lives. The lessons will vary from moment to moment, and sometimes they'll be more accurate than others, but to reap the benefits of an integrated sense of wholeness, the Child's voice needs to be heard.

This means that there is one final and crucial bit of reframing left for us to do. It would be remiss of me to talk at such length about the powerfully suggestive nature of metaphor and not address the central analogy used in this book. No matter how much intellectual understanding we might have about the good intentions of our 'monsters', continuing to call a part of our personality by that name is not likely to send a positive metaphorical message to our unconscious minds.

Fortunately, just as we can improve and update our sense of self without needing to slay any of the individual parts that go into making us, we can also rewrite the monster metaphor without doing away with any of its constituent parts either – we can use an anagram:

$$M.O.N.S.T.E.R \rightarrow M.E.N.T.O.R.S$$

Much better.

Fear, guilt, anger, sadness, grief, shame, and even irritability, grumpiness and fatigue – all of the emotional and physical states that we are most likely to attribute to our 'monsters' – can potentially teach us something that we need to know in order to improve our lives, our relationships and to succeed in what we do. So, here's the thing: there is no big, bad mind monster. Life is just a series of learning experiences, which – when accepted and listened to rather than resisted and loathed – make us stronger and better equipped going forward. Self-sabotage is a teacher, not the enemy, and emotions are its primary teaching tool. Emotions highlight areas of weakness so we can strengthen ourselves; they alert us to danger, they improve our communication skills, they enhance our creativity and they tell us what we love, so that we can bring more of it into our lives. In order to understand and utilise those emotions, we need to have access to the entirety of our experience.

I worked with a client recently who found her younger self in a dark corner of a room, angry and frightened because she thought that her mother was never coming back. As we worked on the memory reframe, my client sat silently for some minutes deciding on what she needed to teach her child self. What she eventually settled on was this: 'When you experience them fully, your feelings transform into knowledge.' I thought this was beautifully put. When we take the time to accept, listen to, nurture and empathise with all parts of the self, our monsters evolve into mentors.

Steve's whole in one

Steve had been passionate about golf from a young age, but for some reason the 'old boys' of the sport had always looked down their noses at him. 'You'll never make it, son,' they told him as he carted his gear around his childhood course. 'Better find something else to do.'

But Steve didn't want to do anything else. And despite their criticism, he progressed swiftly into the professional game before the age of twenty. However, their negative words never really faded from his mind, and by the time he visited me – a decade after turning pro – the old message had grown into what felt like the victimising truth. As a result, Steve was in a near-permanent state of anxious agitation. He could fly into fits of rage behind the wheel of his car, he had started to loathe his training sessions and he was growing increasingly irritated around family and friends. Furthermore, no matter how excellent he might have looked in practice, Steve would consistently underperform whenever it really mattered. His monster was intent on making him look like the failure those bitter older men seemed to want him to become.

Over the first few months of therapy, Steve experienced all the ups and downs that so many people do when they start making an important change. During his sessions he could connect fully to the dejected inner Child who struggled with self-belief, and then he would enjoy a few weeks of calm, self-accepting thinking. When he was on the up, his irritability and road rage would subside, and he found himself beginning to enjoy his training. Yet, whenever a competition loomed, his performance anxiety could drag him rapidly back down into the (dis)comfort of 'not-good-enough' territory again, and he would feel as if he was getting nowhere.

It was the drama of winning v. losing that had enough gravity to pull Steve down. Young Steve, no matter how connected he was able to feel during our sessions, was still hell-bent on proving to the old boys that he could play the game. At the first sign of anything that looked like failure (a wayward drive from the tee, a putt that fell short), that part of his mind would launch into an angry internal rebellion against all his well-meant efforts to stay calm and control his play.

Steve and I have been working together for almost a year at the time of writing this. During those months, he has been through almost every process outlined in this book (some more than once). Our goal has been to reintegrate that hurt and angry little boy, so that Steve can act like a nurturing Parent to himself on the golf course, rather than an exasperated father with a tantrum-throwing teen on his hands. In order to do this, he has worked hard to internalise his locus of control, to let go of his old, resentful need to prove himself and focus instead on all that he loves about his sport.

Two months ago, I received this email:

> I played a tournament today; the first tournament I've ever played where I felt so relaxed and determined just to enjoy myself. I didn't have any of the pre-game anxiety feelings. And guess what? I played really well. I shot five under par (my best ever score in a tournament) and came second, one shot behind the winner.
>
> With two or three holes to play I knew I was in contention and started to get a bit nervous. My first thought was, 'Why are you nervous? This isn't meant to mean anything.' But then I felt a complete calm come over me and I just said to myself, 'You're nervous because you've played well enough to be in this position. So, welcome the nerves. They're a good thing.' If anything, my game went up a notch when the excitement started to kick in. I had this knowledge inside me that I can care enough to let the nerves be a good thing, but not so much that the outcome will have any bearing on my life and how I feel about myself. I was walking the last couple of holes more proud and impressed with my state of mind than how I was playing. I can't tell you how good that made me feel!

On that day, Steve let go of the old drama. He was communicating with himself, rather than battling with old shadows. And by taking ownership of his own emotions, he had evolved his monster into something that could give him positive motivation when he most needed it.

There will still be ups and downs on the golf course for Steve. And, just like the rest of us, he will need to make his positive thinking a practice in order to repeat that level of present-moment fulfilment. But I would love to think that in years to come, he will be able to remember that day as the moment when he first let his monster mentor him into a place where he could enjoy being himself.

Boundaries

One of the most important roles that our emotional mentors have is to act as the guardsmen of our personal boundaries.

Boundaries are a crucial yet often overlooked aspect of self-care. People who know how to honour and respect their own boundaries – and who make a concerted effort to do so – lead healthier and happier lives, and they can enjoy more respectful and nourishing relationships. For years, I would nod knowingly when talking about boundaries with my friends but, if I'm entirely honest, I didn't fully grasp how to live by these principles until I read *Rising Strong* by Brené Brown. Brown's beautifully uncomplicated definition of the concept is this: 'Boundaries are simply our lists of what's okay and what's not okay.'[1]

In order to live the life we want, we have to hold boundaries around our needs, values and general wellbeing. Respecting those boundaries means being aware of our feelings, responding to them autonomously and being brave enough to say what we need to say – very often the 'awkward thing' – in order to stay safely within them. Failure to respect our boundaries can lead us rapidly into a place where we're overworked, stressed or being walked on by others; and we can find ourselves frequently losing sleep, getting ill, feeling depressed or suffering from chronic states of anxiety, resentment and, of course, shame. In other words, failure to respect our own boundaries and self-sabotage are one and the same.

It's the job of the Child mentor to teach us about our boundaries. When we overstep one and find ourselves in the territory of 'not okay', we will experience some kind of emotional pain. That pain – just like the soreness that my 6-foot-5-inch boyfriend feels when he fails to successfully duck under a doorframe – teaches us about our limits. Physical pain tells us where the edges of our bodies are; emotional pain tells us about the edges of our energy, our patience, our input and output, our morals and our emotional involvement.

It's tempting, of course, to blame others for breaching our boundaries: 'She should know better', 'He doesn't have the right', 'They're out of order!' Those things may all be true. However, if we're going to operate out of an internalised locus of control, then how we feel is our responsibility, rather than anyone else's. Yes, we will need to hold accountable those who breach our boundaries (making the breach explicit will usually involve saying the 'awkward thing' that enables us to step away from drama and keep our self-respecting boundaries in place). However, once we have received the emotional message and taken action where possible, our continued entertainment of any residual self-sabotaging emotions – like resentment, anxiety or guilt – is our responsibility. If we continue to suffer from those debilitating emotional states, then it is we who are crossing the line.

Stuck

I once got wedged, shoulder-to-shoulder, inside a doorframe, with someone I had a particularly drama-laden relationship with. This person was my boss, and the Persecutor to my determined little Victim self for some years. One afternoon, he visited my office to pick something up and, as I let him in, somehow we got physically stuck in the entranceway to the building. It only lasted a brief moment, but those few seconds of awkward mumbling and jostling were quite excruciating.

This happened while I was revising for an exam. For at least an hour after The Wedging (I know; retrospectively, it's hilarious) I failed to read beyond a page or two without getting distracted by the memory of our little encounter and having to start again. It could have been a 'say-the-awkward-thing' moment. If it happened now, I might schedule an appointment to discuss our working relationship and iron out the drama in the bigger picture. My unwarranted anguish over the doorframe incident was clearly a message from an inner mentor. I was not standing up for myself with this person and, as a result, I was trampling all over my own boundaries every time I spoke to him. But I was far from ninja-level with my vulnerability skills back then (I'd barely got my white belt), so a full-disclosure conversation was way beyond me. Yet, I had to do something to put an end to my study-sabotaging thinking, so I took to the journal.

This happened long before I started putting the Diving Down technique together (it was even before I had started practising as a therapist), but looking back, I can see why what I wrote worked so well. First, I transcribed my little drama, including a description of the doorframe moment and my frustrations with the relationship as a whole ('What am I thinking?'). I described the way I felt while sitting there failing to read ('What am I feeling?'). And I wrote down how uncomfortable, pathetic and inferior the encounter made me feel ('What is the monster story?'). Then I crumpled up the piece of paper and threw it in the bin, as if to tell myself that it didn't matter.

To my amazement, it turned out that it really didn't matter. At all. Hours went by before I even remembered about the uncomfortable experience. It only occurred to me when I walked past the bin that evening and saw the screwed-up piece of paper sitting atop all the other discarded documents. Granted, the doorframe moment really was a little thing, but my mind was dead set on making it monstrous on the day because it was a metaphor for the much bigger 'stuck' issue in my life at the time.

Projection

The traits we most dislike in others tend to be the things that we least like – or are least willing to see – in ourselves. This phenomenon is called projection. We transfer our self-loathing, fear and shame onto the people around us, rather than experience it directly.

Working mindfully with our projection means that we can channel any drama-like energy into our own personal growth – because whatever we find objectionable about someone else is likely to highlight our own resistance. While someone is suppressing an, 'I'm-weak' limiting belief, for example, they may well find themselves detesting the weakness they see in others. Or if someone is resisting a monster that believes they are stupid, then they might get particularly irritated when their colleagues fail to understand the task at hand. In other words, projection can tell us what to work on; it shows us the dark side of the inner Child.

My door-wedging experience, for example, was with a person who was all about proving his own significance, which was exactly the issue I was struggling with at the time. If I had known to listen to my mentors, rather than make monsters of everyone else, then I might have been able to address my problem earlier, and then see past his resistant behaviours to create a better relationship.

So, what frustrates you the most in others? Do you hate it when people show off? Do you loathe it when people cheat? Do you despise irresponsibility, overt flirtation, childishness or selfishness?

I'm not saying that everyone who really dislikes selfishness in others will necessarily be 'selfish people' themselves. But it could be that they're resisting their own tendencies towards that particular trait (which, let's not forget, is almost certainly a natural occurrence for all of us). With resistance-free awareness, a rogue thought about doing something selfish can be dismissed as an unnecessary idea that the mind just chucked up into your consciousness. Because that's what the mind is for: it's an idea generator. Not all of your ideas will be good ones, and that's fine, especially when you don't act on them. However, if you resist those thoughts, then you could potentially find yourself with a 'selfish monster' on your hands – a destructive part of the personality that inspires you to do the types of egocentric things that you would regret horribly afterwards.

Even if you don't end up sabotaging your own behaviour directly, you could find yourself having very dramatic feelings about the people who exhibit your most resisted traits, and those are the kinds of feelings that can easily handicap a potentially good relationship.

Ultimately, there are very few characteristics that we can avoid completely. Even the most intelligent of people will say silly things sometimes, and even the most virtuous can have a naughty idea. However, most people will agree that, on reflection, it's easier to make the right choice before the act than process the shame that results from stepping outside your boundaries. So, getting real about these potentialities is probably a good move. Your mentors will show you the way if you let them. The key thing to remember is that when it feels as if someone else is breaching a boundary, your mind is potentially telling you about the location of your own.

Learning Our Limits

Unfortunately, we usually need to transgress our boundaries in order to learn where they are. It's possible that we can anticipate a major violation before its occurrence and take action early enough to avoid the pain. However, for the most part, we will only really know where a boundary is once it has been breached at least once. Children, teens and even young adults can't really be expected to know their limits. The first couple of decades of our lives, it seems, are designed for us to stomp all over our boundaries in order to map it all out. We can only learn who we are through trial and error. In that respect, it's the Parent mentor – the experienced part of the self – who must enforce the maintenance of healthy boundaries once they have been identified. However, when there's a breach in progress, it's the Child who will let us know, and the message will be delivered via the medium of emotion.

The pain of a boundary breach is enormously important because it highlights the areas of our life in which we need to take more responsibility for our own self-care. When you find yourself feeling like an angry kid who has had their ice cream taken away, you've probably breached a boundary. When you start feeling afraid in the way that a small, helpless child might do, you've probably breached a boundary. When your relationships start to break down because you've been working too hard, letting someone take advantage of you or said something stupid to someone you love, you've definitely breached a boundary. Ultimately, whenever anything feels 'not okay', we need to quickly ask ourselves what we're going to do in order to step back over into 'okay'. Sometimes the solution will be simple: removing unnecessary commitments from our diary, booking some time off or calling a friend to talk things through. At other times, the solution will be difficult; we may need to end an unhealthy relationship or give up something we feel dependent on. Yet, whatever the breach and whatever the solution, it's always our responsibility to make the move.

Sometimes a little lateral thinking is required because our mentors are fluent in many different tongues. If we fail to recognise the emotional call to action, then the message can come in the form of unwanted behaviours or physical symptoms. If, as the golfer Steve experienced, you're being unusually snappy or grumpy with people you are normally happy to be around, then there may be a boundary breach in progress somewhere in your life (and it will not necessarily involve those people directly). Perhaps your mentors let you know by using an upset stomach, interrupted sleep, back pain, loss of voice, loss of hair, cold sores, a racing heart, twitching eye or any other physiological symptoms, to highlight that something is not as it should be. As I found out all those years ago, what starts with a little niggle can easily grow to terrifying proportions if left unaddressed, so these personalised warning signs are worth getting familiar with. The trick is not to slip into a victim mindset, but to read the message as an important instruction for your decision-making. Whether it is emotional, behavioural or physical, I believe that any (dis)comfortable self-sabotage can function as a signpost to unanswered questions and disrespected boundaries. If we choose to Dive Down into those experiences, we can potentially catch and address the real issues before it's too late.

If we fail to listen to the messages from our inner mentors, however, we'll be destined to keep smashing our foreheads against (or getting stuck inside) the doorframes of this world indefinitely. And if we're really addicted to drama, we might even think that someone else built those doorways a little bit too small for us on purpose.

Growing

Boundaries are not set in stone. Some of them can shift as we develop. Occasionally, things that we used to put in the 'not-okay' category can become an option when we grow. I'm not talking about the big boundary breaches here, like stealing, cheating or abuse. However, there are other things that we might benefit from opening ourselves up to.

A person who does not pay attention when their mentors pipe up is likely to feel large amounts of discomfort during objectively mild breaches (like my wedging incident and Steve's road rage). Once in touch with our authentic emotions, however, the little things can stop feeling like the brink because we know that we will have our own backs when the going gets tough. As a result, we can feel stronger in the face of challenge, and then go to places we wouldn't have dared to visit before or connect with people who might once have felt too intimidating to approach.

It's important to recognise, therefore, that respecting our boundaries is not about going into a defensive state of lock-down. Overly boundaried people have as many problems as those who fail to heed their mentors' warnings. They can come across as closed or cold and, in extreme cases, as heartless and self-serving. Listening to our mentors ultimately leads to growth, change and connection, not protection and retreat.

Inspiration

Mentors, therefore, are more than just guardsmen. The real joy comes when we let them lead us bravely into uncharted waters.

Because our boundaries represent our personal limits, as they shift, so does our sense of identity. Our very idea of what's possible, important and interesting automatically grows and changes when we get faithfully (and curiously) in touch with the emotional language of our gut instinct.

In her book about how to live creatively, Elizabeth Gilbert describes the experience of inspiration like this:

> ... chills ran up my arms. The hairs on the back of my neck stood up for an instant, and I felt a little sick, a little dizzy. I felt like I was falling in love, or had just heard alarming news, or was looking over a precipice at something beautiful and mesmerising, but dangerous.[2]

Do you think someone who religiously resists their emotions could hear this kind of call to action? Almost certainly not. Gilbert's description of inspiration sounds like the experience of an exquisite terror. And the reason it sounds that way is because creativity and fear are bed buddies. To step away from the known – to do or make anything new – is automatically frightening. Without a courageous connection to our feelings, we can neither feel nor follow the urge to create. We have to make friends with our fear in order to even think about going there.

Monsters and Mirages, or Mentors and Magic? Your Choice.

In summary, by accepting the aspects of self that we used to run away from, we can make mentors out of our monster reactions. Then, we can let go of our respective mirages and choose instead to enjoy the process of learning who we really are, what we really want and how we can go about getting it. The reward for listening to our mentors can be that we finally get a taste of whatever it is that we've really been chasing after, because when we cease to fight with ourselves in order to *try* to meet our needs, we usually find that we had everything we needed to do that already.

In a world where it's so easy to get hypnotised into a victim mindset, our mentors can create something for us to trust on the inside. In doing so, they can bring us certainty. Then, they can provide variety by delivering inspiration, as well as the courage to follow it. Because they fuel our personal development and teach us how to be better versions of ourselves, they enable us to feel significant. Finally, because they make authentic, empathetic contact with the Other a possibility, our mentors can also bring us love and connection.

In other words, our mentors can fill the void left by unmet deficiency needs. Therefore, the monster-to-mentor transition means that we can move out of a place of deficit, lack and protection, and into the much more fulfilling and fertile state of growth. Whether we use that to keep growing in the same direction we had been before, or to find a new way, is, of course, entirely up to us.

So how do we ensure that we remain mentor- rather than monster-driven? I think the key principle to keep in mind is this:

Pain does not happen *to* us but *for* us.

Discomfort is an instruction and, if used correctly – sometimes with time – it can also be a gift. No one lives a pain-free life, and some of the pain that we suffer is not that open to change. However, much of what we battle with on a day-to-day basis can be alchemised when we learn how to catch and listen to our discomfort early enough. I don't subscribe to the 'everything-happens-for-a-reason' philosophy because I struggle with the idea of predetermination. However, I do believe that – out of a duty to ourselves – we all have a responsibility to search for meaning inside our darkest moments.

To make the most of our mentors, we need to utilise our internalised sense of control to open up the window of opportunity that sits between stimulus and response – we need to get in the habit of pausing, just for a moment, when things get tough. Then we need to ask a few key questions of ourselves. It's by Diving Down into our challenging moments that we can grasp the opportunity to 'de-hypnotise' ourselves; to break free from the shackles of victimhood, habit and old conditioning to claim the freedom to be who we choose to be.

This all means that self-sabotage can be the very key to our success, our happiness and our growth, because it's only the uncomfortable moments that ever really provide us with the chance to transcend the (dis)comfort zone. We just have to remember to enter willingly into those experiences in order to find the magic that's concealed within them.

Eventually, in times of challenge, we will be able to listen to our mentor rather than the old voice of fear, shame or doubt, to opt out of self-sabotage and into self-acceptance. Only when we operate from a place of self-love can we take control of the mind and its destructive tendencies, and only when we connect with ourselves will we be able to fully connect with others. Ultimately, with self-love, we don't want to harm ourselves. We can choose a better way instead.

Evolution IV

A Metaphor for Wholeness

In this final evolution section, I would like you to create a mental image of what your monster might look like once it has been through its metamorphosis and transformed into a mentor.

We know that it is resistance that makes our monsters monstrous. We know that acceptance is the answer to the resistance problem. And, we know that in order to reach a place of acceptance (especially of the shameful personal fears we have spent so long trying to keep under lock and key), we need to engage with emotional fluidity. So, how do we do that with the aspect of self that we've been calling the 'monster'?

One of my favourite Brené Brown quotes is this:

Empathy is the strongest antidote for shame.[3]

The less we talk about the things that make us feel 'not ... enough', the more power our shame-monsters will have over us. Authentic, empathetic connection, on the other hand, can *heal* the pain of 'not ... enough'. But before we stand a chance of bringing our monsters into the light of inter-personal connection, we need first to empathise with ourselves. We need to learn how to pull our monsters in, listen to their fears, talk to them gently and remind them that everything is going to be OK. This is the solution; to practise radical self-acceptance and to love the whole of the self, monsters and all. In doing this, our inner Children can let go of their destructive behaviours because we're giving them what they needed all along.

What you're about to learn is a means for practising just this — it's a metaphor for empathetic self-connection. But this isn't new, it's something you've been in the process of doing since you started reading this book; first by taking the time to understand your emotional self (Part 1), then by hearing the messages it sends (Part 2) and then by learning how to communicate directly with it (Part 3).

Here, in Part 4, I would like you to bring all of this together into a simple visualisation, so that you can spend a moment observing how your (former) monster can respond to your acceptance. You may already have an idea of what it might look like once it is transformed into a mentor, or your mind might surprise you with the imagery it creates. Either way, I'd suggest you stay open to whatever comes up.

The Visualisation

Before you close your eyes, you will need to have a way of visualising this all-important connection, and I suggest you use a tool that you are already familiar with. Let's make use of your anchored colour.

So, if you're ready to evolve your monster, start by closing your eyes and bringing to mind an image of the part of your personality that inspires your self-sabotage (in whatever way it appears to you now).

Then, as you begin breathing continuously and fluidly, imagine your chosen colour flowing between you and that aspect of self, giving it all the time it needs to transform.

Take a moment to engage with that visualisation now, and just observe what happens.

How does your mentor look when you connect to it in that way? When some people do this they imagine their mentor looking more like a part of themselves. Others see a wise character or something symbolic, like a peaceful lake or a flower in bloom. I've heard stories about demonic faces learning to smile sweetly and gnarly beasts shrinking into fluffy kitten-like creatures.

When I imagine sending a beam of golden light into the shadow that used to represent my monster, I find my five-year-old self emerging from the darkness. The visualisation teaches me that fear of failure is an old and outdated threat, and that regardless of whether I get something right or wrong, I'm still worthy of connection. Ultimately, that golden light enables me to look beyond the old shadow and onto the things that really bring me joy instead: growth, learning, love and the people I can share all of that with.

If you don't yet get the sense that your metaphor has fully evolved, then there's plenty more you can do to encourage your own evolution of self. Perhaps your mentor needs some kind of physical contact before it can settle comfortably into its new role? Or, maybe it needs a message that it can hear as well as see. Consider these options:

* **What was the positive big-picture idea that you delivered to your younger self during your memory reframe (e.g. 'You don't have to win anybody's affection. You're worthy of connection just as you are')?** See what happens when you communicate that same idea to your mentor.
* Maybe your mentor needs to feel accepted by others as well as you. **Who was the significant other you connected with during your memory reframe, and what difference could that interaction make to your mentor?**
* Finally, perhaps your mentor would feel more comfortable if you introduced it to a different environment. If it seems appropriate, you could imagine taking it into the metaphorical story you created in Chapter 10 and encourage it to make its evolution that way.

As this is your story, if you can think of something better to give, show or communicate to this aspect of self to aid its metamorphosis, then you can, of course, go ahead and do it. Take another moment to close your eyes and connect with your mentor in whatever way feels the most powerful. This time, if you like, you can let the communication flow both ways. It may even be that this part of your personality already has something that it could teach you in return for your acceptance.

As always, I'd like you to log what you have imagined here. If you've been drawing (or if you're suddenly overwhelmed by the urge to create now) there's a space allocated for you to represent your mentor on page 349. Or, if you've been using written descriptions, please take a moment to put your mentor visualisation into words before carrying on.

Integrating

Now, if you feel ready to do so, you can take the ultimate step of inviting this part of your personality back into the whole. Here's one last question:

If there were a way for you to imagine reintegrating your mentor, so that it can function as a healthy aspect of your whole self, how would you do that?

Again, go with anything that comes to mind. You might imagine absorbing your mentor right into your physical body; or it could just be that you'd join hands, hug or team up in some other way. You might find that using your anchored colour again here can make an even more powerful suggestion.

Close your eyes and spend a moment visualising your mentor's integration, paying particular attention to how it feels to have welcomed this part of you back.

Finally, you can keep a note of how you imagine the integration taking place on page 348.

Task: Diving Down into Continued Evolution

All of the tools and processes you have learned in this book are here for you to continue coming back to whenever you hit an emotional or behavioural snag in your life, and these visualisations are no different. Just like the anchored colour on its own, you could use the imagery of either your monster's metamorphosis or of your mentor's integration (perhaps both in sequence) as tools to counter self-sabotage and move increasingly closer to a place of wholehearted self-acceptance.

Perhaps the most powerful way of repeating these important suggestions, of course, will be to add them into the Diving Down process. Doing so will mean that with just four questions and a few moments of visualisation, you can achieve all of these things: you will increase your self-awareness; you will ensure that you are not resisting either your emotions or your monster stories; you will challenge your reality map and train your mind to look for solutions; and you will encourage your movement towards a place of integrated self-acceptance. Lovely.

This is the last variation of the technique that we'll look at. Here are the steps:

1. Ask, 'What am I thinking?'
2. Ask, 'What am I feeling?'
3. Ask, 'What is the monster story?'
4. Now breathe ... and evolve your monster.

By now, I'm sure you're more than familiar with the process. However, just in case you'd like a final guided run-through, here's how to use this version of the tool.

Start by choosing your focus: bring to mind a situation or life context that your monster may once have sabotaged.

Step 1: Ask, 'What am I thinking?'

To gain awareness of your surface-level thought processes in relation to your chosen focus, observe and narrate your internal dialogue as you consider the problem situation.

Step 2: Ask, 'What am I feeling?'

Now, drop down into your body to observe the physical presentation of the connected emotions. Pay close attention to how you actually feel those feelings, so you can create a metaphorical symbol to represent them.

Step 3: Ask, 'What is the monster story?'

To make sure that you know what you're dealing with, and that you're taking an internal-locus-of-control perspective, listen to your deeper experience to discern what it is that you're really responding to. Then, complete this sentence:

'I am feeling (X emotion) because a part of my mind wants to believe ... (insert relevant monster story).'

Step 4: Now breathe ... and evolve your monster

Breathe fluidly and comfortably through the ideas that surface for at least three exhalations. As you do that, consciously relax your muscles and observe the emotion (as you see, hear or feel it) in your body.

Then, engage with your evolution imagery by doing one of the following:

a) Imagine connecting to your monster and allowing it to evolve into a mentor by using your anchored colour (or whatever else felt the most powerful for you when you practised this earlier).

b) Imagine integrating your mentor back into the whole.

Finishing up

As always, I'd recommend that you finish by challenging your reality map with the New Territories Question:

'If I were to edit out that monster story, how would I see this differently?'

I have included a run-through of the complete Diving Down process plus all of the different variations that we have discussed (along with one bonus addition) in Appendix 1 (see page 331).

Moving Forward

Finally, before you put this book away, let's explore the question of where your evolution could ultimately lead you. The final chapter of *The Mind Monster Solution* looks at how you could generate a sense of purpose out of the work that you've already done here.

14

(Re)Purpose

Beyond Winning and Losing

Right now, I'm sitting on a balcony overlooking the Forest of Dean in Gloucestershire. Beyond the screen of my laptop there is nothing to be seen but rich, green woodland and a slightly misty early-morning sky.

This is not my home. It's a luxury. I booked this trip instead of a holiday, so that I could focus on the final few chapters of this book in the wholehearted way that I would like. I came in search of the space needed to get the words onto paper and to truly appreciate the process of doing that.

It's beautiful here, impossibly calm. The sun is creeping up from behind the trees, giving them golden halos, and while a sleepy white cloud passes through the cleft of the valley below me, I can pretend that I'm floating in the sky. As I sip my tea and think about how I could best describe this, it occurs to me that I may never before have felt so present.

Yet, it's neither the location nor the view that really brings the magic to this moment. What makes this experience special is that I feel as if I've tuned into something meaningful – something more important than the task of writing a book, and something far bigger than myself. For want of a better word, I am experiencing a sense of purpose.

I do not mention this because I want to sound self-satisfied or smug, nor do I wish to portray the image of the condescending guru, sitting in her lap of luxury, telling everyone else how to live their lives. Have I completely mastered all my self-sabotaging traits? Nope. Have I discovered a state of endless inner serenity and calm? Definitely not. However, I can tell you that I am a great deal happier, healthier, calmer and more confident than I was before, even though I no longer have many of the assets I used to consider mandatory in order to be 'good enough'.

Back in the days when I did have those 'significance badges' – the medals, the thin and muscular body, the social-media posts about recent victories – I also had that permanent, knife-like feeling of anxiety in the centre of my sternum. It was sly and furtive. It told me that I didn't deserve the praise I was so desperate to receive and that I was a pathetic person for seeking it out. I didn't recognise that feeling as fear – for the longest time I didn't recognise it at all – but I know now that it was there because I can feel that it has gone.

These days, no matter whether I'm in the middle of this forest, sat at my kitchen table writing or working with a client in the office, when I search inside my body to learn how I feel, I find a sense of gratitude, enthusiasm and connection. At least, I find those feelings more often than not. The irony is that I have my monster to thank for that. Furthermore, when I then turn my attention away from myself and onto those with whom I can share these new emotions, they only grow stronger. That's a wonderful thing.

Evolution

For me, the therapeutic process led me to a more defined sense of purpose, and I'm lucky enough to have found a way to let it permeate into my career, as well as other areas of my life.

Looking back, I can clearly see that the battle I had with myself was a necessary part of my evolution. If I hadn't been forced to look my 'not … enough' in the eye, I perhaps never would have seen it for what it really was. I almost certainly wouldn't have worked out how to use it.

On that day at the National Boxing Championships, I was able to enjoy my victory because of the sense of togetherness I felt on the inside. But very quickly that internal feeling grew into something even more valuable; something that extended way beyond the boundaries of 'me'. After that, pretty much everything in my life underwent a metamorphosis, much like my monster.

I retired from competition shortly after the Nationals and devoted all of my energy into my therapy practice, instead of juggling the two things at once. I was able to let go of fighting largely because the old need to win no longer gripped me so powerfully. Instead, I found far more meaning and enjoyment in helping others to overcome their 'not … enough' problems.

It's not that I left boxing behind. I still love coaching, and I'll rarely turn down the chance to spar when I'm training. However, my relationship to that part of my world has transformed because it's no longer 'all about me'. As a result of this evolution, I feel like there's a great deal more meaning in my life than there seemed to be when my only mission was to prove myself against an old, fictitious idea that no one but me ever really knew about.

Retrospectively, I can see that none of this would have been possible while my monster was calling the shots. I needed to liberate myself from the shame and angst that monopolised my thinking and kept me at a distance from others. Yet, the sense of purpose that I now feel was also contingent on my having been through what I did; it *grew out of* the challenges my little 'not ... enough' presented me with. These days, with my monster integrated and promoted to the position of mentor, I'm able to do what I love to do and really feel that my contribution is valid and worthwhile.

Purpose

Purpose is the final piece of the happiness puzzle. It adds hope, inspiration and meaning to the self-awareness that we build as a result of working through our problems.

People with a sense of purpose can enjoy higher levels of confidence and self-esteem, and they suffer less from anxiety, boredom and depression. This is the case largely because purpose prevents us from getting drawn inside. Instead, it enables us to look beyond the self – away from the fragile ego – and onto something else.

As important as it is for a sense of wellbeing, however, purpose is something that is often misunderstood. It is easy to assume that possessing a strong sense of purpose means committing to a singular and defined goal, like curing cancer or providing all of Africa with fresh running water. As a result, many of us are likely to feel that 'A Purpose' is something we do not have. However, purpose is a bigger-picture thing than the achievement of a specific goal, no matter how worthy that goal might be. It is a state of being, rather than a state of doing: less about the actions we take or the missions that we choose, and more about our intention. Purpose is the present-moment understanding of *why* we do what we do. Because of this, the feeling of inspiration that it provides can be with us all the way through the journey, not just when we get successfully to the destination.

The importance of facing out

When it comes to the meaning we choose to give our lives, facing out tends to be more fulfilling than facing in. Many people are driven by a sense of purpose that focuses exclusively back on themselves – usually, the desire to be the best they can be at whatever it is that they are doing. While this is clearly preferable to having no sense of purpose, it has a potentially serious shortfall. If we choose this route, we run the risk of missing out on one of our basic requirements for a sense of wellbeing. Only by giving at least some of our attention to something other than ourselves can we meet the sixth (and highest) of the human needs: contribution.

We already know that contribution is a little bit magic. In Chapter 4, when we first looked at the list of needs, I mentioned that this one has a special place because of its capacity to satisfy all the others as well. When we're making a meaningful contribution we find certainty in the consistency of our intent, and in knowing that we're giving back; variety is made easier because when the goal is about more than just ourselves, our paths will be less limited; we get significance from the knowledge that we're making a difference; we get love and connection from the bond created between us and those to whom (or with whom) we contribute; and because all the deficiency needs can be fulfilled, at least in part, we will automatically find ourselves able to focus more on our need for growth.

Giving has also been shown to be good for our physical health. Multiple studies have demonstrated a link between generosity and improvements in chronic illnesses, including HIV and multiple sclerosis,[4] as well as a reduced likelihood of imminent death in the elderly.[5]

And so, when I say that a sense of purpose is the final piece of the happiness puzzle, I really mean that a contributive, Other-focused form of purpose is what we require in order to feel the most healthy, happy and whole.

The role of empathy

Thankfully, both the ability and desire to make a meaningful contribution can come about quite naturally when we choose to make mentors out of our monsters. Learning how to willingly experience all that life has to offer increases our ability to connect because empathy is part and parcel of the process.

Self-awareness makes authentic connection easier because we can not only see other people's monsters and the effect that they have, but we can also see *past* them to the person underneath. So long as we're not under any immediate threat ourselves, empathy inspires us with a very healthy desire to reach out and heal the pain felt by those we interact with. It does this because emotional intelligence blurs the boundaries between Self and Other. With empathy, we can feel their pain almost as if it is our own.

That might sound negative but it's quite the opposite. At the same time as enabling us to understand the suffering of others, empathy heals our own pain by teaching us that we're not alone. In fact, it teaches us that all our emotions are human, natural and, ultimately, quite beautiful – because they are the very things that bring us all together into the same place. This is why empathy is the antidote to shame. We cease to feel the need to hide our feelings for fear of disconnection when we can see that it's our emotions that actually make connection possible.

Empathy doesn't stop at people like us. It doesn't even stop at people. I believe our inner Children can provide us with the ability to connect with the whole of the world and everything it contains if we give them the chance. So it doesn't really matter whether you direct your attention towards individual people, groups of people, animals or the environment; or if you channel your energy into the realm of art, academia, philosophy, literature, sport, science, cooking, crafts or homemaking. So long as at least some part of your day affords you the ability to make a contribution to something that you *feel* to be meaningful, you could find yourself living a happier life.

Dissolving the self

When felt at its strongest, a sense of empathetic connection can direct our awareness away from the self so entirely that we forget about the concept of 'me' altogether (temporarily, at least). This selfless state, where the ego and all of its angst can dissolve away, could be the greatest gift that purpose has to offer.

The psychologist, Steve Taylor, calls this optimal condition the 'trans-purposive state'. This is his description:

> This emerges as we move further beyond an egoic orientation, when our own desires, interests and fears begin to fade in importance, and we connect to a larger superconscious source, for which we become the expression. It's a question of us uncovering a deep, authentic purpose inside us – a purpose which is natural to us, which is an expression of our innate potentials and inclinations – and aligning ourselves to it.[6]

Rather than feeling as though we possess a purpose, the experience of the trans-purposive state is one of being carried forward *by* our purpose. Effortlessly. If finding meaning while chasing mirages and fighting monsters is like swimming upstream, then an alignment with this kind of purpose would feel like turning to swim downstream, with the water. In other words, a sense of empathetic purpose can mean that we step, more often, into a state of flow. Facing out helps us to get fully *involved* in the races we run, the games we play and even the fights we choose to have, without being too *invested* in the outcome. As Csikszentmihalyi demonstrated (see page 48), the more flow moments we experience, the happier our lives will be, but we have to give up the fight first because flow can only really be found in the space beyond winning and losing.

Adding Purpose

Energy cannot be created or destroyed. It can only be changed from one form to another.

The first law of thermodynamics

So, how do we go about uncovering a 'deep, authentic purpose inside us'? I'm not going to give you a process for finding your 'life's purpose' in one short chapter at the end of this book. We'd need way more time for that. However, I do think that we all already have what we need to get in touch with an authentic sense of meaning.

The key, I believe, is to allow the pain that we have experienced personally to motivate us to make a difference. Even better, we can use the (dis)comfort of our own 'not ... enough' to define the type of impact we'd most like to have on the world. It's the ultimate monster evolution: to repurpose the energy we would otherwise have spent fighting the Self, and direct it away from us in a way that can benefit the Other.

Not everyone will do this in quite such an obvious way as I did. We definitely don't all need to become therapists, coaches or to write a self-help book in order to fulfil our need for contribution. Neither does it mean that we all have to drop everything we're doing and devote our lives to some kind of cause. The sense of making a purposeful contribution can arise out of actions large or small, when we just allow ourselves to see (and feel) the effect we have on others. We can achieve a sense of empathetic purpose by writing a letter, calling a relative or taking a moment to be present with someone we know to be struggling; we can feel it when we buy from sustainable sources or make the effort to get hold of energy-saving appliances; and we can build it by joining an evening class to learn about something important to us, or by involving ourselves with a charity or political group that ticks the boxes we most care about.

Expression

In some way, suffering ceases to be suffering at the moment it finds a meaning.

Viktor E. Frankl, Austrian neurologist,
psychiatrist and Holocaust survivor.[7]

A powerful sense of purpose can grow out of authentic, emotional expression. So many people fear the act of communicating their deepest feelings – through any medium – because they simply don't believe that their experience is important enough to share. But no one person feels an emotion that's any more worthy of expression than the next. You could blog, paint, dance or speak from the heart in order to express the way that you feel. You could write poems, music, stories or screenplays. You can be literal about it or entirely abstract, and you don't even have to publish or exhibit what you create in order for it to count. The reason I included sections for you to draw or journal about your thinking as you worked through this book was because in doing so, you would be creatively expressing your feelings. Regardless of whether anyone else sees the results or not, these are all ways of taking pain from the inside and letting it breathe the fresh air on the outside.*

The Diving Down process is a tool that serves the same purpose. By pausing to ask those four key questions, you give yourself the opportunity to express your thoughts, your feelings and your limiting beliefs in the moments when those things matter the most. On the page following this conclusion, I have included a final summary of the Diving Down process along with one new addition, based on the imagery of your younger self. My intention is to provide you with a powerful tool to take away having read this book, so that you have a means of choosing Authorship whenever and wherever you need it.

Communicating

No matter what means of expression you might feel the most comfortable with, choosing to communicate from a place of emotional authenticity can help you to both identify and feel a sense of purpose that is unique to you. You'll also feel vulnerable and exposed, and that's a good thing. Empathy is the antidote to shame, and expression is the means by which empathy happens. It brings our monsters into a space where they can not only heal us, but others too.

Believe me, I'm well aware of how frightening it can be to disclose the things that have made us feel 'not ... enough'. However, when it comes to shame, communication is the very best thing that we can do. We all feel reluctant to share the darkest parts of our experience because our minds believe that it's safer to keep our monsters hidden in the shadows. But that's only because they don't know how beautiful they can be when we bring them into the light.

---

* If you'd like to take the courageous step of sharing your emotional experience online, then I'd love to hear from you. You can tweet or post on Instagram or Facebook using the hashtag: #mindmonsters. Please feel free to share your metaphors, memory reframes, Diving Down findings or monster-to-mentor evolution images. No matter how personal these things can seem, I can guarantee you that you're not alone. Visit mindmonsters.online to view other people's contributions.

Lovable Monsters

Ultimately, whether we perceive our unconscious reactions as monsters or mentors depends entirely on our perspective in the moment. Choosing Authorship means being open to growth, especially when we're experiencing some kind of hurt. It means diving willingly into our painful emotions, rewriting the limiting stories we tell ourselves and constructing better metaphors to live by.

However, as with pretty much everything we've discussed in this book, the switch is not a one-time thing. I believe that no matter how much 'work' we do, we'll always have the odd monster moment. There will always be times when we feel insecure or anxious, and there will probably always be times when we screw ourselves over. But that's OK – because those experiences make us human.

It's perhaps the greatest irony of all that the things we least like about ourselves are the very things that make life purposeful, that make connection possible and that make love worthwhile.

So, don't slay your monster. Please. Love it, learn from it and then send it out into the world where its lessons can make a meaningful difference instead.

Appendix 1

The Complete Diving Down Process

Over the course of this book, we have looked at four different variations of the Diving Down process: in Chapter 8, we looked at the Diving Down technique as a tool for increasing self-awareness and challenging your reality map (see page 194); in Chapter 9, we explored it as a way of creating an emotional shift by introducing metaphorical suggestions (see page 226); in Chapter 12, we integrated your anchored colour into the process, so that you can Dive Down into a state of self-acceptance (see page 278); and in the 'Evolution IV' task section, we added your monster evolution and/or mentor integration imagery into the technique (see page 318).

This section includes a summary of all the variations together, along with the different kinds of situations in which they might each be of the most use. Option iv on page 333 is completely new, so make sure you take a look at that.

The first three steps of the basic process never change:

Step 1: Ask, 'What am I thinking?'

Observe your thought processes and narrate your internal dialogue.

Step 2: Ask, 'What am I feeling?

Drop your awareness right into your body to curiously observe the way you experience the connected emotions.

Step 3: Ask, 'What is the monster story?'

Let the relevant limiting belief or fearful perspective float into your awareness by asking, 'What is it that I'm *really* afraid of right now?' Then create some distance between that idea and reality by inserting the monster story into the following sentence:

'I am feeling (X emotion) because a part of my mind wants to believe ... (insert relevant monster story)'

Step 4: Now breathe ...

We now have a number of different options for this step. They each serve a slightly different function. Here's a summary:

i) Now breathe ... and challenge your reality map

The most basic option is just to breathe and ask the New Territories Question: 'If I were to edit out that monster story, how would I see this differently?'

This version can be used for any situation. The purpose is simply to look beyond the (dis)comfortable norm, and therefore train your mind in finding the Golden Linings. (See page 176 for more detail.)

ii) Now breathe ... and play with the metaphor

This is the variation we took a look at in Chapter 9. Here you can apply some suggestions for a change in your emotional state by playing with the metaphorical representation of your feelings that you created with the question, 'What am I feeling?'

This option will work best at times when an understandable but unnecessarily intense emotion is distracting you from what you'd like to be doing. Common examples include performance anxiety or any other kind of worry, failure to sleep and lingering Drama Triangle emotions like resentment.

As always, start by breathing through your experience and relaxing your muscles. Then, ask yourself this question: 'If there was something that I could do with this symbol, which would encourage a positive shift in the way that I feel, what would that be?'

Close your eyes to focus on the metaphor while you consider and apply the possible answers. Stay relaxed and curious as you play with the options, repeating those that work and continuing the conversation by changing those that aren't accepted. Once you have created the shift you want, ask yourself the New Territories Question to finish: 'If I were to edit out that monster story, how would I see this differently?' (See page 199 for more detail.)

iii) Now breathe ... and fire your anchor

To bring the work you did in Chapter 12 into the process, you can use the colour you anchored to a state of self-acceptance during the memory reframing task. This option will work well as a way to enter into a more peaceful and relaxed state of mind or to direct your awareness away from yourself and onto a better object for your attention (like the person or people you're talking to, or the work you are doing).

Again, start by making sure that you're breathing and relaxing your muscles. Then, either imagine your colour flowing into your own body for a state of calm or out onto whatever or whomever you'd rather be focusing on in a more self-assured way.

After you've finished with that visualisation, as always, you can ask yourself the New Territories Question to make new plans for ways in which you'd like to act or speak differently in the situation you're considering: 'If I were to edit out that monster story, how would I see this differently?' (See page 199 for more detail.)

iv) Now breathe ... and connect to your 'little monster' (new addition)

One of my favourite visualisations for letting go of my fear of failure is the image of my younger self toddling happily through her little race. The reason this is so powerful for me is that I can accept that little girl along with all of her natural and human imperfections. I can see that they make her more loveable, not less. If there was a particular moment in the memory task that could represent a similar kind of unconditional acceptance of your younger self, then you can, of course, use that in the Diving Down process.

Simply call the imagery to mind as you breathe and relax your muscles. Then, challenge your reality map by asking the New Territories Question: 'If I were to edit out that monster story, how would I see this differently?' (See page 275 for original memory-reframing process.)

v) Now breathe ... and evolve your monster

Finally, you can add the imagery you created in the fourth Evolution section. Your options here are to imagine either sending your anchored colour to your monster, so that it makes its metamorphosis into mentor, or you can visualise the process of integrating your mentor back into the whole. Alternatively, you could combine these visualisations into one smooth process.

Every time you make this kind of suggestion, you will compound the idea that when you accept even the most challenging aspects of your experience, you create the opportunity to grow and develop. Because this option is a little more abstract than the others, you can apply it to any kind of situation or issue that you like.

Then, once again, don't forget to ask the New Territories Question: **'If I were to edit out that monster story, how would I see this differently?'**

For the full Evolution process, see page 323.

Taking action

No matter which visualisation you choose, you will want to make sure that you're open to learning whatever your mentor could be there to teach you, and also to taking action. You don't need any new questions to elicit that kind of information. You're already well acquainted with two different ways of considering response-able action:

The Action Question: **'Is there anything I can do about this right now?'**

And perhaps most importantly:

The Golden Linings Question: **'What can I create out of this?'**

As always, if you ever have an answer to either of those questions, the quicker you act, the better. Moving into a place of self-acceptance can make new decisions easier to take, but that doesn't mean they're necessarily going to be easy. The old call to (dis)comfort is still likely to be there, even if it is fainter. But you don't have to keep listening to that same old song now, do you?

Appendix 2

Calibration

Tracking Your Progress

At the beginning of this book, you filled out a form to help you objectively quantify your level of emotional wellbeing. Here it is again. Without looking back at your original scores, complete the form below based on the last two weeks of your life, going with the first rating that comes to mind for each category.

Emotional Wellbeing Scale	0 None of the time	1 Rarely	2 Some of the time	3 Often	4 All of the time
I've been feeling optimistic about the future.					
I've been feeling useful.					
I've been feeling relaxed.					
I've been dealing with problems well.					
I've been thinking clearly.					
I've been feeling close to other people.					
I've been able to make up my own mind about things.					

Emotional Wellbeing Scale	0 None of the time	1 Rarely	2 Some of the time	3 Often	4 All of the time
I've been able to think creatively.					
I've been able to assert my own views and opinions.					
I've been enjoying the things I do.					
I've been feeling as though I'm learning and developing.					
I've been feeling as if I'm contributing to something important.					
Total score:					

Take a look back at your initial scores to compare the two. I'd like to think that you will have created a positive shift in at least one category.

Of course, whether or not you see a significant improvement in your results will depend on how long ago you started the book, how your life was going then and what has happened since. Regardless of what you found this time around, I would recommend you keep this form (along with the Needs Audit on pages 94–6) somewhere safe. Both of these tools can be helpful, both to keep track of how you're doing and to identify the specific life contexts that you could do with focusing a little more attention on.

On that note, just to leave you with one final question, consider this:

Which of the above categories yielded the smallest scores for you, and what measures could you take today to improve those areas of your life?

As always, if you have an answer (or answers) to that question, then you know what to do. It's time to take action.

Monster Evolutions

Another way of getting an idea of the changes you've made, of course, would be to look at your monster drawings or descriptions. Did the way you imagined that part of your personality change over the course of the book? I'd love to know!

Reach out via these channels to show me how your metaphor evolved:

Website: https://www.mindmonsters.online
Twitter: @hazelgale
Medium: @hazelgale
Instagram: @hazel.gale.therapy
Facebook: hazelgalehypnotherapy
You can also join my Facebook group at http://www.facebook.com/groups/fight.thebook.

To either share your own monster drawing or view other people's creations on social media, use the hashtag **#mindmonsters**.

Appendix 3

Task Index

*A List of the Different Tools, Tips
and Processes Included in* The Mind Monster Solution

All of the techniques and tools that you've learned while reading this book are here for your continued use. Below is an index of the interactive sections that you might benefit from repeating whenever you hit a snag.

Page 19: Evolution I
Identifying Self-sabotage
The Evolution sections in this book are not tasks to return to so much as a means of tracking your progress as you read through. However, I will include them in this index for reference regardless. Evolution I was where you were first invited to visualise your monster (the aspect of self that we can hold responsible for your moments of self-sabotage).

Page 44: Analytical Questioning
Questions for Understanding a Particular Issue
These questions are here for you to analyse specific problems. Sometimes, just recognising the boundaries of an issue – its context, the people connected, the kind of thoughts it inspires and the particular feelings it triggers – can help you to get a handle on it. In the cases when a little extra knowledge on its own doesn't help, these questions can give you some clues as to how to delve a little deeper using the other tasks in this book.

Page 76: Taking the Tour
A short process for exploring the ideas associated with your formative years.

Page 78: Rewriting the Future
A visualisation of an improving future.

Page 83: Understanding Your Motivation
A process for identifying your individual motivators (values) in a particular context.

Page 86: The Hierarchy of Importance
A process for arranging your values into their hierarchy of importance.

Page 94: Completing an Overall Needs Audit
Questions to ascertain your levels of needs fulfilment.

Page 101: Considering Better Strategies
Questions for understanding which needs your self-sabotaging behaviours could be attempting to fulfil. Then, questions for identifying which of the deficiency needs appear(s) to be the most problematic in a chosen context, and how you could focus more on the 'growth-and-being' needs to tip the balance.

Page 109: Creating a Driver Symbol
A short process for identifying the specific feeling of your primary driver urge.

Page 113: Monsters and Mirages
Identifying the importance of individual values ('chunking up').

Page 119: Identifying Your Monster's Favourite Stories
A means of recognising the difference between towards and away-from values, and identifying the limiting beliefs hidden within the latter.

Page 126: Challenge It
A task for turning away-from values into towards-focused motivators.

Page 137: Evolution II
Facing the Monster
Here you revisited your monster visualisation. This time you imagined that you could face the most resisted part of your personality.

Page 159: Drama Spotting
Questions for identifying Drama Triangle activity (unhealthy interactions and relationships with other people, habits or situations).

Page 172: The Action Question

A magic question to ask yourself in order to identify necessary behaviours and/or recognise self-sabotaging reactions.

Page 175: The Golden Linings Question

A second magic question to ask yourself in order to discover what you can create out of a moment of challenge. Then, a task for applying that to your life.

Page 176: What Can You Create?

A task for utilising the Golden Linings Question.

Page 186: Choice

Questions for identifying the habits your mind might have learned that allow it to resist your emotions.

Page 190: Breathing Technique

For creating a state of relaxation.

Page 201: Diving Down into Self-awareness

This is the basic Diving Down process. Here you learn to use those four important questions, plus continuous breathing, in order to explore the difference between your conscious and unconscious perception of a challenging moment, and to ensure that you're not resisting your monster's stories.

Page 217: Evolution III
Monster Ownership

Here you face your monster again, but this time you witness it taking ownership of its own stories.

Page 232: Diving Down into Emotional Fluidity

This is the first addition to the Diving Down process. Here you learn how to make metaphorical suggestions for a positive shift in your emotional state.

Page 244: Telling Your Own Story
This is the first of the two in-depth processes in Part 3. Here you create a metaphorical narrative to suggest a certain desired behaviour, outcome or emotional state to your unconscious mind.

Page 254: Accessing the Bigger Picture
An additional task for your metaphorical narrative: viewing the story from different angles.

Page 263: Creating Your Temporal Map
Here you learn how to create a visualisation for the timeline of your life.

Page 280: Earthing Your Live-wires
This is the second in-depth process in Part 3. Here you learn how to reframe your problematic past experiences, so that you can stop your mind from repeating old trauma.

Page 287: A Colourful Anchor
Following on from the previous process, here you learn how to use a certain colour to cue to a feeling of connectedness, love, safety or psychological needs fulfilment.

Page 290: Diving Down into Self-acceptance
Here you learn how to use your anchored colour as an antidote to the shame of self-sabotage, or as a means to connect more fully with others.

Page 316: Evolution IV
A Metaphor for Wholeness
In this final Evolution section, you use your anchor to encourage your mind to accept your monster and allow it to function as a mentor.

Page 319: Diving Down into Continued Evolution
This is the final variation on the Diving Down process. Here you use the imagery from Evolution IV to empathise with and/or reintegrate your monster.

Appendix 4
Evolution Task Drawing Pages

Evolution I

On the opposite page, draw a representation of what you imagined during the visualisation task on pages 21–2.

Consider this question:

If there was something you could give to or do to the self-sabotaging part of your personality that would solve the problem, what would that be?

...... Destroy it ....

....

....

....

....

Avoidance

Procrastinaⁿ

Fear of
failure.

Won't be as good as
anyone
expects.

Evolution II

On the opposite page, draw a representation of what you imagined during the visualisation task on page 138.

Evolution III

On the opposite page, draw a representation of what you imagined during the visualisation task on page 217.

Evolution IV

On the opposite page, draw a representation of what you imagined during the visualisation task on page 317.

Notes on integration:

....

....

....

....

....

Appendix 5

Task Forms

Forms to Fill in for the Chapter 4 and 5 Values Processes

Motivators (Page 83)

Your chosen context:	
1	
2	
3	
4	
5	
6	
7	
8	
9	
10	
11	
12	
13	
14	

Hierarchy of Values (Page 88)

Your chosen context:	
1	
2	
3	
4	
5	
6	
7	
8	
9	
10	
11	
12	
13	
14	

Monsters and Mirages (Page 113)

Question	Answer
Value 1:	
What's important to you about Value 1?	A1:
What's important to you about Answer 1?	A2:
What's important to you about Answer 2?	A3:
Value 2:	
What's important to you about Value 2?	A1:
What's important to you about Answer 1?	A2:
What's important to you about Answer 2?	A3:
Value 3:	
What's important to you about Value 3?	A1:
What's important to you about Answer 1?	A2:
What's important to you about Answer 2?	A3:
Value 4:	
What's important to you about Value 4?	A1:
What's important to you about Answer 1?	A2:
What's important to you about Answer 2?	A3:

Question	Answer
Value 5:	
What's important to you about Value 5?	A1:
What's important to you about Answer 1?	A2:
What's important to you about Answer 2?	A3:
Value 6:	
What's important to you about Value 6?	A1:
What's important to you about Answer 1?	A2:
What's important to you about Answer 2?	A3:
Value 7:	
What's important to you about Value 7?	A1:
What's important to you about Answer 1?	A2:
What's important to you about Answer 2?	A3:
Value 8:	
What's important to you about Value 8?	A1:
What's important to you about Answer 1?	A2:
What's important to you about Answer 2?	A3:

Away-from Statements
and Limiting Beliefs (Page 119)

Away-from Statements:
Potential Limiting Beliefs:

Draw your monster and its favourite stories on the opposite page.

Acknowledgements

I have a long list of people to acknowledge, thank and send my undying love to for the help they've given me while writing this book.

Firstly, I must thank my wonderful boyfriend, Luka Špik, for his endless support, snuggles and cups of tea; and my mother, Sue Gale, and sister, Tess Gale, for putting up with my many ramblings about monsters, mirages and mentors over the past year and a half.

Huge thanks to my agent, Rachel Mills, and editor, Tamsin English, for their help all the way through the process. Also to freelance editor Edward Tripper, who was the one to suggest I write this book in the first place, and who gave me invaluable help in editing and finessing both the proposal and finished product.

My heartfelt gratitude also goes out to my good friend and colleague, Eve Parmiter, for being number one on my speed dial for help with the contents of this book. Also to my equally good friend, Neil Brown, who tirelessly helped me to comb through the detail in the latter stages. Also to freelance editor Annie Mckie, who I met in the Forest of Dean. Annie gave me wonderful and vital feedback when I visited her writing retreat (twice) to immerse myself fully into this process.

My thanks go out to everyone I have trained with as a therapist: first, to the team at the Institute of Clinical Hypnotherapy where I started my therapy training; then to Trevor and Rebecca Silvester for founding the Quest Institute, accepting me as a student, teaching me wonderfully and then lending their ongoing support; and also to my supervisor, Russell Davis, for both his supervision and his excellent coaching as I've been writing this book.

Massive thanks, of course, to Han-Ter Park who put together the lovely illustrations and diagrams included (largely, by all accounts, at approximately two in the morning, fuelled entirely by coffee).

Also, my thanks to Lucy Fry, Henry Johnson, Ellen Price, Alan

Henderson, Jayne Newman, Sharon Cavanagh, Sophie Chisholm, Jonathan Crocker, Sean Heneghan, Joanna West, Lydia Durkin-George, Kyran O'Neill and Simona Dvorackova for their brilliant feedback.

Of course, my thanks go out to everyone who has trained (and trained with) me as a fighter as well. Stuart Lawson et al. at Paragon, where I first found my love of fighting, then the ABA clubs I trained at later as I progressed into boxing – Gator ABC and Islington Boxing Club. A special mention goes to Audi Kinga for being the most wonderful fight coach I've ever met, and to my longstanding training partners, Valerian Spicer and Oriance Lungu, for being my inspiration.

Finally, to all of my clients, without whom I would not understand any of the contents of this book in the way that I do. No matter how incredible the therapy training you undertake is, I'm certain the people you work with will always teach you more. A special thanks to everyone who allowed their story to be printed (some anonymously, some not). You are all amazing human beings.

Get in Contact

Online Resources and Communities

I'd love to hear about your experience of reading this book, completing the tasks and, of course, the changes that you make. If you'd like to reach out, there are various different ways to get in touch.

Facebook community

Share your experience with myself and other readers on the Facebook group: http://www.facebook.com/groups/fight.thebook.

Twitter

Tweet me at @HazelGale

Instagram

There are some (optional) opportunities to draw the visualisations you come up with as you read this book. If you are happy to share, I'd love to see them! You can find me on Instagram here: @hazel.gale.therapy.

#mindmonsters

I will be using #mindmonsters and #fightthebook for online posts relating to this book. If you'd like to join the conversation or share your experience, you can use these hashtags on any social-media platform.

Website

For more information about my practice, or to sign up to my mailing list to hear about lectures, workshops, courses and other events, visit my website: http://hazelgale.com. This is also where you can find the guided meditations that accompany each part of the book (see page 5 for all the links).

Visit https://www.mindmonsters.online to view a gallery of other people's mind monster visualisations, hear the monsters' stories and *take part*.

Bibliography

Banville, John, *The Sea* (Pan Macmillan, 2008)

Bass, Ellen and Davis, Laura, *The Courage to Heal: A Guide for Women Survivors of Child Sexual Abuse* (Random House, 2002)

Brown, Brené, *Daring Greatly: How the Courage to be Vulnerable Transforms the Way We Live, Love, Parent and Lead* (Portfolio Penguin, 2013)

Brown, Brené, *The Gifts of Imperfection: Let Go of Who You Think You're Supposed to Be and Embrace Who You Are* (Hazelden Publishing, 2010)

Brown, Brené, *I Thought It Was Just Me (but it isn't): Making the Journey from "What Will People Think?" to "I Am Enough"* (Penguin, 2007)

Brown, Brené, *Rising Strong* (Vermilion, an imprint of Ebury Publishing, Penguin Random House, 2015)

Brown, Oliver, 'Rio 2016: Newly relaxed Michael Phelps determined to enjoy his Olympic swansong', *Telegraph* (7 August 2016) <http://www.telegraph.co.uk/olympics/2016/08/07/rio-2016-newly-relaxed-michael-phelps-determined-to-enjoy-his-ol/>

Carson, Richard David, *Taming Your Gremlin: A Surprisingly Simple Method for Getting Out of Your Own Way* (William Morrow, an imprint of HarperCollins Publishers, 2003)

Chandler, Steve, *Reinventing Yourself: How To Become the Person You've Always Wanted to Be* (Career Press, 2005)

Csikszentmihalyi, Mihaly, *Flow: The Classic Work on How to Achieve Happiness* (revised edition: Rider, an imprint of the Random House Group, 2002)

Dweck, Dr Carol S., *Mindset: How You Can Fulfil Your Potential* (Robinson, 2012)

Forrest, Lynne, *The Three Faces of Victim – An Overview of the Drama Triangle* (lynneforrest.com)

Frankl, Viktor E., *Man's Search For Meaning* (reprint, Simon and Schuster, 1985)

Freud, Sigmund, *Oxford Dictionary of Medical Quotations*, Pete Mcdonald, ed. (OUP, 2004), p. 37

Gendlin, Eugine T., *Focusing: How to Gain Direct Access to Your Body's Knowledge* (first published in 1978 by Everest House; updated edition: Rider, an imprint of Ebury Press, Random House, 2003)

Gibbs Jr, Raymond W., 'Categorization and Metaphor Understanding', *Psychological Review*, vol. 99, issue 3 (1992).

Gilbert, Elizabeth, *Eat, Pray, Love: One Woman's Search for Everything Across Italy, India and Indonesia* (Bloomsbury Publishing, 2007)

Gilbert, Elizabeth, *Big Magic: Creative Living Beyond Fear* (Bloomsbury Publishing, 2015)

Gottschall, Jonathan, *The Storytelling Animal: How Stories Make Us Human* (Mariner Books, an imprint of Houghton Mifflin Harcourt Publishing Company, 2013)

Heller, Steven, Ph.D. and Steele, Terry, *Monsters and Magical Sticks: There is No Such Thing as Hypnosis* (New Falcon Publications, 1991)

Hendricks, Gay, *The Big Leap: Conquer Your Hidden Fear and Take Life to the Next Level* (HarperOne, an imprint of HarperCollins, 2010)

Jung, Dr Carl G., *The Archetypes and the Collective Unconscious (Second Edition)* (first published in England by Routledge & Kegan Paul Ltd, 1959; second edition, 1968)

Jung, Dr Carl G., *The Undiscovered Self* with *Symbols and the Interpretation of Dreams* from *The Collected Works of C. G. Jung* (Princeton University Press, 1990)

Kurzweil, Ray, *How to Create a Mind: The Secret of Human Thought Revealed* (Duckworth Overlook, 2013)

Lakoff, George and Johnson, Mark, *Metaphors We Live By* (The University of Chicago Press, 2003)

Landau, Mark and Sullivan, Daniel of the University of Kansas, and Greenberg, Jeff of the University of Arizona, 'Evidence That Self-Relevant Motives and Metaphoric Framing Interact to Influence Political and Social Attitudes', *Psychological Science* 20(7) (November, 2009), 1421–7

LeDoux, Joseph E., 'Manipulating Memory', published in *The Scientist*, March 2009

Lehrer, Jonah, *The Decisive Moment: How the Brain Makes Up its Mind* (Canongate Books Ltd, 2010)

Mcdonald, Pete, ed., *Oxford Dictionary of Medical Quotations*, (OUP, 2004)

Mountcastle, Vernon B., 'The View from Within: Pathways to the Study of Perception,' *Johns Hopkins Medical Journal*, 136 (1975), 109–31

Nader, Karim, Schafe, Glenn E. and LeDoux, Joseph E., 'Fear memories require protein synthesis in the amygdala for reconsolidation after retrieval', published in *Nature* 406 (2000), 722–6

Neisser, U. and Harsch, N. (1992), 'Phantom flashbulbs: False Recollections of Hearing the News about Challenger'. In Winograd, E. and Neisser U. (eds.), *Emory Symposia in Cognition, 4. Affect and Accuracy in Recall: Studies of 'Flashbulb' Memories* (CUP, 2010)

Nhat Hanh, Thich, *Fear: Essential Wisdom for Getting Through the Storm* (Random House, 2012)

Nørretranders, Tor, *The User Illusion: Cutting Consciousness Down to Size* (Penguin Books, 1999)

Oman, Doug of the University of California, Berkeley, Thoresen, Carl E. and Mcmahon, Kay, 'Volunteerism and Mortality among the Community-dwelling Elderly', published in the *Journal of Health Psychology*, vol. 4, issue 3 (1 May 1999), 301–16

Pennebaker, James W. Ph.D. and Evans, John E., Ed.D., *Expressive Writing: Words that Heal* (Idyll Arbor, Inc., 2014)

Post, Stephen, *Why Good Things Happen to Good People* (Crown/Archetype, 2007)

Rich, Adrienne, *'Claiming an Education,' a talk given at the Douglass College convocation in 1977*, first printed in the magazine *The Common Woman*, 1977

Russell, Bertrand, *The Basic Writings of Bertrand Russell* (Routledge, 2009)

Sapolsky, Robert, 'This is Your Brain on Metaphors', *New York Times* (14 November 2010)

Schneider, Pat, *How the Light Gets In: Writing as a Spiritual Practice* (OUP USA, 2013)

Shaw, George Bernard, *Back to Methuselah* (The Floating Press, 2010)

Silvester, Trevor, *Cognitive Hypnotherapy: 'What's that about and how can I use it?'* (Matador, an imprint of Troubador Publishing, 2010)

Silvester, Trevor, *How to Click: How to Date and Find Love with Confidence* (Hachette UK, 2015)

Silvester, Trevor. *The Question is the Answer: Focusing on Solutions with Cognitive Hypnotherapy* (The Quest Institute, 2006)

Silvester, Trevor, *Wordweaving: The Science of Suggestion* (The Quest Institute, 2003)

Steiner, Claud M. *Scripts People Live: Transactional Analysis of Life Scripts* (New York: Grove Press, 1990)

Sullivan, Wendy and Rees, Judy, *Clean Language: Revealing Metaphors and Opening Minds* (Crown House Publishing, 2008)

Taylor, Steve Ph.D., *A Model of Purpose: From Survival To Transpersonal Purpose*, published in the *Transpersonal Psychology Review*, vol. 18, no. 1 (spring 2016)

Tolle, Eckhart, *A New Earth: Create a Better Life* (Penguin UK, 2009)

Wolinsky, Stephen, Ph.D., *Trances People Live: Healing Approaches in Quantum Psychology* (Bramble Books, 1991)

Endnotes

Introduction

1 Koschwanez, H.E., Kerse, N., Darragh, M., Jarrett, P., Booth, R.J., and Broadbent, E., 'Expressive writing and wound healing in older adults: A randomized controlled trial', *Psychosomatic Medicine*, vol. 75, issue 6, (2013), pp. 581–590;
Pennebaker, J.W., Kiecolt-Glasser, J.K., and Glasser, R., 'Disclosure of traumas and immune function: health implications for psychotherapy', *Journal of Consulting and Clinical Psychology*, vol. 56, (1988), pp. 239–245;
Lumley, M.A., Leisen, J.C., Partridge, R.T., Meyer, T.M., Radcliffe, A.M., Macklem, D.J., and Granda, J.L., 'Does emotional disclosure about stress improve health in rheumatoid arthritis? Randomized, controlled trials of written and spoken disclosure', *Pain*, vol. 152, issue 4, (2011), pp. 866–877.

2 Smyth, J.M., and Arigo, D., 'Recent evidence supports emotion-regulation interventions for improving health in at-risk and clinical populations', *Current Opinion in Psychiatry*, vol. 22, issue 2, (2009), pp. 205–210;
Smyth, J.M., Stone A.A., Hurewitz, A., and Kaell, A., 'Effects of writing about stressful experiences on symptom reduction in patients with asthma or rheumatoid arthritis: a randomized trial', *Journal of American Medical Association*, vol. 281, (1999), pp. 1304–1309.

3 Petrie, K.P., Fontanilla, I., Thomas, M.G., Booth, R.J., and Pennebaker. J.W., 'Effect of written emotional expression on immune function in patients with HIV infection: A randomized trial', *Psychosomatic Medicine*, vol. 66, (2004), pp. 272–275.

4 Halpert, A., Rybin, D., and Doros, G. 'Expressive writing is a promising therapeutic modality for the management of IBS: a pilot study', *American Journal of Gastroenterology*, vol. 105, issue 11, (2010), pp. 2440–2448.

5 Henry, E.A., Schlegel, R.J., Talley, A.E., Molix, L.A., and Bettencourt, B.A., 'The feasibility and effectiveness of expressive writing for rural and urban breast cancer survivors', *Oncology Nursing Forum*, vol. 37, issue 6, (2010), pp. 749–757;

Low, C.A., Stanton, A.L., Bower, J.E., and Gyllenhammer, L., 'A randomized controlled trial of emotionally expressive writing for women with metastatic breast cancer', *Health Psychology*, vol. 29, issue 4, (2010), pp. 460–466;

De Moor, C., Sterner, J., Hall, M., Warneke, C., Gilani, Z., Amato, R., et al, 'A pilot study of the effects of expressive writing on psychological and behavioural adjustment in patients enrolled in a phase II trial of vaccine therapy for metastatic renal cell carcinoma', *Health Psychology*, vol. 21, (2002), pp. 615–619; Rosenberg, MA, H.J., Rosenberg, PhD, S.D., Ernstoff, MD, M.S., Wolford. PhD, G.I., Amdur, MD, R.J., Elshamy, AMP, M.R., and Pennebaker, PhD, J.W., 'Expressive disclosure and health outcomes in a prostate cancer population', *International Journal of Psychiatry in Medicine*, vol. 32, issue 1, (2002), pp. 37–53.

6 Barclay, L.J., and Skarlicki, D.P., 'Healing the wounds of organizational injustice: Examining the benefits of expressive writing', *Journal of Applied Psychology*, vol. 94, issue 2, (2009), p. 511.

7 Lepore, S.J., 'Expressive writing moderates the relation between intrusive thoughts and depressive symptoms', *Journal of Personality and Social Psychology*, vol. 73, pp. 1030–1037.

8 Lumley, M.A., and Provenzano, K.M., 'Stress management through emotional disclosure improves academic performance among college students with physical symptoms', *Journal of Educational Psychology*, vol. 95, (2003), pp. 641–649;

Cameron, L.D., and Nicholls, G., 'Expression of stressful experiences through writing: Effects of a self- regulation manipulation for pessimists and optimists', *Health Psychology*, vol. 17, (1998), pp. 84–92; Pennebaker, J.W., Colder, M., and Sharp, L.K., 'Accelerating the coping process', *Journal of Personality and Social Psychology*, vol. 58, (1990), pp. 528–537.

9 Klein, K., and Boals, A. 'Expressive writing can increase working memory capacity', *Journal of Experimental Psychology: General*, vol. 130, (2001), pp. 520–533.

10 Pennebaker, J.W., and Graybeal, A., 'Patterns of natural language use:

Disclosure, personality, and social integration', *Current Directions in Psychological Science*, vol. 10, (2001), pp. 90–93;

Baddeley, J.L., and Pennebaker, J.W. 'A postdeployment expressive writing intervention for military couples: a randomized controlled trial', *The Journal of Trauma Stress*, vol. 24, issue 5, (2011), pp. 581–585.

Part 1: Perception

1 Nørretranders, Tor, *The User Illusion: Cutting Consciousness Down to Size* (Penguin Books, 1999)

2 Nørretranders, Tor, op. cit.

3 Nørretranders, Tor, op. cit.

4 Csikszentmihalyi, Mihaly. *Flow: The Classic Work on How to Achieve Happiness* (revised edition: Rider, an imprint of the Random House Group, 2002), p. 71.

5 Brown, Brené, *Daring Greatly: How the Courage to be Vulnerable Transforms the Way We Live, Love, Parent and Lead* (Portfolio Penguin, 2013), pp. 68–9.

6 Kappes, H.B., and Oettingen, G., 'Positive fantasies about idealized futures sap energy', *Journal of Experimental Social Psychology*, vol. 47, issue 4, (2011), pp. 719–729.

7 Phelps, Michael, in interview on NBC's *Dateline*, following the 2012 Olympic Games in London

8 Brown, Oliver, 'Rio 2016: Newly relaxed Michael Phelps determined to enjoy his Olympic swansong', *Telegraph* (7 August 2016) <http://www.telegraph.co.uk/olympics/2016/08/07/rio-2016-newly-relaxed-michael-phelps-determined-to-enjoy-his-ol/>

Part 2: Power

1 Frankl, Viktor E., *Man's Search for Meaning* (Beacon Press, 2006), p. 86.

Part 3: Play

1 Lakoff, George and Johnson, Mark, in the Afterword of *Metaphors We Live By*, written some two decades later than the original publication in 1980 (University of Chicago Press, 2003)

2 Gibbs, Raymond W., Jr, 'Categorization and Metaphor Understanding', *Psychological Review*, vol. 99, issue 3 (1992)

3 Sapolsky, Robert, 'This Is Your Brain on Metaphors,' *New York Times* (November, 2010)

4 Landau, Mark and Sullivan, Daniel of the University of Kansas and Greenberg, Jeff of the University of Arizona, 'Evidence That Self-Relevant Motives and Metaphoric Framing Interact to Influence Political and Social Attitudes', *Psychological Science* 20(7) (November, 2009), pp. 1421–7.

5 Gottschall, Jonathan, op. cit., p. 49.

6 Gottschall, Jonathan, op. cit., p. 56.

7 Neisser, U. and Harsch, N. 'Phantom flashbulbs: False Recollections of Hearing the News about Challenger' (1992), in Winograd, E. and Neisser, U. (eds), Emory Symposia in Cognition, 4, *Affect and Accuracy in Recall: Studies of "Flashbulb" Memories* (CUP, 2010)

8 Nader, Karim, Schafe, Glenn E. and LeDoux, Joseph E., 'Fear memories require protein synthesis in the amygdala for reconsolidation after retrieval', *Nature* 406 (2000), pp. 722–6.

Part 4: Purpose

1 Brown, Brené, *Rising Strong* (Vermillion, 2015), p. 126. You may have noticed that Brown has been a great influence; her studies on shame and vulnerability were nothing short of life changing for me. This definition of boundaries is one she developed after reading a blog post by artist, teacher and entrepreneur, Kelly Rae Roberts. The post was titled, *What Is and Is Not Okay.*

2 Gilbert, Elizabeth, *Big Magic: Living Creatively Beyond Fear* (Bloomsbury, 2015), p. 33.

3 Brown, Brené, *I Thought It Was Just Me (but it isn't): Making the Journey from "What Will People Think?" to "I Am Enough"* (Penguin, 2007); full quote: 'Over and over, the women I interviewed explained how *empathy* is the strongest antidote for shame. It's not just about having our needs for empathy met; shame resilience requires us to be able to respond empathetically to others. Women with high levels of shame resilience were both givers and receivers of empathy.'

4 Post, Stephen, *Why Good Things Happen to Good People* (Crown/ Archetype, 2007), p. 48.

5 'Volunteerism and Mortality among the Community-dwelling Elderly', a study led by Doug Oman of the University of California, Berkeley, the results of which found that elderly people who volunteered for two or more organisations had 63 per cent lower mortality than non-volunteers; Oman, Doug, Thoresen, Carl E. and Mcmahon, Kay, *Journal of Health Psychology*, vol. 4, issue 3 (1 May 1999), pp. 301–16.

6 Taylor, Steve, Ph.D., 'A Model of Purpose: From Survival to Transpersonal Purpose', *Transpersonal Psychology Review*, vol. 18, no. 1 (spring 2016)

7 Frankl, Viktor E., op. cit.

Index

A

acceptance
  change vs acceptance 208–9
  diving down into continued
    evolution (task) 319–21
  self-acceptance 18, 287, 290–1,
    316–17
  visualisation 317–19
achievement 121
  overachievement 60–1
  sense of 18–19, 71, 300–1
  underachievement 70–2
action
  the action question 172–5
  taking action 80, 171–6
addictive behaviour 100, 185–7
Adler, Alfred 56–7
the adult (Transactional Analysis)
  301
advertising, hypnotic effects of
  34
amnesia 71
analytical questioning 44–5, 338
anchoring 277
  and colour 287–90
  diving down into self-accept-
    ance (task) 290–1
  firing your anchor 287–9
  practice using 291–2

testing your anchor 289–90
  visualisation of mentors 317–19
anger 24, 31, 74, 146, 245. see also
  blaming others
anxiety 53, 73–4, 173–4
  low-level 29
  performance anxiety 191–4,
    270
authenticity in relationships
  156–9, 183, 328–9
authorship 28, 182–3
  bad habits 185–7, 211
  breathing and relaxation
    189–90
  breathing technique (task)
    190–1
  and certainty 188–9
  change vs acceptance 208–9
  choosing 205–9
  diving down into self-aware-
    ness (task) 201–4, 211–12
  emotional intelligence 183–5,
    211
  feeling emotions 188
  going with the flow 187–90
  and reflection ('diving down')
    194–200, 201–4
autonomy 167, 168, 169
awareness 30–3

conscious understanding 31
conscious vs unconscious 32–3
unconscious understanding
31–2
away-from values 115, 116–18,
132
and limiting beliefs 118–20,
355
the 'awkward thing', saying 157,
308

B
bad habits 185–7, 211
Be Perfect driver 106
Be Strong driver 107–8
behaviour. *see also* conscious
mind; self-sabotage;
unconscious mind
addictive 100, 185–7
analytical questioning task
44–5
bad habits 185–7, 211
drivers 105–11
improvements after journaling
7
trance behaviours 34–5
beliefs 38–9. *see also* limiting
beliefs
and actions 52–3
childhood origins 29, 35–6,
54–5, 170
and fear 51–3
and reality 37, 38–9, 40–1
self-beliefs 49, 51, 58, 75–6
training a better belief system
170–1
and truth 26, 51

unconscious flow 48–50
and visual illusions 40–1
binary thinking 54, 55
blaming others 74, 147, 154–5,
159, 166, 198
blaming ourselves 143
blind spot and unique reality
39–40
body-image issues 73
body language and space/time
264
boundaries 307–10
breaching 311–12
changing with growth 312–13
the brain
and metaphor 221–3, 237–8
neuroplasticity 143–5
breathing 189–90
breathing technique (task)
190–1
Brown, Brené 58, 303, 307,
316
Brown, Roger 257

C
calibration 8–9, 335–7
call to action 26
calmness: using anchoring colour
to increase 288
the captain (conscious understanding) 31–2, 42–3, 116,
130, 218, 222, 227, 251, 271,
301
certainty 91–2, 98–9, 169
and authorship 188–9
challenges of life
authorship of 28

the hero's journey 27–8
victims of 27–8
challenging the norm 75–6
changes
change vs acceptance 208–9
submodality changes 230
taking action 80
the child (Transactional Analysis)
301, 302–3. *see also* limiting
beliefs; monsters of self-sabotage; self-sabotage
and boundaries 311
learning from 303–7
listening to 303–7
childhood. *see also* 'live-wire'
memories; reframing
memories
and beliefs 29, 35–6, 54–6,
170
benefits of writing about 6–7
relationship with parents 35–6,
55–6, 76–8
resisting negative messages
56–7
self-centredness 55–6
a tour of your childhood world
76–8
choice 186–7. *see also* authorship
chronic fatigue 43, 139–40
classical conditioning 277
Clean Language 246
co-dependency 151–3. *see also* The
Drama Triangle;
Transactional Analysis
cognitive development: processing
54–5
cognitive hypnotherapy 34–5

colours
anchoring 287–90
reframing memories 283–4,
285, 286, 287–90
visualisation of mentor 317–19
communicating 32, 288, 329. *see
also* emotions; metaphor
and purpose 329
saying the 'awkward thing' 157,
308
Transactional Analysis 301–3
with your mentor 317–19
with your younger self 280–6
comparison with others 73
complaining 74
confidence 288, 324
conflict, internal. *see also*
conscious mind; limiting
beliefs; self-sabotage; unconscious mind
analytical questioning task
44–5, 338
connection (relationships) 93, 325
authenticity in 156–9, 183,
328–9
childhood 35–6, 76–8
co-dependency 151–3
and disconnection 58–60, 77
The Drama Triangle 149–63
honesty in 156–9, 183
with parents 35–6, 76–8
and projection 309–10
and reframing memories 278,
282–4
self-connection 284–5
using anchoring colour to
improve 288

conscious awareness 30, 31
conscious mind 19, 30-2
    capacity for information 37
    conscious vs unconscious
        32-3
    values 86-9
conscious understanding 31-2,
        42-3, 116, 130, 218, 222,
        227, 251, 271, 301
consumerism 147
contribution 94, 99-100, 325
control 164-5. see also fears
    feeling out of 20
    internalising 180-1
    locus of 166-9, 170-6,
        210-11
    and needs fulfilment 168-9
    and responsibility 165-6
    what can you create? (task)
        176-7
control continuum 171
conversing 231
coping mechanisms 4, 129, 185-7,
        211
creative metaphor 230
creativity 278, 304, 328-9
the crew (unconscious under-
        standing) 31-2, 42-3, 116,
        218, 271
Csikszentmihalyi, Mihaly 48, 327

D
deficiency needs 98-9, 131, 325
    met by mentors 314
    strategies 102-3
dependency culture 147
(dis)comfort 69

(dis)comfort zone 67-72, 70, 130,
        314-15
    expanding 75-80
    and happiness 72-5
    lifting the lid on your beliefs
        75-80
    rewriting the future 78-80
    second-place syndrome 70-2
disconnection (relationships)
        58-60, 77, 325
Diving Down process 194-200,
        201-4, 329, 331-4
    diving down into continued
        evolution (task) 319-21, 341
    diving down into emotional
        fluidity (task) 232-3, 293,
        340
    diving down into self-accept-
        ance (task) 290-1, 294
    diving down into self-aware-
        ness (task) 201-4, 211-12,
        226, 228-31, 340
The Drama Triangle 210. see also
        Transactional Analysis
    drama spotting (task) 159-61
    and honesty 156-9
    opting out of 156-61
    The 'Persecutor' victim 154,
        159
    The 'Rescuer' victim 151-3,
        157-9
    and responsibility 166
    the triangular mind 162-3
    the 'Victim' victim 150-1, 159
    victimhood 149-63
drawing: monster of self-sabotage
        22, 138, 342-3

drivers 105–8, 131
  awareness of 108–9
  Be Perfect 106
  Be Strong 107–8
  counter commands 111
  creating a driver symbol (task)
    109–11
  Hurry Up 107
  and limiting beliefs 109
  as needs fulfilment 108
  Please Others 107
  primary 110
  Try Hard 108

E
eating disorders 43
  as resistance to limiting beliefs
    59–60
ego 155, 301, 324, 327
emotional intelligence 183–5, 211
emotional resistance 184–5, 189
emotional wellbeing, measuring
  8–9
Emotional Wellbeing Scale 8–9
emotions
  Be Strong driver 107–8
  diving down into emotional
    fluidity (task) 232–3, 293
  and empathy 326
  expression of 328–9
  feeling 188
  known resistance to 206–8
  metaphorical emotions 225–7,
    230–1, 238
  and metaphorical fluidity
    226–7
  and needs 184

playing with your feelings
  227–31
remembering moments of
  self-sabotage 20–1
and self-awareness 194–200,
  201–4, 227–31
and shame 184–5
empathy
  and emotions 326
  and mirror neurons 145
  with monsters of self-sabotage
    316–17
  and purpose 326
  and shame 326
  visualisation 317–19
enough: fear of being not enough
  50–1, 56–7, 58, 61, 69, 109,
  122–3
equivalence 223–5, 293
Evans, J.F. Expressive writing 7
expression of emotions 328–9
expressive writing 6–7
external locus of control 167

F
facing out, importance of 325,
  327
failure, fear of 23, 50–3, 177–80
families. see relationships
fathers, relationship with 35–6
fatigue, chronic 139–40
fears. see also call to action
  and anxiety 53
  of being not enough 50–1,
    56–7, 58, 61, 69, 109, 122–3
  countering 271
  fear and belief 51–3

fear of disconnection 58–60
fear of failure 23, 50–3, 177–80
fight or flight response 65–6,
    116
feelings. *see also* emotions
    diving down into emotional
        fluidity (task) 232–3, 293
    metaphorical emotions 225–7
    playing with 227–31
fight or flight response 65–6, 116
flashbulb memories 257–8
flow 327
    blocks to 49–50
    going with 140–2, 182, 187–90
    unconscious 48–50
fluidity, emotional 232–3, 293,
    316
focus
    challenging (task) 126–8
    choosing 3–4
food as resistance to limiting
    beliefs 59–60
foreboding, sense of 29
Frankl, Viktor E. 209
free will 32
Freud, Sigmund 115–16
Freudian slips 222–3
future
    fear and anxiety 53
    rewriting 78–80

G
Gale, Hazel
    beginning of boxing career
        17–18
    burnout 112–13, 139, 141–3
    challenges faced 18

childhood and emotion
    206–8
childhood and winning 256–7,
    260–2, 269–71, 272
chronic fatigue 43, 139–43
cognitive hypnotherapy 142–3
doorframe incident 308–9
drive to succeed 81–2
early values 84–5, 97
eating disorder 43
fear of failure 23, 25–6
flying fish narrative 235–7,
    238–9, 251, 253–4
going with the flow 140–2,
    182
insomnia 228–9
lioness metaphor 219–20,
    224–5
lost aggression 219–20, 224–5
ocean encounter 140–2, 182
pivotal boxing matches 15–17,
    18, 225, 299–300
relationship with family 207–8,
    260
relationship with father 207–8,
    256–7, 261–2, 270–2
(re)purposed 322–4
self-acceptance 299–300
self-awareness 182
self-belief 15–17, 18
self-doubt 25–6
shame 61–2, 63–4, 83
striving for perfection 82–3
taking back control 164–5
timeline 269–71
use of metaphor 219–20,
    224–5

victimhood 148, 308–9
World Championship wins
    63–4
generalisation 66–7
Gilbert, Elizabeth 313
glass ceiling 68, 69–70
    example 70–2
golden linings question 175–7
Gottschall, Jonathan 240–1
Groves, David 246
growth 93–4, 99–100
    and changing boundaries
        312–13
    state of 116–18
growth needs 99–100, 126–8, 131,
        325
    strategies 102–3

H
habits, bad 185–7, 211
happiness
    and the (dis)comfort zone
        72–5
    and purpose 324–7
    and success 124
health, physical 7, 325. see also
    wellbeing
health, psychological 7, 8–9,
        324–7
the hero's journey 27–8
hierarchy of importance (task)
        86–8, 352
honesty in relationships 156–9,
        183
Human Givens 'Needs Audit'
        94–6
Hurry Up driver 107

hypnosis 33–6
    cognitive hypnotherapy 34–5
    Quest Cognitive Hypnotherapy
        1
    stage hypnosis 34
hypnotic states: unconscious flow
        48–9

I
identity 140
    and boundaries 313
    the personality construct
        41–2
imagery. see metaphor
important other 278, 282–4
insomnia 29, 228–9
inspiration 313
    and purpose 324–7
internal locus of control 168,
        180–1
    the 'action question' 172–5
    the 'golden linings question'
        175–7
    and needs fulfilment 168–9
interpersonal connection. see rela-
    tionships
interval processing 54

J
Johnson, Mark 220
journaling 6–7
Jung, Carl 19, 57

K
Kahler, Taibi 105
Karpman, Stephen 149
Kulik, James 257

L
Lakoff, George 220
language: use of metaphor 221–3
Lawson, Stuart 46–8
LeDoux, Joseph 258–9
Libet, Benjamin 32
limiting beliefs 26–7, 129. *see also*
    beliefs; reframing memories
    and away-from values 118–20,
        355
    challenging the norm 75–6
    childhood beliefs 29, 35–6,
        54–6, 170
    and children 54
    and drivers 109
    and generalisation 66–7
    impair needs fulfilment 100–1,
        122–3
    importance of identifying
        120–2
    lifting the lid on 75–80
    making the unconscious
        conscious 77–8, 100–1
    owning the story (task) 217–18
    resisting 56–7, 59–60, 67–8
    and self-fulfilling prophecy
        52–3
    tracing 118–20
'live-wire' memories 64–6, 130
    earthing your live-wires (task)
        280–6, 294
    example 262–3
    finding 280
    locating 275–6
    reframing 268, 269–71, 272,
        275–8
    resisting 67–8

locus of control 166–9, 210–11
    external 167
    internal 168, 180–1
    mastering 170–1
    taking action 171–6
love and connection 93, 98–9,
    100, 325

M
marijuana, smoking 35–6
Maslow, Abraham *Hierarchy of
    needs* 91
memories. *see also* reframing
    memories
    earthing your live-wires (task)
        280–6, 294
    flashbulb memories 257–8
    'live-wire' memories 64–6, 130,
        262–3, 275–6
    making the unconscious
        conscious 77–8
    of self-sabotage 20–1
    unlearning 258–9
memory
    amnesia 71
    metaphorical nature of 257–8,
        260–5
    plasticity of 257–8, 260, 268
    Reconsolidation Theory 258–9
    and resistance 267–8
mentors 304–5. *see also* the child
    (Transactional Analysis)
    benefits of 313–15
    and boundaries 307–10
    and deficiency needs 314
    diving down into continued
        evolution (task) 319–21

example 305–7
and growth 312–13
integrating 318–19
visualisation 317–19
metaphor 219–23, 293
    conversing 231
    creative metaphor 230
    diversity of 240
    diving down into emotional
        fluidity (task) 232–3,
        293
    and diving down into
        self-awareness (task) 201–4,
        211–12, 226, 228–31
    equivalence 223–5, 293
    getting past the 'can't' 224–5
    mapping to reality 251–2
    memory as 257–8, 260–5
    metaphorical emotions 225–7,
        230–1, 238
    metaphorical fluidity 226–7
    metaphorical suggestions and
        diving down task 228–30
    playing with your feelings
        227–31
    and problem solving 238–40,
        241–3
    spatial metaphor for time 264
    and storytelling 237–8
    telling your own story (task)
        244–50
    timelines 265–7
    vehicles of meaning 220–3
Metaphors we live by 220
the mind
    awareness 30–3
    capacity for information 37

conscious mind 19, 30–2, 37,
    86–9
conscious vs unconscious 32–3
creating your temporal map
    (task) 263–7
hypnosis 33–6
limiting beliefs 26–8
and metaphorical equivalences
    223–5
'normality' 28–9
trance states 35
unconscious mind 19, 30, 31–2,
    65–70
and unique reality 36–42
'mirages' 121–3, 132
mirror neurons 144–5
and storytelling 241
monsters of self-sabotage 22–4,
    38–9. see also limiting
    beliefs; negative thoughts;
    reframing memories;
    self-sabotage
the child (Transactional
    Analysis) 302–7, 311
dealing with/solutions 24
diving down into continued
    evolution (task) 319–21, 341
drawing 22, 138, 342–3
empathy with 316–17
evolutions of 337
making use of 28
meeting the monster eye to eye
    (task) 137–8
as mentors 304–5
owning the story (task) 217–18
and personality 21–4, 57,
    58–60

reconnecting with 275–8
and the unconscious mind
   32
visualisation of 21–2, 137–8,
   317–19, 344
motivation 82. *see also* values
and performance 116–18
types of 115–18
unconscious motivators 101
understanding your motivation
   (task) 83–4, 351
motivators. *see* values

N
Nader, Karim 258–9
narrative 235–7, 293
accessing the bigger picture
   (task) 254–5
different angles of 253–4
mapping metaphors to reality
   251–2
metaphor and storytelling
   237–8
problem solving using
   metaphor 238–40, 241–3
telling your own story (task)
   244–50
working through troubles
   240–1
'nearly-there effect' 68, 70–2
needs 90–4, 131
audit 94–6, 339
certainty 91–2, 98–9, 169
considering better strategies
   (task) 101–2
contribution 94, 99–100, 325
and control 168–9

deficiency needs 98–9, 102–3,
   131, 325
and drivers 108
and emotions 184
fulfilment 96–101, 108, 122–3,
   125, 168–9
growth 93–4, 99–100, 312–13
growth needs 99–100, 102–3,
   126–8, 131, 325
and internal locus of control
   168–9
and limiting beliefs 100–1,
   122–3
love and connection 93, 98–9,
   100, 325
significance 92–3, 98–9, 325
variety 92, 98–9, 325
negative beliefs. *see* limiting
   beliefs
negative messages, resisting 56–7,
   59
negative thoughts. *see also*
   limiting beliefs; monsters
   of self-sabotage; self-
   sabotage
power of writing them down
   6
Neuro-linguistic programming
   115, 230, 277
neuroplasticity 143–5
New Territories Question
   199–200, 203, 208
nominal processing 54, 55
normality 28–9, 41
challenging the norm 75–6
Nørretranders, Tor, *The user
   illusion* 39, 40

O
ordinal processing 54
overachievement as resistance to
limiting beliefs 60–1

P
parent, adult and child 301–3. *see also* The Drama Triangle
the parent (Transactional Analysis) 301
and boundaries 311
parents
divorcing 55–6
relationships with 35–6, 76–8
Pennebaker, J.W. *Expressive writing* 7
people-pleasing 74, 107
perfection 106, 121–2
Be Perfect driver 106
performance and motivation 116–18
performance anxiety 191–4, 270
The Persecutor (Drama Triangle) 154, 159
personality
the personality construct 41–2
self-sabotaging element of 21–4, 57, 58–60. *see also* monsters of self-sabotage
Phelps, Michael 123–4
physical health 7, 325
Piaget, Jean 54–5
Please Others driver 107
The Pleasure Principle 115–16, 131
positive self-beliefs 75–6
powerlessness, feelings of 20. *see also* fears

problem solving using metaphor 238–40, 241–3
telling your own story (task) 244–50
projection 309–10
protection, state of 116–18
psychological health 7, 8–9, 324–7
purpose 324–7
adding 327–8
communicating 329
dissolving the self 326–7
and empathy 326
expression 328–9
and happiness 324–7
importance of facing out 325
(re)purpose 319–21

Q
Quest Cognitive Hypnotherapy 1
questions to ask 211
action question 172–5
golden linings question 175–7
New Territories Question 199–200, 203, 208

R
ratio processing 54–5
rational thinking 31
reality
the blind spot 39–40
challenging the norm 75–6
and narrative 251–2
and pre-existing beliefs 37, 38–9, 40–1
subjective reality 129
your unique reality 36–42, 75–6

reality filter 37–9. *see also* beliefs;
    drivers; limiting beliefs;
    memories; needs; uncon-
    scious mind; values
reconnecting
    anchoring 277, 287–90
    with childhood memories
        269–74, 276–8
    choosing your focus 279–80
    colours and feelings 283–4,
        285, 286, 287–90
    earthing your live-wires (task)
        280–6, 294
    finding a live-wire 280
    the future 286
    interpersonal connection 278,
        282–4
    with monsters of self-sabotage
        275–8
    new lessons 281–2
    observing the memory 281
    positive messages 285
    and relationships 278, 282–4
    self-connection 284–5
    visualisation of mentors 317–19
Reconsolidation Theory 258–9
reflection ('diving down')
        194–200, 201–4, 329, 331–4
reframing memories 269–71, 272
    anchoring 277, 287–90
    choosing your focus 279–80
    colours and feelings 283–4,
        285, 286, 287–90
    earthing your live-wires (task)
        280–6, 294
    example 272–4
    finding a live-wire 280

the future 286
interpersonal connection
    282–4
new lessons 281–2
observing the memory 281
process 275–8
and relationships 278, 282–4
self-connection 284–5
relationships 93. *see also* The
    Drama Triangle
    authenticity in 156–9, 183,
        328–9
    childhood 35–6, 55–6, 76–8
    co-dependency 151–3
    connection 93, 325
    disconnection 58–60, 77, 325
    honesty in 156–9, 183
    with parents 35–6, 76–8
    and projection 309–10
    and reframing memories 278,
        282–4
    using anchoring colour to
        improve 288
relaxation 189–90
remembering moments of
    self-sabotage 20–1. *see also*
    memories
(re)purpose 319–21
The Rescuer (Drama Triangle)
    151–3, 157–9
resentment 74
resistance
    emotional resistance 184–5,
        189
    known resistance 206–8
    and memory 267–8
    and negative messages 56–7, 59

resisting limiting beliefs 56–7, 59, 67–8, 128
responsibility 165–6
Robbins, Tony 91
Robins, Mel 173

S
Sapolsky, Robert 237
Sathian, Krish 221
Schafe, G.E. 258–9
second-place syndrome 70–2
the self 182, 301–3, 304–5, 311, 324
  dissolving 326–7
self-acceptance 18, 287, 316–17. see also anchoring
  change vs acceptance 208–9
  diving down into self-acceptance (task) 290–1, 294
  visualisation 317–19
self-awareness 194–200, 211–12, 326
  diving down into continued evolution (task) 319–21, 341
  diving down into emotional fluidity (task) 232–3, 293, 340
  diving down into self-acceptance (task) 290–1, 294
  diving down into self-awareness (task) 201–4, 211–12, 226, 228–31, 340
  and emotions 194–200, 201–4, 227–31
  and purpose 324–7
self-belief 49, 51, 75–6. see also beliefs

self-beliefs 58
self-confidence 288, 324
self-connection 284–5
self-doubt 49–50, 51. see also failure, fear of
self-fulfilling prophecy 52–3
self-sabotage 3–4, 70. see also limiting beliefs; monsters of self-sabotage; negative thoughts
  analytical questioning 44–5, 338
  analytical questioning task 44–5
  by anger, blame and complaining 74
  and boundaries 307–10
  the child (Transactional Analysis) 302–3
  by comparison 73
  considering better strategies (task) 101–2
  identifying 19–24
  by people-pleasing 74, 107
  and performance 116–18
  remembering moments of 20–1
  using anchoring colour to counter 288–9
  by worry and anxiety 73–4
self-talk 29. see also limiting beliefs; negative messages
self-worth 36
  and comparison with others 73
  example 177–80
sensory stimuli, connecting 277

shame 58–60, 130
    and emotions 184–5
    and empathy 326
significance 92–3, 98–9, 325
Silvester, Trevor 260, 279
situations: remembering
        moments of self-sabotage
        20–1
smoking: marijuana 35–6
social-media addiction 73
solutions, focusing on 78–80
spatial metaphor for time 264
stage hypnosis 34
state of growth 116–18
state of protection 116–18
stimuli
    connecting sensory stimuli
        277
    triggering 'live wire' memories
        66–7
stories. see narrative
The storytelling animal 240–1
strategies
    considering better strategies
        (task) 101–2
    values strategies (task)
        102–3
stress 27, 29
    and need fulfilment 90
striving 57, 70. see also resisting
        limiting beliefs
    connection with fear, belief and
        shame 50
    for conscious control 49
subjective reality 129
submodality changes 230
substance abuse 93

success
    desperation for 124
    and flow state 50
    visions of 121–3, 132
survival mechanisms 116
    certainty 91–2
    fight or flight response 65–6,
        116
symbolism. see metaphor
synaptic paths 143–5

T
Taylor, Steve 327
temporal maps: creating your
        temporal map (task) 263–7
time. see also timelines
    creating your temporal map
        (task) 263–7
    spatial metaphor for 264
    subjectivity of 267–8
    taking control of 265–6
timelines 294
    and emotional states 266–7
    organisation of 265
    and reframing memories
        275–6, 280
    taking control of time 265–6
    tracing live-wire memories
        275–6
    towards values 115, 116–18, 132
trances 34–5
trans-purposive state 327
Transactional Analysis 105, 111,
        301–3
trauma, childhood: benefits of
        writing about 6–7
triangular mind 162–3

troubles and narrative 240–1
truth and belief 26, 51
Try Hard driver 108

U
unconscious awareness 31–2
unconscious flow 48–50
  blocks to 49–50
unconscious mind 19, 30, 31–2.
    see also limiting beliefs;
    monsters of self-sabotage;
    self-sabotage
  capacity for information
    37
  comfort zone of 69–70, 70
  conscious vs unconscious
    32–3
  fight or flight response 65–6,
    116
  Freudian slips 222–3
  and generalisation 66–7
  metaphor and problem solving
    239
  needs 90–4, 100–1
  self-sabotaging effect of 68–9,
    69, 70
  and trance states 35
  values 86–9, 100–1
unconscious motivators 101
unconscious understanding 31–2,
    42–3, 116, 218, 271
underachievement: example 70–2
unique reality 36–42
  the blind spot 39–40
  challenging the norm 75–6
  and pre-existing beliefs 40–1
  reality filter 37–9

V
values 85–6, 130–1
  analysing 113–14, 353–4
  away-from values 115, 116–20,
    132, 355
  changing for the sake of differ-
    ence 88–9
  example 89–90, 103–5
  the hierarchy of importance
    (task) 86–8, 352
  identifying your monster's
    favourite stories (task)
    119–20, 355
  importance of individual values
    (task) 113–14, 353–4
  and limiting beliefs 119–20
  as strategies for needs fulfil-
    ment 96–100
  strategies (task) 102–3
  towards values 115, 116–18, 132
  types of motivation 115–18
  unconscious mind 86–9, 100–1
  unconscious motivators 101
  understanding your motivation
    (task) 83–4, 351
variety 92, 98–9, 325
The Victim (Drama Triangle)
    150–1, 159
victimhood 27, 139–40, 210
  drama spotting (task) 159–61
  The Drama Triangle 149–63
  external locus of control 167
  fortifying helplessness 149
  language of 148
  mastering your locus of control
    170–1
  neuroplasticity 143–5

playing the victim 145–6
resistance to 162–3
and responsibility 165–6
taking action 171–6
victim culture 146–9
visual illusions and pre-existing
    beliefs 40–1
visualisation. *see also* Diving
    Down process
creative visualisation 20–2
of drivers 110
and metaphor 227–9
outcome-focused 121–2
of the process 126–8
reconnecting with your
    younger self 280–6

self-sabotage moments 20–2
self-sabotage 'monster' 21–4,
    137–8, 178–80, 344
timelines 264–6
visualising the future 79–80

W
wellbeing
    emotional 8–9
    and purpose 324–7
worrying 29, 53, 73–4, 173–4
writing 6–7
    rewriting the future 78–80

Y
'Yes, but...' conversations 152–3